The West Indian Fiction

The West Indian Fiction

edited by

R.K. DHAWAN

Sangam Books

SANGAM BOOKS LIMITED
57 London Fruit Exchange
Brushfield Street
London E1 6EP, U.K.

By arrangement with
PRESTIGE BOOKS
3/28, East Patel Nagar
New Delhi 110 008

Published by Sangam Books Limited, 1999

ISBN 0 86132 418 8

Composed by Pivot Computers, Delhi 110 006
Printed by Dhawan Industries Offset, New Delhi 110 028

Contents

Short Fiction

Contributors

MADHUMALATI ADHIKARI	Maharani Durgavati Univ. Jabalpur
URBASHI BARAT	Maharani Durgavati Univ. Jabalpur
T.S. BORATE	University of Poona Poona
N. RAMA DEVI	S.K. University Anantapur
R.K. DHAWAN	S.B.S. College University of Delhi
GILLIAN DOOLEY	Flinders University South Australia
VEENA JAIN	Mittal Girls School Sardarshahr
C.L.L. JAYAPRADA	Andhra University Visakhapatnam
ANNAMMA JOSEPH	University College Trivandrum
R.K. KAUL	Rajasthan University Jaipur
A.J. KHAN	Christ College Cuttack
VINEY KIRPAL	Poona Formerly at I.I.T., Bombay
RAMA KUNDU	University of Budwan
I.K. MASIH	Ranchi
RAMA NAIR	Osmania University Hyderabad
R.S. PATHAK	Dr. H.S. Gour University Sagar
S. RAMASWAMY	Formerly at Bangalore Univ. Bangalore
NIRUPA RANI	Andhra University Visakhapatnam
S.S. SHARMA	M.L.N. (E) College University of Delhi
ROOPALI SIRCAR	S.V. College University of Delhi

The West Indian Fiction: An Introduction

R.K. DHAWAN

West Indian writers have produced some of the most enduring literary pieces by any standards in the world. It was duly recognized in the recent years when Derek Walcott was awarded the Nobel Prize for his contribution to literature. Perhaps the most significant feature of the West Indian writing is that it is deeply rooted in its culture. It is especially true of the fiction produced there. A noteworthy function of the West Indian novel is that it aims primarily at investigating and projecting the inner consciousness of the West Indian community. This view was expressed by George Lamming in *The Pleasures of Exile* (1960). But only two years later, after the publication of this remark, the still-born West Indian Federation was finally declared dead. Since then, Guyana, Jamaica, Trinidad and Barbados, the larger territories of the English-speaking Caribbean have become independent nations.

In spite of the island nationalisms that have arisen, we continue to recognize a West Indian community. It is persistent of some common features in the arts in general and in the literatures of the new separate nations in particular that contribute most to the sense of a unity. Readers and scholars continue to share certain values and concerns that have assumed cultural significance. In the world of sports, these islands represent a unified and consolidated West Indies cricket team.

II

Roger Mais is a Jamaican, born in 1905. He was educated at Calabar High School. He worked as civil servant, journalist and photographer. He was associated with the political activist Norman W. Manley in the 1930s and 40s. He was imprisoned for six months in 1944 for his anti-colonial essay. He died in 1955. His works include *And Most of All Men* (stories & verse) (1939), *Face and Other Stories* (1942).

The Hills Were Joyful Together (1953), *Brother Man* (1954) and *Black Lightning* (1955). In an article on Mais's *Brother Man*, Gillian Dooley analyzes patterns of communication in this work. The novel anatomizes three relationships quite closely, and sketches several others. It is structured in five parts, and in each of these, communication and the nature of communication is of utmost importance. The novel thus has greater significance as a work of psychology rather than of sociology or political ideology.

III

Cyril Dabydeen was born in Guyana in 1945 but moved to Canada in 1970. Currently, he teaches English at the University of Ottawa. He is essentially a poet but has published some collections of short stories and two short novels namely *The Wizard Swami* (1989) and *Dark Swirl* (1989). Dabydeen's diasporic consciousness expressed itself throughout his writings. For him, the diaspora is a reiterative experience: the movement of his ancestors from India to Guyana is, in a way, re-enacted by his own immigration to Canada. In an illuminating essay on Dabydeen's *Dark Swirl*. Annamma Joseph analyzes the novel as a work of resistance culture. Set against a context of struggle for personal and national identity, *Dark Swirl* draws on raw material from the author's early years in the Caribbean before he migrated to Canada.

IV

Samuel Selvon was born in Trinidad on 20 May 1923. He served as a wireless operator with the Trinidad Royal Naval Volunteer Reserve from 1940 to 1945. He worked as a journalist in *Trinidad Guardian* from 1946 to 1950. He joined civil service in the High Commission, London, in 1950. In 1954, he took to full-time writing. He received Guggenheim Fellowship in 1954 and 1968, Society of Authors Travelling Scholarship in 1958, Trinidad Government Scholarship in 1962, Arts Council of Great Britain grant in 1967 and 1968, and Humming Bird Medal, Trinidad, in 1969. His novels include *A Brighter Sun* (1952), *An Island is a World* (1955), *The Lonely Londoners* (1956), *Turn Again Tiger* (1959), *I Hear Thunder* (1963), *The Housing Lark* (1965), *The Plains of Caroni* (1970), *Those Who Eat the Cascadura* (1972) and *Moses Ascending* (1975). While *A Brighter Sun* and *Turn Against Tiger* deal with the life of an East Indian family in the Caribbean, *The Lonely Londoners* presents the plight of West Indian immigrants in London.

In her article entitled "Two Faces of Solitude," C.L.L. Jayaprada makes a comparative study of Samuel Selvon and the Australian writer Henry Lawson. Both these writers depict the lonely men, fighting the battle of life under nightmarish circumstances trying to find a meaning in an essentially fragmented world. The lone battlers and underdogs fighting for survival are the central figures both in the faceless city of London portrayed by Selvon in *The Lonely Londoners* and in the daunting spaces of bush depicted in Lawson's various stories.

Selvon is best-known for his short stories which are collected in *Ways of Sunlight* (1958) and *Foreday Morning* (1989). In her scholarly article, Nirupa Rani gives a critical survey of Selvon's short stories. According to her, the stories of Selvon can be grouped into four categories: immigrant stories; personal stories dealing with love; stories set in rural Trinidad containing characters of Indian origin and stories set in the city or suburbs containing characters of African origin. S. Ramaswamy, in his article, "Innocence and Experience: Colonial Consciousness in Two Caribbean Stories" compares Selvon's "Brackley and the Bed" with A.L. Hendricks's "Jamaican Fragment." In both the stories, he argues, we find the essence of colonial consciousness.

V

Wilson Harris was born in New Amsterdam, British Guiana, now Guyana, on 24 March 1921. He was educated at Green's College, Georgetown. He worked as Government Surveyor in the 1940s and Senior Surveyor of the Government of British Guiana from 1955 to 1958. He was a Visiting Lecturer at State University of New York at Buffalo in 1970. In the same year, he was Writer-in-Residence at Scarborough College, University of Toronto. He was the Commonwealth Fellow in Caribbean Literature at Leeds University, Yorkshire in 1971. He was the Visiting Professor at the University of Texas at Austin in 1972, University of Mysore in 1978 and Yale University, New Haven, Connecticut in 1979. He received Arts Council grant in 1968 and 1970, Guggenheim Fellowship in 1973, Henfield Writing Fellowship in 1974 and Southern Arts Writing Fellowship in 1976. His novels include *Palace of the Peacock* (1960), *The Far Journey of Oudin* (1961), *The Whole Armour* (1962), *The Secret Ladder* (1963), *Heartland* (1964), *The Eye of the Scarecrow* (1965), *The Waiting Room* (1967), *Tumatumari* (1968), *Ascent to Omai* (1970), *Black Marsden* (1972), *Companions of the Day and Night* (1975), *Genesis of the Clowns* (1977) and *The Tree of the Sun* (1978).

In his essay "Topography of the Heartland: An Approach to the Novels of Wilson Harris," S. Ramaswamy investigates the meaning and significance of the word "Heartland" with reference to five novels of Harris. According to this critic, Harris used the word to include a number of things. At the literal level, the 'Heartland' is Guiana itself which he explores in his novels. 'Heartland' also refers to the human heart and it is the unique way in which Harris explores the 'heartland' that gives his fiction universal appeal.

VI

Jean Rhys was born in Windward Islands, Dominica, in 1894. Her father was a Welsh doctor and her mother a Creole—that is, a white West Indian. At the age of 16, she emigrated to England to attend the Royal Academy of Dramatic Art, London. Her father's death, after one term, put a stop to further training. She joined the touring company of *Our Miss Gibbs* and worked on stage. At the end of the First World War, she married a Dutch poet and lived in Paris between the Wars. She met Ernest Hemingway, James Joyce and Ford Madox Ford and started writing in *Transatlantic Review*. Her first book *The Left Bank* contained studies and sketches of Bohemian Paris. In the "Preface" to the volume, Ford Madox Ford writes that Rhys has a singular instinct for form possessed by singularly few writers of English and almost no English women writers.

Jean Rhys has written five novels to-date: *Posters* (1928) was later published as *Quartet* in New York; *After Leaving Mr. Mackenzie* (1931); *Voyage in the Dark* (1934); *Good Morning, Midnight* (1939); and after a gap of twenty-seven years *Wide Sargasso Sea* (1966). The sparse and repetitive narratives of her five novels are variations on the themes of failure and rejection. Rhys's recurrent heroine is a beautiful, young woman, generally Creole in origin, and artistic in leanings. Hopelessly and helplessly at sea in her relations with men, she is a passive victim, doomed to destruction. Like schizophrenics, she experiences the world as a hostile environment and leads a life of isolation.

Wide Sargasso Sea derives its leading characters and their situation from another work of art, namely Charlotte Bronte's novel *Jane Eyre*. The heroine and the narrator of the greater part of *Wide Sargasso Sea* is Bertha Mason—the first Mrs. Rochester in Bronte's novel whose sudden appearance at the wedding ceremony prevents Mr. Rochester's marriage to Jane Eyre. Jean Rhys fills in the details of her character and vividly renders life in Jamaica in the early nineteenth century after the emancipation of the slaves. The blurb on the paperback edition describes the work as "a novel of unforgettable romance and terror. A 'triumph' of Caribbean Gothic!"

It is her fifth and award-winning novel *Wide Sargasso Sea* that has caught the attention of the various Indian critics in this anthology. There are as many as four articles on this masterpiece. Madhumalati Adhikari discusses the 'archetypal confrontations' in this novel which draws heavily from Rhys's childhood ordeals of Jamaica and the agonizing adult experiences of England. She makes the familiar world of women and her conflicts transparent for our viewing. Another scholar Urbashi Barat discusses *Wide Sargasso Sea* in terms of Rhys's colonial experience. In her article, she suggests that our understanding of the novel is enriched if we read it not just as a woman's novel but as an exploration of the colonial experience. Veena Jain considers *Wide Sargasso Sea* as an attempt to re-write history. She approaches the novel from the historical point of view looking at it from the angle of reworking of the colonial past of the West Indies. By linking history to personal consciousness, Rhys enlarges the panorama of human experience. Rama Kundu, in her scholarly article, makes a comparison of the treatment of black woman servant figure in the American and Caribbean contexts respectively with particular focus on the character of Dilsey in Faulkner's *The Sound and the Fury* and of Christophine in Rhys's *Wide Sargasso Sea*. Dilsey and Christophine, she argues, represent the marginalized and oppressed victims of racism/sexism/imperialism in the two countries.

VII

George Lamming was born in Barbados in 1927. He taught in Trinidad and Venezuela. He hosted a book review programme for the West Indian service of the BBC, London in 1951. He received both Guggenheim Fellowship and *Kenyon Review* Fellowship in 1954 and Maugham Award in 1957. His novels include *In the Castle of My Skin* (1953), *The Emigrants* (1954), *Of Age and Innocence* (1958), *Season of Adventure* (1960), *Water with Berries* (1971) and *Natives of My Person* (1972). He has written some short stories also.

In the Castle of My Skin is not only an autobiography of a childhood, it is also a collective autobiography of a Barbadian village moving through the break-up of the old plantation system dominated by the Great House and into the new age of nationalism, industrial unrest and colonial repression. Set in the Barbados of the 1930s and 40s, the story is largely narrated by a young boy whose growth to manhood corresponds with the gradual disintegration of the social ethos in which he grows up. In an illuminating essay in this book "Make me a captive, Lord, and I shall be free," Roopali Sircar, like Ngugi, argues that the novel is "a study of colonial revolt." The boy 'G' actually experiences the non-existence of ties and his inquisitiveness on his ninth birthday, regarding father and relations, hints at an exodus, an aspect of West Indian life, that touches all classes of society and all races. In this novel, Lamming demythologizes Prospero and allows Caliban to grow out of a stultifying relationship. In doing so, says Roopali Sircar, Lamming's West Indies is seen through the eyes of Caliban and not Prospero.

Lamming's other significant novel, *Of Age and Innocence*, is set in San Cristobal, a fictional Caribbean colony, in the 1940s and 50s, rapidly approaching independence. It depicts the West Indian struggle for independence which had just begun on the island. Isaac Shephard, a native of Negro origin, returns to the island after a long stay in England, and raises the slogan of a basic West Indian identity. The slogan unites the people against the colonial forces on the island. Shephard joins Aly Singh's Indian freedom party and gets it renamed as the Peoples' Communal Movement. In the novel, the conflict is represented as the conflict of two generations. While highlighting facets of the novel, eminent Indian critic Viney Kirpal argues that it has not received the attention it deserves. She says although the theme of the novel is essentially political, community life is evoked by Lamming with genuine feeling and authenticity. And the most striking quality of the novel, she continues, is its sensuousness.

VIII

V.S. Naipaul was born in Chaguanas, an island of Trinidad, on 17 August 1932. Chaguanas was an Indian village re-created by indentured labourers brought over to work in the fields. Naipaul was educated at Queen's Royal College, Port of Spain, Trinidad, 1943-48, and University College of Oxford, 1950-54. After obtaining a degree in English Literature from Oxford, Naipaul went to London and worked as Editor of "Caribbean Voices" for the BBC Caribbean Service during 1954-56 and as Fiction Reviewer in *New Statesman*, London, 1957-61. He received Rhys Memorial prize in 1958, Maugham Award in 1961, Phoenix Trust Award in 1962, Hawthornden Prize in 1964, Smith Literary Award in 1968, Arts Council grant in 1969, Booker Prize in 1971 and Bennett Award (Hudson Review, New York) in 1980.

Naipaul writes about the Caribbean, more in the tradition of the English rather than the West Indian novel. His first three books of fiction were: *The Mystic Masseur* (1957), *The Suffrage of Elvira* (1958) and *Miguel Street* (1959). *The Mystic Masseur*, the best of these, is a satire on a man who rises, through use of popular superstition, from failed masseur in Trinidad to an English-named and decorated mystic and politician. The novel evokes the Port of Spain of Naipaul's boyhood.

While *The Mystic Masseur* won critical acclaim, it was *A House for Mr. Biswas* (1962) which established Naipaul as a truly major novelist. The novel is set in Trinidad, over three generations. However, it does not celebrate the vitality of Caribbean life; it is a satire on life there that it is on life anywhere. S.S. Sharma's article entitled "The Theme of Selfhood in Naipaul's *A House for Mr. Biswas*" points out that the novel, more than anything else, is the portrayal of a single individual's search for identity, his struggle to arrive at authentic selfhood.

Place and displacement are recurrent themes in postcolonial literature. The crisis of identity is related more to placelessness than to rootlessness. Rama Nair's article "'Island' as a Metaphor of Creativity" makes a comparative analysis of this search for belonging and identity in Mr. Biswas and Ralph Singh, the central protagonists of Naipaul's *A House for Mr. Biswas* and *The Mimic Men*. The historical, ideological and cultural circumstances that entrap Mr. Biswas and Ralph Singh in closed worlds of despair and loneliness are re-examined and re-aligned to symbolize the beginning of a creative process.

In her article, N. Rama Devi makes a comparative study of the satire and structure in V.S. Naipaul and R.K. Narayan. Thus she places Naipaul in the tradition of Indian literature by virtue of Indian names, customs and cultural ideas that proliferate in his works. In his scholarly essay "Disorder within, Disorder without," R.S. Pathak finds a powerful expression of colonial consciousness in the writings of Naipaul. In his delineation of human problems, Naipaul is under a profound indebtedness to Joseph Conrad.

In his article, A.J. Khan takes up the travel writings of Naipaul. In his opinion, V.S. Naipaul in his non-fiction has been able to adopt an altogether new narrative technique and express his ideas in a startling and arresting way. Following this method, the writer describes things in a seemingly journalistic manner but his statements have a touch of universal truth, which gives a deep philosophical touch to the entire work.

I.K. Masih critically examines Naipaul's *An Area of Darkness* and challenges many of the writer's ideas expressed in this work. India may be a land of darkness for Naipaul, says the critic, but for him, "it is an area of light and will remain so." T.S. Borate evaluates the changing Indian critical response to *An Area of Darkness*. He analyzes the varied response to the book, from condemnation and outright rejection to appreciation and acceptance of the book as a work of art.

According to R.K. Kaul, in *The Loss of El Dorado*, Naipaul traces the history of expeditions to Trinidad, Guiana, Venezuela and the neighbouring islands. Naipaul directs his wrath especially against the Western media which treat the coloured people as playthings.

IX

Significant works continue to make additions to the richness of the West Indian fiction. In the late nineties, many new novels have appeared. Notable amongst these is one by Opal Palmer Adisa's first novel, entitled *It Begins with Tears*. Drawing on the Jamaican folklore, it is set in rural Jamaica and deals with the return of young woman to the community of Kristoff village. Another recently published novel is *The Festival of San Joaquin* by the author of well-known novel *Beka Lamb*, Zee Edgell.

Patterns of Communication in Roger Mais's *Brother Man*

GILLIAN DOOLEY

Communication, and failure to communicate, is at the basis of human relationships: find out about the nature of communication that exists between two people, and you will find out a great deal about the nature of that relationship. In *Brother Man*, Roger Mais anatomizes three relationships quite closely, and sketches several others. The plot of the novel is simple three story-lines which are essentially independent—and the interest lies mainly in the exploration of the dynamics between the three couples: Girlie and Papacita; Jesmina and Cordelia; and Brother Man and Minette; and, looking beyond that, of the nature of Brother Man's relations with his community. The three plot-lines are not closely interlinked: they offer points of comparison and contrast with each other, and enhance the psychological authenticity of Mais's characters, without providing the main driving force behind the narrative. And despite the claims of some critics that he was a social realist,[1] psychology rather than sociology or political ideology is his chief interest in *Brother Man*.

The novel is structured in five parts, each beginning with a "Chorus of People in the Lane." The need to communicate is thus a basic undertow in the novel. People gather to exchange gossip. It passes the time, it's free, and it entertains and distracts them from their own troubles: "There are those with an accounting of troubles the same and equal to and over and beyond the ones they tell. . . . It is their own story over that they tell in secret, overlaying it with the likeness of slander, licking their own ancient scrofulous sores."[2] This gossip is partly communication in self-defence—people's attempt to deflect the pity and shame of their own situations on others they can imagine as even more unfortunate than themselves. When Cordelia complains "Ah shame fo' walk down de street. De women stare, dem shame me, can 'most hear dem a-whisper, whisper, *dem tek-up Jonas fo' ganga, hush, see Cordy de a go-long down de street. . .* " (17) she knows what people are saying because she has no doubt said the same things about others, before her own misfortune. She now feels ostracised: as the subject of gossip, she can no longer participate in it.

The scene straight after the first Chorus shows, almost cinematically, Girlie and Papacita. The tension between them is so great that everything either of them does in the other's presence is a form of communication, even when they are pretending to ignore each other:

> Girlie was idly turning the pages of magazine when Papacita came in through the door. She did not look up. He closed the door quietly—too quietly—behind him, without taking his eyes off her, came cat-footing across the room.
>
> He noticed that a corner of the page picturing Ingrid Bergman in Kodakcolor trembled a little between her fingers. Something tickled him at the back of his throat. He wanted to cough.
>
> He said: "*Hm*!" trying to clear it.
>
> She turned the page, slowly, put her other hand up to her back-hair.
>
> He went past her, across to the window overlooking the lane, threw it open with a bang, and said, angrily:
>
> 'It's like a furnace in here.'
>
> She went on turning the pages of the magazine she held across her knee. She put a finger up to her lips, wet the tip of it with her tongue, raised her eyes slowly to look at him, as though aware of his presence for the first time, saw him without recognition, without change of expression, and brought her eyes back slowly to the page.
>
> He leaned against the window and stood to look at her a moment, shrugged, turned away, went across to the bed, sat down, started pulling off his shoes.
>
> 'Lousy bum,' she said, causing, as though she was speaking to herself, just turning her thoughts out to air. (9-10)

What follows is obviously a scene which has been played out before. Papacita tells Girlie, "I know you're jus' bustin' with things to say. Why n't I come home las' night, hey? Don't you want to know?" (10) The fight continues with withering scorn and sarcasm on Girlie's part, and frustration and, presumably, lies on Papacita's part. What is most obvious about their relationship is that there is no trust between them. Their verbal sparring turns physical, and they fight until he can overcome her resistance. He forces her to have sex which gives them both "deep physical satisfaction that was like nothing else on earth," (28) but any healing, reconciling effect of their love-making is short-lived. It seems that Girlie is not fulfilled by the "deep physical satisfaction," she wants more, and this fact is "there between them, not to be dismissed." (28) This interrupts their communication, which for a short time has been wordless and deep.

> . . . they tried to talk around it, but every time it came back at tail-end of everything they said, and it was like a secret embarrassment between them. It was a goad and a taunt to him, to her a great barrenness and a void in her flesh. (34-35)

Embarrassment is almost as detrimental to communication as the hostility and mistrust which usually characterizes their relationship, and the fight resumes, ending with Papacita walking out, bleeding from a knife wound. This is the pattern of their communication. They have moments of great tenderness, for example the scene in the night-club when Girlie sings, but their bond cannot survive Papacita's need to escape commitment, aggravated by Girlie's jealousy, which eventually leads her to murder him.

Girlie and Papacita use words as weapons: they are far from inarticulate. Jesmina, on the other hand, often cannot even formulate her thoughts, let alone express them. Nameless fears impede her, and she is troubled by the power of words: when Cordelia says, "wish ah was dead," Jesmina replies, "Don't say it, Sis. Hush, do! Is a sin." (15) Her reluctance to express her feelings is justified here, when she bites her lip to hold in her tears (17), as she does not want to upset her sick sister. However, her inability to express herself to Shine causes trouble in their relationship at first:

> . . . even when he pressed her she wasn't able to give her secret fears, forebodings, concrete form. So that in truth she was unable to tell him, though she would, if just to set his own mind at rest.
>
> And presently they got up and left the ice-cream parlour with that feeling between them that something had come into their lives to set them apart.
>
> He was hurt that a thing like this could have happened to them already, hurt and puzzled, not knowing what this thing might be, and like a child he wanted to kick it down and stride across the ruins, but her own silence thwarted him, cancelled him out like a digit, and he was hurt and angered and dumb. (86)

In their case, though, the need for love overcomes the communication barrier. In their last scene together, he asks her if she feels like talking, and she declines, but "she felt, suddenly, it was loving more than anything she wanted; that alone had any meaning out of all the tumult and confusion." (156) After this, Jesmina seems to lose the fear that had constrained her. She confronts Cordelia with her betrayal of Brother Man, and comes to understand the value of communication, talking to Minette and Brother Man:

> They sat for a long time talking it over, the three of them.
>
> Jesmina, all her primitive, intuitive fears now resolved and confirmed in her mind, told them all she had seen. She said she would never forgive herself for not speaking about them before. (169)

Brother Man seems to stand out as the ablest communicator in the novel:

> . . . somehow the words didn't sound banal, coming from him. He spoke with such simple directness that it seemed to give a new import to everything he said. It was as though the common words of everyday usage meant something more, coming from his lips, than they did in the casual giving and taking of change in conversation, the way it was with other folks. (24)

But he is certainly not perfect in this respect. Communication is a two-way process, and involves understanding others as well as making them understand. It is clear from the frustration Minette feels with Brother Man at first that he is completely successful in neither way. Although he gives "a new import to everything" he says, Minette still doesn't "understand a word of all this." (24) On the other hand, "she was young, and things were stirring inside her, and she couldn't make him understand, or aware of her in that way at all," (32) meaning in a sexual way. When she asks him directly why he has never married, he finds himself "stumbling for words." (40) It is not until he responds to Minette's love, and "something that went without words" (137) passed between them, that communication between them is finally completely open, allowing them to move ahead to a hopeful future at the end of the novel:

> 'They'll all come crawlin' to you yet, an' beg to you forgive them.'
>
> He just bowed his head before her. His heart was too full to speak.

He saw all things that lay before him in a vision of certitude, and he was alone no longer.

'Look at me,' he said.

Her gaze met his, unfaltering.

'You see it, out there, too?'

She looked up above the rooftops where that great light glowed across the sky.

She said: 'Yes, John, I have seen it.'

'Good,' he said, and again, 'Good.'

He moved away from the window, back into the cool dimness of the room beyond.

And she went before him, carrying herself proudly, shielding the little flame of the candle with her hand. (190-91)

Brother Man is a good man, but he is far from omnipotent. He preaches to the crowd which gathers around him at the height of his popularity, telling them simply "that they were to turn away from evil and to follow after righteousness," but he knows that they will not be able to fast for three days as he instructs them; and when he is accused of counterfeiting money, the community quickly turns against him. His powers of communication are useless: he tries to reason with them, but "his voice was downed in the shrieks and curses of the mob," (185) and they attack and defile him. He has, at any rate, the capacity to appeal to the emotions of people but not to change their basic attitudes: he can soothe Cordelia, for example, so that her mind is "bright and clear" (134) for ten minutes, but "her thoughts muddied and clouded again, and things that were straight and simple before seemed blurred and complex." (134) Mais's point is perhaps that good cannot overcome evil, but that they can nevertheless co-exist. Brother Man does not have the influence one would expect from a Christ figure, despite the obvious parallels between his experience and the crucifixion and resurrection; but the survival of the pure and good, even if it is weak in terms of temporal power, is surely intended as a sign of hope for the world.

NOTES

1. Evelyn J. Hawthorne, *The Writer in Transition: Roger Mais and the Decolonization of Caribbean Culture* (New York: P. Lang, 1989), p. xiii.
2. Roger Mais, *Brother Man* (Oxford: Heinemann, 1974), pp. 8-9.

Cyril Dabydeen's *Dark Swirl*: A Study in Resistance Culture

ANNAMMA JOSEPH

Set against a context of struggle for national and personal identity, *Dark Swirl* draws on raw material from the author's childhood and youth in the Caribbean before he migrated to Canada, probably in search of a wider audience and easier access to publishers. It has not only a Guyanese setting, but also has characters and situations whose social correlates are immediately recognizable as belonging to that region.

Cyril Dabydeen was born in the Canje district in Guyana, South America. About twenty miles inland there are fertile plantations of sugarcane converted from mangrove swamps by settlers. Beyond these there lies the rocky hilly Plateau covered with impenetrable forests. The scanty population living on the coast or on the banks of the rivers consists of Negroes, indentured labour, brought from India, and some native Indians. They live in perfect harmony with the abundant animal life found in the rivers and forests in the form of alligators, fish of innumerable species, reptiles, insects, and colourfully plumed birds. It is in this geographical area where landscape and people offer a mixture of the exotic and the savage, that Dabydeen places his village without a name, where the action of the novel takes place.

In an autobiographical piece, the author relives his childhood in such a village: "I grew up breathing in the scent of rotten sugarcane and inhaling the aroma of molasses mingling with the vague air of mollusc, crab, and shrimp floating up from the Atlantic all along the Guyana coastland, all the while as the giant cane factory hummed, throbbed."[1] This nostalgic special landscape becomes within the novel, the landscape of the mind of the colonized at a time when the narrative of the colonized is about to be subsumed by the metanarrative of the colonizer.

The village where the action takes place, derives its identity from the Dark Swirl, a muddy creek which sustains its communal life, forming the centre of its culture and its religion, and holding together its values. The dynamic presence animating this centre, which is mysterious, yet tangible for the villagers, is the Massacouraman, a leviathan who resides within the depths of the swirl and visits the villagers sometimes in their dreams. The Dark Swirl thus forms the inspiriting centre of a tightly structured cohesive and concentric social structure, with the "pool of origins" at the centre, the children swimming within it, and the grown-ups moving around it. The story traces how the intrusion of strange and conflicting values into the life of the village shakes the placid calm of the pool and its imaginary inhabitant, and how the tenacious centre holds on without letting things fall apart. This drama of colonization is presented through the responses of a central consciousness, a sensitive and introspective mind, whose dilemma is not only how to interrogate and interpret the impact of a new culture, and how to validate and authenticate the old against the new, and how through a process of enquiry arrive at a personal and national identity, but also how to go about it without the help of the language and thought structure of the oppressor.

The owner of this eccentric mind is Josh, a ten-year-old village boy, who is obviously the author's surrogate. Josh, who starts on a journey from awareness to articulation, finds himself in a situation exactly similar to what the author found himself within his own village environment, where he says, "nothing was really private, save for our innermost thoughts, though we were already cultivating the sense of awareness of 'the pool of origins' deep within us."[2]

Josh acquires a distinct identity, and the right to have a name of his own—a right he shares with his father Ghulam, by his overwhelming desire to probe into the mysteries the Dark Swirl hides within it. In marked contrast, the other members of the community accept it as a vital part of their existence. Their unselfconscious attitude is conveyed by the children of the village: "This time he [Josh] saw the other children swimming, as they did when the sun was hottest; saw the brown and black bodies, naked and half naked; slim waisted, lithe, whipping in and out of water, hands jutting out in mock truculence or glee, in the glimmer of sun against faces, backs and buttocks."[3] They take to the creek instinctively. And when within the creek they have the same rank smell of rotten leaves mixed with mud, which is the smell of the creek.

Josh's mother represents the adult members of the village community who are not equally native or uncontaminated, but are subject to alien thoughts at unguarded moments, unchecked by the necessity of conforming to tradition: "Like almost everyone else in the village she had her suspicions. Nearly everyone, at one time or another, had imagined strange reptiles crawling out of the creek at nights and inhabiting the space under their beds, or even crawling into the beds and lying next to them." (8) She also understands and admits that Josh has arrived at what she has only vaguely sensed: "'That chile . . .' she murmured to herself. 'He in' like the rest o' them. . . . Maybe he know t'ings 'bout dat creek that none of the rest o' we know'." (8)

Josh's awareness of a presence which is more than what meets the eye slowly advances into an inner compulsion to interrogate it. The author sketches out this compulsive obsession: "Josh stood at his familiar spot by the window, staring out over the creek, unable to look away, wishing the water was clear enough to see exactly what was at the bottom. . . . He did this day after day." (7) The unconscious possesses its own rationale and its own logic of reality, as psychoanalysis points out. Discarding the instinctual and the intuitive sources which alone could lead him to those mysterious depths of the mind, Josh resorts to Western methods of analyzing knowledge, when he attempts to bring the unconscious to the conscious level and bound it within a framework of scientific rationality. The framing of the unthought and the uncommunicable within language and reason is suggested by the window behind which Josh stands to look at the pool, and the scientific objectivity by the distance he always keeps between himself and the swirl.

It is suggestive that, while the children of the village swim with abandon in the swirl, Josh refuses to be initiated into its mysteries in that most natural manner, which is a great source of worry for his parents. A parallel process of evolution and growth is mentioned by Dabydeen in his autobiographical reminiscences. He remembers how "in the pervasive bellyache of socialism all around us, the logical and the ratiocinative would take over even as we grappled with dogs and ideology supplanting the purely numinous."[4]

Josh's positioning himself as the central authorizing subject attempting to mould the unconscious into a recognizable form using its observing, ordering, and recording powers, traces the evolution of the man among many, into the artist or writer who works in isolation. In the struggle to reach the cathartic experience of creatively bodying forth his vision of reality, the artist in Josh understands that he cannot do without the tools offered by the West. It is, however, with great reluctance that he admits them into his world of mighty leviathans, primordial alligators, and black water creeks: "Now and again his eyes strayed beyond the creek: to the houses, to the lush sugarcane fields, to the widening horizon: a different world altogether. But he always looked back into the creek, familiar ground." (7)

This world which Josh would rather push out of his thoughts comes in uninvited, in the form of the White visitor to the village. He represents what is beyond the horizon, the challenge posed by the theoretical positions held by a faraway and totally unsympathetic society to the tenacious hold of the native on his tribal beliefs and traditions.

It is his interest in the exotic animals and reptiles from a scientific point of view that brings the White Man to this remote village. The space assigned to him is on the other side of the creek. The villagers watch him with suspicion as he peers into the odd places at the edge of the creek. He is everything that they are not. "He in' like we; he skin white—white an' yellow too. . . . He in' like we—he pale like root!" (15)

This difference, which is more than just skin-deep, is substantiated and highlighted by the animal symbolism which is pervasive throughout the work. Apart from the dominant symbol of the Massacouraman, the plentiful presence and proximity of animals of all variety, thins the line of demarcation between the world of the animal and the human, in this remarkable world of nascent priomordial nature. It is often difficult to distinguish between the reptiles within the Swirl and the naked brown and black bodies of the children as they whip in and out of it, intertwining and whirling about exposed to the glare of the sun. This interdependent relationship between the human and the animal world as a feature of an unspoilt natural situation is suggested by the two quotations which form the prologue. One is from Ted Hughes's "Gog," a poem about a mythical race of giants, and the second, from Konrad Lorenz's poem "King Solomon's Ring," which is about a thinking fish. These make us breath the air of a world outside history, of a time when man totally identified himself with the animal world, sharing not only power and dynamism, but even his reasoning power.

The White Man violates this sacred relationship by seeing animals as objects of scientific study. He traps the animals and keeps them in cages in his room ready to be transported to the zoos in different parts of the 'civilized' world. This tampering with a fundamental law of nature is a prelude to the trapping of the subjective world of the native objectified through the Massacouraman, and the use of his culture as a showpiece from a bygone past, whose interest lies in its irrelevance to the present.

In addition to the racial compartmentalisation, the trapping of animals also suggests the acquisitiveness of the coloniser. Self-interested economic motives have been pointed out as the primary motive of the empire builder, compared to which self-interested political considerations are only secondary.[5] The animals here are hence the counterparts of the gold in West Africa, diamonds in South West Africa, copper in Congo and Rhodesia, etc. The White Man's identification with the colonizer becomes complete when he sees the possibility of converting the village into a continuous enterprise of the empire supported by cheap local labour. He offers the villagers money for trapping animals for him. He jingles a few coins in his pocket and tells them, "Just let me know. . . . If you see strange toads, fish, animals—whatever—I'm willing to pay." (13)

Imperialism need not be achieved by force, but could be achieved by political, social, economic, or cultural dependence or collaboration. There is an absence of force in the collaboration between Josh and the White Man. It starts with the incident of the White Man rescuing Josh from being forcefully pushed into the swirl by the village boys. For the first time, while coming to the help of Josh, the White Man crosses over the unchartered boundary between the divergent cultures. This incident brings the two closer. The White Man, in the hope of getting from Josh some information about the creature which scared him, strikes a friendship with him. He dreams of a time when that strange creature will be shown off in the zoos of Europe and America, as the crowning achievement of his career.

The villagers, however, feel uncomfortable about Josh's increasing friendship with the White Man. They attribute to his machinations the changes that have come over Josh, as they find him becoming more and more withdrawn, refusing to partake in the life of the community, even refusing to eat, and having terrible nightmares which make him moan at night. He even falls sick. "Maybe is the stranger. He do somet'ing to Josh! He put spirit in de watta," (22) is how they explain it, in a spontaneous identification of the subjective self of the boy with the water of the swirl. The terrible misgivings expressed by them fall on deaf ears. Josh only draws closer to the White Man. The frontiers of the two worlds stretch bringing into existence an overlapping area of collaboration as Josh tells the White Man his secret fears and how he actually saw the monster, secrets which no amount of coaxing by the villagers would bring out. The White Man does not make fun of his hallucinations. Instead he pours over his books mulling over theory after theory in a vain effort to find out at least some hints about such a creature.

The Massacouraman is obviously the objective correlative for what Homi Bhabha would term as the "ominous silence that utters an archaic colonial 'otherness,' that speaks in riddles."[6] It is the inscription "of an uncertain colonial silence that mocks the social performance of language with its nonsense; that baffles the communicable verities of culture with its refusal to translate."[7] It is this refusal to translate itself using the communicable verities of culture which makes the Massacouraman elude the White Man, while Ghulam's refusal to mix up the numinous and the secular brings his quest to fruition. How language fails in its social performance while trying to articulate nonsense and how it has to resort to speaking in riddles and half lost and deformed expressions is seen in the following description of Massacouraman's being brought out of its habitat between the human and not-human into the consciousness of Ghulam:

> He saw something. He wasn't sure what it was. . . . He saw commotion next. He could feel it too, as if it was inside his own bloodstream . . . hot, burning, rioting in his veins.
>
> Ripples spread from one side of the creek to the other. What was it? He looked towards the centre of the commotion. He felt nausea rising in his throat. "Oh Gadd!" he cried our soundlessly. Wha' happenin'?"
>
> Suddenly the middle of the creek rose up like a great mountain, upsetting the vegetation on both banks; even the brush shook and heaved.
>
> "Oh Gadd!" he cried again, out loud this time.
>
> The flashlight fell from his hand, but he could still see the water lifting up, like a living being. A head next, its eyes . . . looking back at him! (40)

The White Man has to go a long way in his understanding of the native to locate the colonial otherness or to understand the question of cultural choice posed by this senseless signifier, namely the Massacouraman. But unknown to himself the journey has already started. He finds that part of his mind which refuses to be ordered by reason, slipping into thoughts his training as a scientist would never endorse. The anteater and the small monkey waiting to be transported arouses metaphysical speculations in him.

Meanwhile the tentacles of the coloniser spread through the society. The village elders cross over to go and peep into the hut of the White Man and ask for Western medicines. Their faith in the healing ripples of the swirl is disturbed. They start looking for strange clues. Assumptions start turning into questions. The Massacouraman's presence is something that they have never addressed before. Now it becomes a question mark: "Was it more than a myth? Real? Something that would appear before their eyes? A mighty snake, crocodile. . . ?" It was no longer something which appeared in their dreams, which they heard at night splashing: "It writhed in their entrails, pain showing in their eyes." (23)

Finally they rise in revolt, their anger snowballing into rebellion when they come upon the caged animals in the White Man's hut. Even Josh and Ghulam, the only persons who recognize the possibility of some good in the White Man, become alienated when they imagine the ultimate horror of the Massacouraman thrashing about in a cage. A second reason is the White Man's declaration that the Massacouraman is dead. It stemmed from them and in a way defined them. It was part of their identity, of what made them odd yet recognizable. The White Man's assertion would mean the colonizer's success in destroying the existing social system, which began with the symbolic trapping of the smaller animals, with a view to replace it with another. Hence they wanted it to be alive. If the choice is between the White Man and the Massacouraman, they would choose the latter.

The White Man's attempt to identify and place within its structure of reality, the colonial consciousness, results in a disturbance, a displacement in the empire's work itself. The foregrouding of the language of the colonial nonsense displaces the dualities into which the colonial space is traditionally divided. In other words, the attempt to study the relationship between the West and its dominated cultural "other" becomes, for the White Man, a point of entry into an understanding of the formation and meaning of Western cultural practices resulting in a disorienting change in his perception of the West-non-West relationship.

In spite of his conscious effort to retain his ties with the Western civilization and its scientific rationalism, he finds himself undergoing a process of evolution towards becoming one with the natives. He is shocked to find himself to have undergone a physical change: "He scowled—he was a scientist! This change of colour would be merely temporary." He becomes dark like a Negro which makes Josh exclaim, "You become like one of we." (34) He finally reaches the point when the conflict within himself becomes unbearable. He desperately needs to separate what is real from what is not. As if to say he has reached the end of his quest, comes his encounter with the monster. He feels the two halves of his self becoming one in his awareness of its terrible beauty. He learns to step out of the self and participate in the sacrament of ritual life. He makes the plunge of initiation into the creek and passes through the village with his clothes covered with mud. All conflicts are removed as he comes to the conclusion: "Why not let things remain the way they were, retaining their mystery, their malevolence too, all through the centuries?" (78)

The change pervades all realms of life. The caged animals have all been set free. Josh plunges into the creek and swims in it as if he has been born in it. The water itself is no longer black. Its opacity gives way to crystalline clarity. And the White Man leaves the village, as it was before his arrival, leaving only a memory behind him. The focus shifts back from the individual to the communal, from the conscious to the instinctual, making the reaffirmation of the native's past, complex, proud, dignified and faithbound, which dwarfs the western sensibility, with its arrogance born out of a superior hold on reason and a sense of mastery over knowledge.

Like the novels of Achebe, or other African novelists like Soyinka or Okara, this novel also chooses as its canvas the testing ground for the native's residence in the context of the collision between two opposing value systems. As a rule, such situations end in the tragedy of the elimination of the less sophisticated, the less ruthless and the less efficient. Even the village around the Dark Swirl faces the threat of being overpowered and exterminated. But almost on the point of no return, the otherness of the native, nurtured and strengthened by long isolation from the processes of civilization, reasserts itself upsetting the relative status of the binary opposites into which colonial space is divided, like nature/culture.

What has been said above more than justifies the study of *Dark Swirl* in the context of Postcolonial Resistance Discourse with which it shares many issues and characteristics. However what it does not share with other works of the genre is what makes the work unique as a study in resistance culture, which is a form of resistance marked by the absorption or subsuming of the colonizer and not by his rejection, resulting in the dominated other becoming the only one reality. The White Man ends up discarding the set of assumed notions, stances, and roles he had brought with him, as part of a process of self discovery. An aesthetic understanding of the native leads dismantling of his prejudices. The White's suppositions about the tribals as savage and inferior fade with an increasing sense of the native's superior hold on his instinctive faculties. Moreover he is required to confront himself as the representative of a culture and race accused of crimes of violence and suppression. "The stranger was no longer a stranger, in mood or spirit." (90)

Thus in a land beyond time and space, the author manipulates reality and illusion to arrest the metaphysical basis of existence as an effective tool of resistance in a context of confrontation between the victim and the victimizer, and stretches the frontiers of the fiction of the colonized by recreating the Utopia of the native.

NOTES

1. Cyril Dabydeen, "Where Doth the Berbice Run," *World Literature Today*, Summer 1994, p. 451.
2. *Ibid.*, p. 454.
3. Cyril Dabydeen, *Dark Swirl* (Yorkshire: Peepal Tree Press, 1987), p. 61.
4. "Where Doth the Berbice run," p. 455.
5. D.C.R.A. Goonetilleke, *Images of the Raj: South Asia in the Literature of the Empire* (London: Macmillan, 1988), p. 5.
6. Homi K. Bhabha, "Articulating the Archaic: Notes on Colonial Non-sense," *Literary Theory Today*, ed. Peter Collier and Helga Geyer-Ryan (Cambridge: Polity Press, 1990), p. 203.
7. *Ibid.*, p. 204.

Two Faces of Solitude: Lawson and Selvon

C.L.L. JAYAPRADA

Two writers with such diverse backgrounds as Lawson who was a second generation settler in Australia and Selvon who is an East-Indian born in West Indies and settled first in England and later in Canada have surprizingly common preoccupations. The lone battlers and underdogs fighting for survival are the central figures both in the faceless city of London portrayed by Selvon and in the daunting spaces of bush depicted in Lawson's short stories. Both the writers are the masters of the use of colloquial language that reflects intimately the rhythms of the lives of these stragglers (or hustlers, to use Selvon's term) and they are also seriously concerned with the existing form of short story, sketch and fiction. The paper proposes to make a comparative study of the themes, language and technique of Lawson and Selvon in their struggle to make a place for themselves in the developing literary traditions.

Lawson was born in 1867 to a father who was a German selector battling to make a living in the Australian bush and a mother whose literary aspirations were being progressively frustrated in the wilderness. The mother was a distant figure in all sketches of childhood by Lawson and perhaps it was she who instilled in him a yearning for higher things in life. Living and working in the bush in grinding poverty and making continual shifts 'to make a go,' Lawson pursued his literary efforts, kept in touch with the literary world and was also forced to do much of hack writing to support himself. He wrote sketches, short stories, journalistic pieces and poetry though his best talent was exhibited in his sketches. Much of the despair that was involved in his struggle to write and sustain his creativity in harrowing circumstances found expression in the images of solitary men battling out in the bush under the grand Australian sun.

The literary situation too was riddled with contradictions in Australia. Harry Heseltine says: "Thrust as it were into a cultural vacuum, without the support of a sanctioned tradition, his central task became that of authenticating his own uncertain self in an unfamiliar world."[1]

There was no known significant literary tradition in Australia when Lawson started writing. At that time, half of the best known writers were English—Henry Kingsley, Marcus Clarke and Gordon—who saw Australia through strangers' eyes and the other half like Henry Kendall, Rolf Bolderwood still wrote unconsciously for the English readership. After Lawson, several significant works were published by Henry Handel Richardson, Kenneth Slessor, Katherine Susanna Prichard and Louis Esson. Lawson was at the centre of the developing literary tradition and for generations of writers he was the most representative Australian writer. He delineated the life of the nation and its characteristics. Both his technique and attitudes contributed to a distinctive national tradition.

Though born in a different clime and time, Selvon also faced similar though not the same contradictions before he achieved a literary identity. Born in 1923 in Trinidad to East Indian working class parents, Selvon worked as a wireless operator with the Royal Naval Reserve in war before he became a journalist. Later he completely devoted himself to creative writing and wrote short stories, novels, T.V. and Radio plays and film scripts.

Apart from personal struggle to rise above limiting circumstances, Selvon also faced severe constrictions and contradictions. The Caribbean islands lack an indigenous culture and the people of different races from various countries of Africa and Asia were brought here as slaves and indentured labour and the people from America and Germany migrated during the world wars. The mingling of several races, cultures and language created a Creole community. The heterogeneity of people, lack of cohesive precolonial history and cultural ambivalence created a sense of uncertainty among the Caribbean writers. The four major writers found different ways to achieve a sense of identity. V.S. Naipaul saw himself as a metropolitan writer and claimed to be a world citizen. George Lamming avowed negritude which became a major theme in his fiction while Wilson Harrison explored the metaphysical questions which are by nature distant from the social reality. Selvon opted for folk tradition which offered to him a wide scope to deal with the 'fluid variety of the West-Indian personality' and it could adequately express the multi-layered identities of the Caribbean consciousness. Selvon's unique contribution to the West Indian literature lies in his powerful blending of folk and oral traditions with the alien language and a distinctively modern form. *The Lonely Londoners* is significant in its use of calypsonian tradition, with its distanced narrator and an episodic structure in the novel form.

In the novel a single narrator Moses Aloetta, one of the early immigrants, tells us genially about various other Caribbean immigrants, their struggle to get work and a place and also to retain their identity in the face of metropolitan pressures. The oppressive winter of London expressed in the bizarre image of "sun without heat hangs in the sky like a force-ripe orange," the indifference or hostility of the whites to coloured people, sometimes overt and sometimes covert, the frustrating efforts to find a job and keep oneself in a job turn many solitary men eccentric or ratty. One can say Selvon's men are bushed in London, which is indifferent to their travails. The narrator while telling us about Galahad, Tolroy, Lewis, Captain, Harris and Small Change brings out their peculiarities and eccentricities. The older immigrants develop a sense of wry and laconic humour and are not far from playing a lark on one of the new immigrants. Moses tells Lewis for fun that the women carry on with the other men, when their husbands go out for night work. Lewis slowly goes berserk being eaten by an unconfirmed suspicion and wrecks his marriage with Agnes while Moses remains ignorant of the effect of his words. In Lawson's story "Iron Bark Chip," the mates play a trick on the Government inspector to deceive him into believing that the wood they are using is iron-bark which the Government requires them to use. There are also many other tricksters who live by their wits and on the friends in straightened up circumstances. For example there are Captain in London and Jim and Stiffner in the bush. These men are of course accepted by their mates because the fun, the tricks and the elaborate pretences (the way they try to pull down Harris at his party) make their otherwise dreary lives bearable. The thoughts of home are not far from the minds of these 'hustlers' in London—the thoughts of rising in life, the possibility of going home rich to a settled life and a re-union with the family, these thoughts make the present misery of these men more poignant.

Similar are the travails of lone battlers in the bush of Henry Lawson. The selector, the drover, the itinerant worker, the larrikin, the sun-downer, the confidence man and the bush philosopher are the images of every man and they are victims of the inhospitable landscape. Some of them face the drought, floods, bush fires one after the other and the experiences and privations leave a mark on the gaunt hungry faces of men, an aged stoic look on the faces of children and hardened lines on the faces of women who lose the charm and bloom of youth too soon. They think of brighter days ahead and hope to return to a nearby town or city to settle one day. The vast bush, the pitiless sun which frustrates human efforts to cultivate the land and the grinding poverty disorient some of the men. The ragged old man in "The Bush Undertaker" talking to the corpse of an old mate, while preparing the dried up corpse for a bush burial is a potent symbol of isolation.

> "Brummy," he said at last, "it's all over now; nothin' matters now—nothin didn't ever matter, nor—nor don't. You uster say as how it 'ud be all right termorrer (pause); termerrer's come, Brummy—come fur you—it ain't come fur me yet, but—it's a comin'."[2]

Galahad finds himself in a similar position in the *Lonely Londoners.* The honesty, sincerity and hard work do not make the coloured people even socially acceptable and the economic discrimination shown in employment is obvious. This puzzles many a new immigrant. When his efforts to talk to a child at a bus stop are subtly rebuffed, Galahad, so named by Moses for showing a brave front always, momentarily loses his head and starts talking to his hand. "Colour, is you that causing all this, you know. Why the hell you can't be blue, or red or green, if you can't be white? You know is you that cause a lot of misery in the world. Is not me, you know, is you, I ain't do anything to infuriate people and them, is you! Look at you, you so black and innocent, and this time so you causing misery all over the world."[3]

The striking rhythms of colloquial speech evoke the berserk figures in the reader's mind and leave behind an imprint. The illiterate speech of the old man and Galahad makes their bewilderment authentic and convincing because they fail to understand the larger forces behind what is happening, and intellectual or philosophical consolations are not available to them.

Lawson and Selvon also depict the depths of degradation to which men can be reduced to by poverty, hunger and isolation. Galahad in winter is reduced to catching pigeons and eating them. To assuage his own guilt, he makes Moses also do so. The bush undertaker, quietly having his dinner while his mate's corpse is perhaps being eaten away in his shanty by an iguana, is of course dehumanized and the image evokes horror.

Sexual frustration too is dominant in the lives of the Londoners and bush figures. Selvon's men are cut off from the families and it would take years of work and saving before they hope to settle down to a married life. They pursue women relentlessly but relations do not mean anything beyond sex. Lawson's men leave behind their women and children in suburbs. When they settle with the women in bush, the travails work on them in such a way that they slowly drift apart in Joe Wilson's stories. Sexual frustrations are depicted by Lawson through powerful images in "Rats." The three travellers sight a man wrestling with another. When they realize it is a woman, they run forward dropping their swags. They encourage the ratty old man to fight with his swag and later humour him when he starts fishing in imagined waters. The wrestling match and the fishing are powerful images and the mates's enthusiastic participation in a neurotic man's activities can be attributed to "displaced male sexuality." (Heseltine, 51)

Thus both Lawson and Selvon depict the lonely men, fighting the battle of life under nightmarish circumstances trying to find a meaning in an essentially fragmented world. Both have exploited the resources of the spoken rhythms, colloquial idiom, non-standard syntax, nicknames for characters (Big City and Small Change in Selvon, Barco-Rot, One-Eyed Regan and the Oracle in Lawson) to authenticate the perspective of the narrator. The presentation in both is dependent on a lean bare style and a controlled selection of facts for sharpening the focus and maximizing the effect. This narrative strategy is related from their conscious rejection of romantic literary conventions. They deliberately debunk popular myths about bush and the blacks.

Lawson's narrative is more in the form of a sketch and he depends more on graphic description of persons and places for evoking a whole perspective of life than on a plot with cause and effect and chronology. Selvon's novel on the other hand, can be seen as a cycle of sketches in which an older immigrant tells us about many others and reminisces about his own first experience of London. The outer and inner links to the sketches are provided by the narrator and the thematic continuity. Selvon also avoids the omniscient mode and presents these lives of the immigrants from the point of view of the narrator or the characters through their own limited vision. Thus through their respective narrative modes and fictional techniques, both Lawson and Selvon bring out the acute loneliness and bewilderment of the men around them and lay bare their fragmented psyche.

NOTES

1. Harry Heseltine, *The Uncertain Self* (Melbourne: Oxford University Press, 1986), p. 2.
2. Brain Kiernan, *Henry Lawson* (St. Lucia: University of Queensland Press, 1976), p. 110.
3. Samuel Selvon, *The Lonely Londoners* (Essex: Longmans, 1956), p. 88.

Topography of the Heartland: An Approach to the Novels of Wilson Harris

S. RAMASWAMY

> Beneath him lay the chasm of the river, volcanic and subdued Above him stood the mountains of lava, worshipful and brooding, a subsidiary ridge of temperament thrusting—as he felt—towards loops of sky and bush. Topography of the heartland.
>
> Wilson Harris, *Ascent to Omai*

I

Wilson Harris uses the word "heartland" to include a number of different things. Nothing is simple and straightforward in the writing of Harris—not even the "simple" act of eating: "He sprinkled the sugar on the biscuits (discarding the mildewed bread) and ate like one conducting a ravenous inward dialogue with a strange principle and sentiment."[1] Naturally, anything which has to do with the "heart" is a much more complex affair, which is what is probed in this essay.

At the literal level the "Heartland" is Guiana itself—the heartland of this Guianan writer, which he explores in his novels:

> A woman had come abruptly out of the bush, Amerindian, midnight hair on her shoulders, so jet-black it looked as if her head-dress was one perpetual plait of stroke of mourning. Her eyes were sad, blacker than numerals of ink and yet devoid of the sinister humour of self-pity. It was a feature of unsentimentality she had inherited from her mother's tribe in the Brazilian/Guianan heartland. (62)

"Heartland" also refers to the human heart itself and it is the unique way in which Harris explores this "heartland" that gives his fiction a universal appeal as well as a special place among novelists for his extraordinarily individualistic approach to language as well as experience and makes him one of the most significant novelists writing today. Speaking of the central character of this novel Harris says: "The barren fear grew in him that he might be inwardly consenting to an improvident thick which dispossessed him of everything and everyone transcendental and there might be nothing at all within the storehouse of the heartland." (28) It is this "barren fear" that harasses the characters of Harris so that they fear that their "heartland" is a wasteland: "This was the controversial question of subsistence—in the significant consciousness of every observer—wasteland or heartland." (72)

The nature of the "dream" of "every dreamer"—the characters of Wilson Harris—is explored by him in "the language of the heartland":

> The open-and-closed shutter of dream, the bitter cry in the night, the language of the heartland, relying as it did upon a curious jigsaw of intangible resources, set in viable perspective, matching darkness and light, by the recurring implosion of a sound or a word, was capable of claiming the unique eye and voice of the animal in the mind, drawing one to an appreciation of constructive mission or creative meaning which lay in consuming every total act of self-evident choice of precipitate order, chaos or diversity. (88)

This provides a clue to the approach to the language of Wilson Harris in his novels. Thus "heartland" refers to the exploration of Guiana and the exploration of the human heartland of emotions. Guiana is both geographical entity—an external reality as well as interior landscape in the novels of Harris. We find, for example:

> There was a poor village he knew on the Pomeroon (if one scanned the map of Guiana one might find it) named Charity.[2]
>
> The Empyre of Guiana is directly cast from Peru towards the sea and lieth under the Equinoctial line and it hath more abundance of Golde than any part of Peru and as many more great Cities than ever Peru had when it flourished most: it is governed by the same lawes and the Emperor and people observe the same religion and the same forme and policies in government as was used in Peru, not differing in any part: and as I have been assured by such of the Spanyardes as have seen Manoa the emperiall Citie of Guiana, which the Spanyardes call El Dorado, that for the greatnes, for the riches and for the excellent seate, it farre exceedest any of the world, at least such of the world as is known to the

> Spanish nation: it is founded upon a lake of salt water of 200 leagues long like Vuto mare Caspin.[3]

This device of giving the historical, tourist-guide description of Guiana leads inevitably to the Guiana of the heartland:

> Perhaps it had started at the very outset when he and Petra (she had given herself this new name, Amerindians were famous for adopting a diversity of titles) were struggling across a faint landscape in the dream like company of ghostly pursuers. A faint landscape it was because of the eclipse of time, the end of a long hazardous phase of discovery and conquest, an eclipse which allowed a light otherwise too reticent for brightness to illumine the pilot of the mind. This faintness was akin to a constellation of renewal and rebirth appearing for this age and time in the underworld sky of the jungle and upon a horizon which coincided with the end of empires when the darkness of rule becomes the absolute light of consciousness. Such involuntary associations—subtler than conventional upbringing and station would allow—were real for the woman she was: real in the way every symbolic jungle becomes to those who are steeped in the intimate species of its inhabitants until the vision of what is buried and alive suddenly transcends a fixed limb or region of historical value. (66-67)

Sometimes the two levels—the external and the internal—are telescoped together:

> "Pomeroon is the best place to be born to know this whole country, the whole of Guiana, British, Dutch, French, everything." He waved his hands. "First, to know we're all mixed up, East, West, North, South, every race under the sun, second, to know that what we possess comes from the ground up—cocoanut, copra, plantain, banana, wood-grant, sawmill (don't forget Pomeroon is a nursery of boatbuilders, think of the lively schooners as well as the sturdy seamen) . . . we've got to pick up the seeds again where they left off. It's no use worshipping the rottenest tacouba and tree-trunk in the historic top-soil. There's a whole world of branches and sensation we've missed and we've got to start again from the roots up if they look like nothing. Blood, sap, flesh, veins, arteries, lungs, heart, the heartland. We're the first potential parents who can contain the ancestral house.[4]

This is an exceptionally straightforward, "emotional" passage about the "heartland" in what has been described as a "political" novel, *The Whole Armour*. After this speech of Cristo, Harris writes, "He had forgotten himself, waving his hands gesticulàting. He stopped all of a sudden, his heart racing wild." This is perhaps what has happened to Harris at this point because he rarely "forgets himself' if ever! A few pages after this:

> Cristo roused himself. It wasn't Pomeroon I was in a far forest. The earth looked like Cuyuni . . . really heartland ground. . . .
>
> "The heartland, I see."
>
> "I don't know. Must have been Pomeroon after all. But far above and inside." (119)

Yes, the heartland of Harris is "above" as well as "inside." But it is really the "inside" that Harris is primarily concerned with. At the end of his novel *Heartland*, he has a "Postscript":

> Zechariah Stevenson disappeared somewhere in the Guianan/Venezuelan/Brazilian jungles that lie between the headwaters of the Cuyuni and Potaro rivers.
>
> In the half-burnt down shell of the small resthouse where he was last seen by a couple of pork-knockers was found a bundle of scorched papers: when pieced together they grew into fragments of letters to one Maria—three shattered poems, two (*Troy* and *Amazon*) practically destroyed and the other (*Behring Straits*) so browned by fire that some of the lines were indistinguishable. (93)

However, four lines from the poem *Amazon* may be quoted here as being relevant in the present context:

> This living jungle is too filled with voices
> not to be aware of collectivity
> and too swift with unseen wings
> to capture certainty. (95)

It is with this "living jungle too filled with voices," and "too swift with unseen wings to capture certainty" that we can concern ourselves now in the exploration of the heartland—through characterization in Harris.

In the "Postscript" to the Author's Note of *The Waiting Room*, Harris writes: "In the text following I have used inverted commas around 'he' to emphasize that the lover in Susan's memory was indeed sheer phenomenon of sensibility rather than identical character in the conventional sense."[5] This is typical of the characters in Harris because they are more easily decipherable as "phenomena of sensibility" rather than characters in the "conventional" sense. There is a great deal of fluidity in Harris's approach. The characters live in a fusion of the past and the present and the extraordinary liberties that Harris takes with the concepts of time and place, Illusion/Intuition and Reality that even his central "characters" can only be talked about as the central sensibility of the novel. As Ramchand puts it, "Harris has no interest in his central figures as individuals."[6] In his *Ascent to Omai* "all roles were interchangeable—judge, judged, victor, victim, Adam etc., as parts of a broken translation and legacy of history." (83) The characters of Harris are placed in that "emptied out condition on the edge of self-discovery" which is worked out "through a process of memory."[7] When we look at the movement in Harris's fiction, it seems as though his characters become less and less real as we move from *Palace of the Peacock* (1960) to *Ascent to Omai* (1970) through *The Whole Armour* (1962), *Heartland* (1964) and *The Waiting Room* (1967).

II

A reference to just two passages from *Palace of the Peacock* is enough to illustrate characterization in this novel. The boat's crew that beats its way up-river through the Guianese jungles and rapids towards an Amerindian settlement is described at the beginning of the novel:

> The crew swarmed like upright spiders, half-naked, scrambling under a burden of cargo they were carrying ashore. First I picked and counted the da-Silva twins of Sorrow Hill, long-legged, fair-skinned, of Portuguese extraction. Then I spotted old Schomburgh also of Sorrow Hill, agile and swift as a monkey for all his seasoned years. Donne prized Schomburgh as a bowman, the best in all the world his epitaph boasted and read. There was Vigilance, black-haired Indian, sparkling and shrewd of eye, reading the river's mysterious book. Vigilance had recommended Carroll, his cousin, a thick-set young Negro boy gifted with his paddle as if it were a violin and sword together in paradise. My eye fell on Cameron, brick-red face, slow feet, faster than a snake in the forest with his hands; and Jennings, the mechanic, young, solemn featured, carved out of still wood, it seemed, sweating still the

> dew of his tears, cursing and reproving his whirling engine and toy in the unearthly terrifying grip in the water. Lastly I counted Wishrop, assistant bowman and captain's understudy.[8]

This is as clear, graphic and straightforward a description as can be found in any novel dealing with a boat crew—in Melville or Conrad. The attention to physical detail and the accuracy with which the background of each character is sketched shows Harris as a gifted describer of realistic detail. This approach is still evident in his description of the Amerindian woman who is forced to be the guide for the crew:

> We had in our midst a new member sitting crumpled-looking, like a curious ball, old and wrinkled. Her long black hair—with the faintest glimmer of silvery grey—hung in two plaits down to her waist. She sat still as a bowing statue, the stillness and surrender of the American Indian of Guiana in reflective pose. Her small eyes winked and blinked a little. It was an emotionless face. The stiff brooding materiality and expression of youth had vanished and now—in old age—there remained no sign of former feeling. There was almost an air of crumpled pointlessness in her expression, the air of wisdom that a millennium was past, a long timeless journey was finished without appearing to have begun and no show of malice, enmity and overt desire to overcome oppression and evil mattered any longer. She belonged to a race that neither forgave nor forgot. (71)

It is this kind of fairly conventional attitude to characterization that gradually gives place to what can be recognized as the typical Harris approach.

There are six characters in *The Whole Armour* who are in search of the author Harris—Abram, Magda, Cristo, Peet, Mattias and Sharon of whom Magda is the most impressive and almost awe-inspiring. She is introduced right at the beginning of the novel:

> A strong black skin of a woman, polished like mahogany, approaching forty. Chinese eyes, emotionless in expression and filled with the blackest unshed tears. Barefoot. The columns of her legs were sculptured to stand out from the loose formless miraculous stone of her dark body and dress, unadorned and plain. (12)

Soon we become aware of her toughness, her "black disdainful smile,"

(28) "her studied casualness," "cruel bitterness," her "unpredictable style of a great cat," (33) "black ingenuity and brutal pride" (39)—all of which congeal into her "brutal maternal instinct" (42) which is the guiding force of her entire character. Her son Cristo "was of medium height, slenderly built, poise of a dancer. High questioning cheek-bones, penetrating eyes, a restless way of shaking hands and wrists, the sensitive, nervous shuddering joints and limbs of a sprinter, at the start of a race." (16) The accuracy of this description at the beginning is realized by the reader when he understands that Cristo is really the man on the run. He is running throughout the novel—literally as well as metaphorically. The "slender build" and the "limbs of a sprinter" along with the "poise of a dancer" are naturally important in a novel in which the "tiger" and the jaguar play such an important symbolic role. In about two-dozen references to the "tiger" throughout the novel—incidentally, one of the mottos Harris chooses for Book Three of his novel "Time of the Tiger" is the first two lines of Blake's famous poem. However this prototype of the running man becomes "the universal bridegroom of love, pierced by all the ecstacy of constructive innocence." (78)

Peet is the third interesting character of the novel. His story is quietly tucked away in a paragraph towards the end of the novel because the "facts" of a story are not important for Harris. It is a characteristic of the narrative technique of Harris that one has to search carefully in his novels if one insists on finding the story line.

> Peet knew he had failed in some profound inexplicable way and he returned with his mind full of the gnawing spirit of disaster. The entire expedition took their cue from him and turned back. He came home to learn that while he was away his wife (whom he jealously loved and madly adored) had slipped and fallen heavily upon the landing by the river. She was a delicate woman, six to seven months gone in pregnancy. She had been rushed to the Government Hospital at Suddie on the Arabian coast. At first it had seemed she would be all right, then a variety of complications developed like a whiff of one's breath—the spirit of mother and child had gone. (85)

This straightforward narration—which is rare in Harris—leads us to the realization that this individual is also a type—"a hearty old school pioneer." (86) Thus not merely do we realize that even comparatively straight "characters" serve a double purpose but these characters are double people! Characters have a way of "sliding" into each other in

Harris—Abram and Peet, Madga and Sharon, and Cristo and Mattias.

> Time had stopped, he thought with a premonition of the future, looking into Peet's extinguished eyes; it started again with a gasp as if the mask of Abram had returned to play once again an evolving and still accusing part. *It was Abram who stood before him.* Mattias closed his eyes. When he opened them again Peet was replying to the remark about the drought in the Pomeroon as though there had been no interval whatever of monstrous identity and the eternal bridge stretched across limbo—from the "dead" to the "living"—had always been there, conjoint with time and eternity. (68)

> Sharon could not help shrinking a little in her skin at the memory of her every limb and bond of extremity, as when the serial dreadful vision of Magda and herself fused into one. It had all melted with tenderness and she had gained the reins of freedom. (81)

> "Mattias's father worshipped him," Sharon said unsmilingly. "And Magda worshipped you. One was father's boy and the other was mother's boy. Something magnetic and psychological in that." "The unstable twins, eh? Ah well the old folk are saying it." (107)

Thus in Harris, characterization does not work only at the level of describing individuals but the individuals fuse into complex types peculiar to the region and finally there is a perfect fusion of landscape, cultural history and life of man in one unified sensibility.

> It was along this very mysterious backbone and watershed—between ancient terror and new-born love—that the frightful jaguar of death had roamed, leaping across emotional tumbling rivers from crag to crag, across Devil's Hole Rapids and the Nameless Falls, greenheart ravines steaming with mist, blue mountains frowning in cloud, coming from as far as the heart of Brazil into Venezuela's Orinoco and Guiana's Potaro, Mazaruni, Cuyuni and Pomeroon. Her fingers travelled across the map of Cristo's skin, stroking the veins in every ancestor's body. It sought to establish the encounter with the lost soul of all generations, the tiger roaming through the trackless paths, rapping at every jungle door, calling to the sweet meat belonging to the dead sleeping flesh of

> night, pausing by every pool of meditation. (82)

This passage amply illustrates the nature and place of characterization in his novels. Added to this level, he also fuses the myth and legend of the area with the literary associations drawn from his enormous repertoire of English literature. In his novel, *The Whole Armour*, for example, he has used Blake's "Tiger" most effectively by fusing it with the legendary "tiger" of the geographical area about which he is writing. Nor merely is Book Three of his novel entitled "Time of the Tiger" with the motto from Blake's poem—"Tiger, tiger, burning bright/In the forests of the night"—but throughout the novel—in about twenty-five references to the tiger—he has explored to the full all the possible ways in which symbol, metaphor, myth, legend, literary allusion and historical perspective can be fused into an extremely "poetical" statement about the condition of man. This is evident in the way in which he has handled the character of Petra in *Heartland*:

> Here was a strong and primitive woman, with the strength of rock and of naked eloquence and element only the truly inarticulate possess because they are capable of invoking the image of every man's conception and misconception of misfortune. . . . Thus it was—like a numinous boulder informed by legs and arms as well as by the universal heart of man—Petra struggled to rise and resume the journey of the past which had begun the very day she crossed the everlasting plateau. (71)

The Waiting Room has three "characters"—Susan Forrestal, her husband and her lover. But this is a very strange *menage a trois* situation in fiction because Harris's fiction itself is "strange." As he himself puts it: "By fiction I do not mean to deny certain literal foundations but rather to affirm these absolutely as a mutual bank or living construction of events." (9) The nature of characterization in this novel can be understood in terms of the narrative technique adopted by Harris here:

> *The Waiting Room* is based on the disjoined diary of the Forrestals which came into my hands many years ago. Susan Forrestal described this diary in one section as "her husband's log book" but it would appear that she and possibly others were engaged in an art of fiction peculiar to themselves. (9)

This novel is introduced by Harris himself in what he calls the

"Author's Note." Complicated as his other novels are plot-wise and structurally, this novel would be even more complex without the Note. However, we realize that this note is an integral part of the narrative technique of Harris and not an "external" explanation of what happens in the novel. The novel is printed in three different lettering—the usual, the capitals and the italics. Though this in itself is not unusual in a Harris novel the italics here, among other things, are important to understand the character of Susan as the "present" action is parenthetically indicated by the use of the italics—e.g., "Susan drew the palm of her hand slowly across her face as if it had turned to stone," (17) "Susan made an involuntary gesture upon the page of her book," (33) "Susan lit a match and placed it against the eyes of the *living* doll still lying at her feet," (35) "Susan fished for the glasses which she had laid aside an hour or two ago," (38) "Susan moved—inclined her head a little and listened to the sudden disconcerting impact of silence—savage as a blow in itself—which had fallen all at once upon her in *The Waiting Room*." (38) These references to Susan in the novel punctuate the narrative flow and make Susan come alive as a "real" person and the reader's reverie of Susan's reverie is given a local habitation and a name. This is necessary because the lover is Susan's memory of him. He is referred to as "he" in inverted commas and "his" habitat is inside Susan's skull. As Harris puts it, "Through the blind or curtained window where 'he' sat and watched FROM WITHIN HER SKULL, the tops of vehicles could be seen as they passed." (15) The lover is "dumb": "If she was blind it was fitting that he should be dumb." (35) The form of this novel, indeed the clue to the art of Harris in this novel cannot be better expressed than in Harris's own words in his Note:

> Susan and her husband (mention of whom does not clearly occur until Book 2) died in an explosion which wrecked their home and much of their belongings, antiques, ornaments, etc. The log book survived though certain sections were half obliterated. . . . But this—while apparently depleting continuity—only served to enhance the essential composition of the manuscript that involved accidental deletions or deliberate erasures, reappraisals, marginal notes, dissociations of likely material (as well as associations of unlikely material) to confirm and blend into, a natural medium of invocation in its own right. And this disproportionate, sometimes shocking condition, was the world in particular of Susan Forrestal. (10)

Indeed, the world of Susan Forrestal couldn't be explored in any other manner than the way Harris has done. We know that "Susan suffered from an incurable complaint of the eyes and after three operations became almost totally blind." (9) But this is interesting in the context of characters sliding into each other in Harris, referred to earlier in *The Whole Armour*. Here the doctor and lover are rolled into one and the non-realistic/symbolic level of characterization in Harris becomes clear:

> Doctor and lover rolled into one. He approached her, pistol in hand, dealer in menaces and self-deceptions whose object it was to sell her to the highest bidder—shatter her, riddle her, grind her—lens as well as drum, eye of crystal and crunch of bone, deck of reality, ship of illusion. And she appeared to submit to him—to his craft of fire and nature—in order to unfurl a new sail and conviction: she drew him in, held him up, thicket of storm, as if he were her eternal sculpture of overcoming fear and she his eternal flag and quarry—LADY OF THE BEASTS.(43)

The "log-book" of the "husband"—to which there are half a dozen references in the novel—is a part of the design of *The Waiting Room* as has been inferred from a reference to it in the Author's Note. But the nature of the log book itself is important as the nature of the title—to which there are twenty references in the novel—itself is. For the nature of the experience of Harris's characters—how much of it is happening in the external phenomenal world and how much of it is all in their mind, in their memory safely locked—only Harris holds the key.

> She began to trace the narrative title upon a further page of the log-book. . . . The borderline features which she summoned, part-veiled, part-exposed, were half-subject, half-object of each other—displayed by each other within "living" room, "waiting" room, equally substantial as frail, animate as inanimate within a yielding train of capacity that erected "objective" goals, "subjective" barriers, whose "inner" openness and "outer" obduracy of conviction was but one involuntary spectre. (63)

About the significance of the "waiting room" only one reference out of a score of them in the novel should suffice.

> The "waiting" room—part-present, part-past, part-future, it

> seemed—was falling through the dust of space, axe of memory, chopping sea, flying chip or vessel whose strain, leash, trough and course had become participle of its own crust and loaf—headless plunge . . . ocean . . . devouring perspective, joint, ground (mill of the gods), "vanished" species, felled season. (54)

The proper approach the reader should make to this novel is indicated in the novel itself:

> And in fact sometimes it appeared to her that time had grown to design the log-book to achieve this very end in time—to assume the symbolic proportions of a raft which she was grateful to the past and the present for establishing in the phenomenal tide of a medium of cleavage existing in its own true abandoned structure and right. (61-62)

Right at the beginning of this novel we find a short passage in between two asterisk marks: "She drew him closer still within the skin of another incongruous skeleton they shared, flesh or wood, swimming in the glass of their shop window within and without. Antique display. Waiting Room." (17) This passage is repeated word for word right at the end of the novel. In fact this is the last sentence of the novel with a title "Page 17." (80) This gives a rounding-off effect to the novel indicating that our end is our beginning. It is interesting indeed that Wilson Harris uses this very expression—from Eliot in the novel, "In our end is our beginning." (70) In fact, one of the mottos for this novel is a line from T.S. Eliot: "a moment of exhaustion, of appeasement, of absolution, and of something very near annihilation." (6)

But it is really in *Ascent to Omai* that the non-realistic approach to the novel ascends into the completely symbolic. In the middle of the novel, there is a figure—a figure of concentric circles. It is this figure that figuratively "explores the horizons of stone". because the "stone" is in the midst of all. These "horizons" are represented by the eight concentric circles round the stone. The figure is explained by Harris himself in the novel when he writes: "victor's immersion, in constructing the tree of night was symbolic of spaces—sea, land, air: unchartered seas upon which the drama of puberty visualized half-obscurely, half-clearly all the concentric horizons of the stone—petticoat, whale, rose, iron-mask, parrot, raven, baboon, madonna." (101)

In the final section of the novel entitled "Dance of the Stone," Harris explores this symbolic structure. Only two of these, the fourth and the fifth—the parrot and the raven—will be mentioned here. Harris writes, "The fourth and fifth movements of the dance of the stone (popularly called parrot and raven) have also been adumbrated in this novel as complex heralds of landscape of time." (119-20) There are many such "complex heralds" in the novels of Harris. In fact, the entire curve of Harris is one "complex herald." However, it is this preoccupation with Time—one of the major themes of modern fiction from James Joyce to Faulkner—that makes the work of Harris fascinating. A brief reference to the theme of Time in *Ascent to Omai* is in order at this point in time! The just quoted reference to the "landscape of time" is followed by this passage:

> The judge's cards and sketches were a symbolic equivalent to the Mexican sheaf of time, series of time. . . . There was, however, a profound distinction the judge wished to imply in his vision of time vis-a-vis the ancient Mexican obsession with a sheaf or game. The distinction was an important one. It could be stated in this way: the Mexicans—precisely because they wished to conscript time on a material base—were drawn every fifty two years by their fear that time had to be manufactured afresh (the game needed to commence afresh) or it would slip from their grasp forever.
>
> Thus they seized on a victim—on flesh and blood as their fortress or factory of time—and tore the living heart out as from a rabbit, stuffed rabbit. Then by firing this base they greeted the bank of the sun as a new dawn, newly-minted time. . . . The judge on the other hand, precisely because he wished a qualitative illumination to emerge in his novel history rather than a quantitative bank of time, saw—beforehand into the unique density and transparency of his victim (spectral character and dust) and refrained therefore from inflicting a senseless ordeal on what was in essence the ghost of the universe, serial participation in time, universal subsistence of memory. (120-21)

This entire passage, word for word is found earlier in the same novel. (84-85) This is surely not just an illustration of "subsistence of memory!" But an illustration of Harris's more than "Mexican" obsession with time. Besides, repetition of one of his own passages later is not new in Harris—a similar occurrence has been referred to earlier with reference to *The Waiting Room*. However, the more than half a dozen references to Time in various ways in this novel alone, taken in the context of his concept of time in his various novels, leaves one in no doubt about Harris's "disregard for the usual conventions of time."[9] The tyranny of Time is referred to by calling it a "spectre of humanity." This same expression used more than once in the novel (80) and humanity is a "prisoner of time." (81) Harris refers to the "fear or longing that time, obscure time, would bring all things to a close. Obscure time." (83-84) He also talks about "a material predilection for storing time as well as *angst* at the leakage of time." He mentions "soaring higher in a curious chamber of time," (84) and he tries to make a distinction between "dead time" and "living time":

> Dead time is stored energy which may have a catastrophic explosive significance (in terms of overlong repression, depression, oppression): living time is that power or medium of presence one can summon at any stage to commune with and compensate the past. They begin to learn, as it were, that the spectre of time is something they cannot conscript whatever stamp or seal they manufacture. (108)

Harris's preoccupation with Time is present even in his earliest work referred to in this essay, *Palace of the Peacock*, though the language in which it is expressed is different: "It was as if something had snapped again, a prison door, a chain and a rush and flight of appearances jostled each other—past, present and future in one constantly vanishing and reappearing cloud and mist." (48) Or, "Time had no meaning. The room was as old as a cave and as new as a study. The walls—whether of glass or stone or wood—were thicker than the stratosphere." (133) The completely symbolic and metaphorical level of the novel *Ascent to Omai* cannot be better illustrated than by making a reference to the title itself and what it means. There are some twenty-five references to this in the novel but only three of them will be picked here for purposes of illustration:

> OH MY, Victor laughed like a man bereft of his wits yet same as a clown. OMAI. . . .
> OH MY was a mushroom settlement far beneath the spectral watershed of Guyana, Amazon/Orinoco. Some said it was really OMAI—an Amerindian root word—subconscious foreboding. Others that a clown like Victor had invoked the substitution of OH MY/OMAI. To forge a treaty of sensibility. English/Amerindian. Conquerer/conquered. Free/Enslaved. Richman/Porknocker. Translation of the stigmata of the watershed. Was it a mirage of the

> senses, ruined faculty but therapeutic lighthouse, OPUS CONTRA NATURAM? (20)

This single quotation shows the nature of the writing of Harris—his remarkable powers of compression and working through the evocation of the association of ideas. It is the use of the final Latin expression that leads us to the further definition of the scope of "omai":

> This was a prison of reality (or irreality) in which Adam dwelt. Futuristic robot. Ruined porknocker. Insensible soul, insensible insurrection, insensible bone, insensible nerve. It was as if he had already ceased to exist and Victor's journey in search of him possessed an order of fatality—"immaterial" adventure of the soul, OPUS CONTRA NATURAM. (42)

It is this "adventure of the soul" that is expressed in the third quotation:

> The longest seas inundate his negative body, the spiritual explorer
> by many shores of memory: the bright wares are light
> like feathers upon his wide eyes.
>   Darkness falls in strange alarms
> like bells off San Salvador (music he heard in
>   imagination reached Columbus
> was like a chorus of the dead
> reiterating old crimes for new discovery)
>   And sunset or sunrise
> was discovered equally guarding the mountain of his heart. (24)

The quintessential words here are "the spiritual explorer," "shores of memory" and "the mountain of his heart." This is indeed what Harris is doing in his novels. He is the spiritual explorer who is taking us along on this journey, voyage, ascent, descent—after all "the mind has mountains, sheer fall, no man fathomed"—through shores of memory—our associations literal as well as literary—to the mountain of the exploration of the heartland.

III

The achievement of Wilson Harris as a novelist can be understood in terms of his own intentions and what he wants to do. This can be summed up in two stages—one, through appropriate quotations from his novel *Ascent to Omai* where he makes one of his characters give expression to his idea of the novel and secondly by quoting Harris's direct statement in his "Tradition and the West Indian Novel." First let us look at a few sentences in his novel *Ascent to Omai*.

> My intention, in part, is to repudiate the vicarious novel . . . where the writer, following a certain canon of clarity, claims to enter the most obscure and difficult terrain of experience without incurring a necessary burden of authenticity, obscurity or difficulty at the same time. (96)

> He wanted, he knew, to write a kind of novel or novel history in which the spectre of time was the main character and the art of narrative the obsessed ground/lighthouse of security/insecurity. (83)

The intention of writing this kind of a novel results in tackling a subject matter which had "Something to do with the buried tongues of consciousness, African, Manoan ancestors, limbo dancers of Albouystown, the masked dead of several continents and centuries." (91) In this exploration, Harris's characters assume a very unusual aspect:

> The judge shuffled his sketches and cards. There stood Victor within schooldoor marked prospects and futures: Alternatives. Shuffled his sketches again. There—thought the judge—stands primary mask and clown, scholar: life-mask death-mask. Born during World War in a British Colony on the coastlands of South America. Steeped in the three R's. One foot in two M's—(mathematics and mythology), the other in a single L (Latin)—residual functions of Pythagoras and Homer. Caesar and Hannibal. Shuffled his sketches again. One hand on an expurgated series, English history and literature. The other on limbo pavement—East Indian/African folk tales, stories of porknocker/sailor/welder/El Dorado, charcoal limbs, artist's wall in the market place. (124-25)

This is truly Wilson Harris the novelist shuffling his cards. In order to record "silent voices he felt beneath everyone and everything: mute sensations (Cezanne would have called them 'ma petite sensation')." (78) Harris deliberately chooses an approach to language which is all his own: "Language for him, therefore, was a vision of consciousness as if what one dreams of in the past is there with a new reality never so expressive before because nothing stands now to block the essential intercourse of its parts, however mute, however irrelevant." (78)

These passages from his novel *Ascent to Omai*, give us an idea of Harris's approach to fiction. However, let us turn to the direct statement that Harris himself has made in his lecture entitled "Tradition and the West Indian Novel":

> The novel of persuasion rests on grounds of apparent commonsense: a certain 'selection' is made by the writer, the selection of items, manners, uniform conversation, historical situations etc., all lending themselves to build and present an individual span of life which yields self-conscious and fashionable judgements, self-conscious and fashionable moralities. The tension which emerges is the tension of individuals—great or small—on an accepted plane of society we are persuaded has an inevitable existence.[10]

Wilson Harris is not interested in writing this kind of a novel. As Ramchand points out:

> The novel of persuasion, Harris might argue, with its commitment to ordinary linear time, to the creation of finite characters and to the portrayal of a self-sufficient social world with reference to which characters are valued, indulges a one-sided view of human life, a restricted vision of human capacities. Harris's disregard for the usual conventions (time, character, social realism) in the novel arises from an almost literal-minded obsession with expressing intuitions about the "person." . . . He sees these intuitions, however, as being of particular and immediate concern in the West Indies. . . . Harris would hardly imagine this to be an exclusive West Indian property, but such a conception of the person seems natural in the West Indies where so many different cultures and peoples have interacted on each other.[11]

It is this "heartland" that has been explored by Harris in his novels. We have seen at the beginning of this essay how the word "heartland" is used in a number of different ways. After having explored these with reference to five of his novels we conclude our visit to the heartland of Harris, "the landscape of history is constructed by a daemon of the heartland." (18) From this "landscape of history" we move to meet "the ruined porknocker face to face, *doppelganger* of the heartland." (19) This "landscape" and this "porknocker" are explored through the unique style of Harris, "A trail which moved within humid and arid cycles of memory. Forbidden Cycles of the Heartland." (23) As a result of this survey of the novels of Harris, we too, like the judge in *Ascent to Omai* get an aerial view of "silver pavement, gold pavement, sulphur pavement, continent or heartland washed by a sea of cloud" (125) in short, the topography of the Heartland.

NOTES

1. Wilson Harris, *Heartland* (Faber and Faber), pp. 86-87.
2. Wilson Harris, *Ascent to Omai* (Faber and Faber), p. 19.
3. *Ibid*., pp. 57-58.
4. Wilson Harris, *The Whole Armour* (Faber and Faber), pp. 108-10.
5. Wilson Harris, *The Waiting Room* (Faber and Faber), p. 11.
6. Kenneth Ramchand, *The West Indian Novel and Its Background* (Faber and Faber), p. 11.
7. *Ibid.*
8. Wilson Harris, *Palace of the Peacock* (Faber and Faber), pp. 22-23.
9. Kenneth Ramchand, "Preface" to *Palace of the Peacock*, p. 3.
10. "Tradition and the West Indian Novel," *Tradition, the Writer and Society* (New Beacon, 1967), quoted by Kenneth Ramchand, "Preface" *Palace of the Peacock*, pp. 1-2.
11. Ramchand, "Preface," *Palace of the Peacock*, p. 3.

Archetypal Confrontations: Jean Rhys's *Wide Sargasso Sea*

MADHUMALATI ADHIKARI

Charlotte Bronte, the original conceiver of Antoinette Cosway Rochester subscribes to Emily Dickinson's view and places her marginal character Bertha/Antoinette with the female players of an archetypal tune:

> I told my soul to sing—
> She said her Strings were snapt—
> Her bow—to Atoms blown. "The First Day's Night"[1]

Contrarily, Jean Rhys in *Wide Sargasso Sea* reconstructs and modifies the image of her female protagonist Antoinette and moves her from the periphery to the centre believing in: "Woman/you not a noplace/anonymous/girl."[2] The portrait of Bertha/Antoinette in *Jane Eyre* as "a self-immolating colonial subject for the glorification of the colonizer"[3] is erased by Rhys who was moved by Bertha Rochester's story: "I thought I'd try to write her a life."[4] Even though Rhys has concentrated on depicting "the world outside which, say what you like, can be a black and cruel world," (146) yet she has not circumscribed her experience and awareness within this narrow enclosure. The story narrated from the point of view of three characters, Antoinette, Rochester and Grace Poole (Bertha's caretaker in Thornfield), remarkably widens the perspective. It is true that Bertha's fate is sealed by Bronte and yet, Rhys succeeds in universalizing the problems of Antoinette and Rochester, the twin victims caught in the diversity of archetypal confrontations.

Rhys combines personal experiences with psychological and emotional awareness to portray various forms of contrariety between Man and Woman, black and white, the hunter and the hunted, the master and the slave, the rich and the poor, the colonizer and the colony and good and evil. The perception from the standpoint of the "self" and the "other" cannot but stand in opposition. Various patterns of antagonisms related to race, sex, culture, class, power and temperament, to name a few, spring from the primal competition and jealousy between the privileged and the under-privileged. This paper intends to scrutinize the heterogeneity of archetypal conflicts of man in society as mirrored by Rhys in *Wide Sargasso Sea*. Thus, it is not limited by the feminist point of view.

Wide Sargasso Sea, a psycho-historical novel, draws heavily from Rhys's childhood ordeals of Jamaica and the agonizing adult experiences of England. The title itself evokes the memory of the treacherous patriarchy, apparently inviting like the Sargasso Sea but latently subverting and suffocating. A woman's life, more often than not, is encircled by a metaphorical Sargasso sea but in this novel, the man is also caught in its turbulent waters.

Jean Rhys, in the novel, vindicates the stand of a white Creole woman Antoinette and reconstructs her life to win back our sympathy lost in *Jane Eyre*. She, a daughter of a slave owning West Indian Creole family faces alienation, isolation and animosity from different quarters as her social position and psychological condition is eroded by the abolition of the plantation culture, a result of the Emancipation Bill of 1834. A product of the decadent culture, she is resented by the recently freed slaves. The racial and cultural distancing takes horrendous dimensions. Her widowed mother Annette remarries Mr. Mason in desperation. Antoinette's lonely childhood in restored Coulibri partially remains safe till it is burnt down by the blacks in a fit of frenzy. Her imbecile younger brother is burnt alive and her mother becomes mad due to the shock. Uprooted from the soul nourishing environment, she an "outcaste" and an "outsider" is sent to a convent. For sometime, it remains her "refuge" but despite its "shimmering colour," she "soon forgets about happiness" as it is very often overwhelmed with "shadows." (47) At the age of seventeen, she is again destabilized and the parental veto compels her to marry an impoverished Englishman, Edward Rochester who turns out to be a fortune hunter. His conflict with his wife is aggravated because of a deep cultural separation and his incompetency in coping with her sexuality. Poisoned by gossips, he attempts to negate her identity by rechristening her as Bertha Rochester. Her removal to Thornfield, his country house, in cold England is his abject manipulation to undermine his wife's confidence and to restore his damaged ego. Imprisoned Antoinette sets fire to the house, leaps from the battlements of Thornfield to meet Tia, the black girl from her childhood.

Jean Rhys has projected the mythical generality of trapped mankind through the specific conflicts in the text. The objectifying power of art finds expression through subtle images that frames various encounters.

Wide Sargasso Sea mirrors not only women's predicaments (though it is the dominant theme) but also a man's confrontation with society at different levels. For the sake of convenience, I will like to divide my contentions in two components: the first intimately related with Antoinette and the second with Rochester.

I

Part one of the novel is narrated by the female protagonist Antoinette. She begins, "They say when trouble comes close ranks, and so the white people did." (15) The black community identifies the white people with trouble. The very second sentence is "We [Antoinette and her mother] were not in the ranks." (15) The statement reveals clearly their isolation and peripheral position in society. Unfortunately, they are ignored by the whites and the blacks because of their poor financial condition, "they notice clothes, they know about money." (16) The black natives often torment them by yelling, "White cockroaches, go away, go away. No body want you." (20) She the "white nigger often wonder[s] who I am and where is my country and where do I belong, and why was I ever born at all." (85) She gets the taste of the dangerous form of racial antagonism as her home is burnt down by the black mob. She runs towards her coloured friend Tia for emotional and physical support, "I saw Tia . . . and I ran to her. . . . As I ran, I thought, I will live with Tia and be like her. . . . When I was close, I saw the jagged stone in her hand but I did not see her throw it." (38) The very next moment she could feel and taste blood. The attack and her rejection may have been precipitated by the political turmoil but the psychology of racial antagonism between the colony and the colonizer has always been explosive from the age of Caliban. Antoinette's remoteness from Tia is not the aftermath of touching Caulibri. In fact, there never has been any merging through friendship as we find in Toni Morrison's *Sula*. Tia was introduced into the family to become Antoinette's friend but from the very beginning Tia had learnt to cheat the white girl. In rage, Antoinette had called her a "cheating nigger." (21) Tia had retorted that they were poor as beggars and not rich as Antoinette posed. The conflict was apparently racial but it also had the undercurrent of economic inequality sprouting from the revenge motif of the exploited. This can be identified with the eternal conditions of this earth.

Antoinette's Garden of Eden had turned "wild." (16) From one loveless existence she is moved to the other in the convent. The poor uprooted girl feels the weight of 'veils' and 'shadows' and 'not so safe.'

(48) The alien atmosphere comforts her but cannot offer the adequate gigantic proportions because of her mother's rejection of the girl-child. Annette the mother nearly disowns Antoinette, "She [mother] had decided once for all that I was useless to her." (17) She has to fight the ancient patriarchal attitude embedded in women that girls are a burden, a botheration and thus worthless. A girl child is identified with the women of the third world. Rhys attaches a negative concept of motherhood with the island. The mother and the island both fail to nourish her, the child. This metaphorical and the literal material difference is clearly identified to develop the selfish nature of the mother/country to its child/colony. Poor Antoinette has to bear the indifference of the mother and the mother-country. Interestingly enough, Rhys's angle of seeing motherhood in the culture varies from whites to blacks. Annette frames the negative picture and Christophine (the black surrogate mother) projects the positive view. Antoinette too never becomes identified with any creativity. But one is not inclined to put the blame on Antoinette. Rochester's coldness, his sexual incompatibility with his wife, his psychological and physical efficiency lead to the tragic state of affairs. Rhys implicitly passes strictures on the male partner. These irreconcilable differences constitute specific oppositions.

Antoinette's impending departure from the reasonably agreeable convent is a second reminder of her refugee status. The fear of being 'outside' makes her dream of a terrible man who compels her to walk in the forest:

> He turns and looks at me, his face black with *hatred*. . . . He smiles *slyly*. . . . Here in here, a *strange* voice said. And I follow him weeping. . . . We are no longer in the forest but in an enclosed *garden* surrounded by a *stone wall* and the *trees are different*. (50, my italics)

Rhys foreshadows Antoinette's future in an "archetypal enclosure of marriage."[5] She grows down and not up. She has a premonition of a strange man, cunning and full of black hatred who would transplant her to a new locale where the trees are strange (being English) and the garden is surrounded by a stone wall like a prison house. It is undoubtedly Rochester and his Thornfield. Here the English law/patriarchal authority, beggars her in all possible manner; she is turned into an "economic imbecile," an impotent subject of man. Her body language, her likes and dislikes are intentionally silenced. Stripped of her name/identity by the British colonizer, she turns into a "prototypal mad wife."[6] Indirectly,

Rhys suggests that the "negative image"[7] associated with woman's unabashed sexuality is really not the chief cause of Antoinette's later insanity. It is a construct of male hegemony. Rhys reconstructs the image of woman as an Angel in the House. She is one of the earliest of the female writers to dilate upon a woman's need of physical love. Patriarchy restrains and punishes an exhibition of passion in women. In a male hero the desire for sexual fulfillment is never fatal.[8]

The plundering of the Creole heiress's riches, dignity and name takes place after her marriage and the story is narrated from Rochester's point of view, in Part II of the novel. Money, name and dignity empower woman to fight for selfhood. The dominant culture constantly aborts the endeavour of the subculture through "ties" of "enduring values as well as accommodations."[9] This is one of the causes of age-old sexual antagonism. The fortune hunter Rochester and Antoinette's coloured half-brother spin the web of her destruction. The malice of the opposite forces is concretized through the differences of needs, motivation and exposure to some primordial situations. Antoinette and her mother Annette are the symbolic nineteenth century Creole girls to be colonized by fortune hunting English men. Antoinette's property and sexuality is bartered for a socially approved name. Psychologically and physically vulnerable Antoinette becomes under-privileged.

Antoinette's honeymoon begins on an inauspicious note. She loves the 'wildness' of Granbois, an estate that once belonged to her mother. For Rochester, "everything is too much. . . . Too much blue, too much purple, too much green." (61) The difference of taste is a symptom of temperamental opposition. Woman is archetypally associated with wildness, romance and imagination and man is a typical representative of order, fact and reason. Antoinette is expected to make all the compromises. For Rochester, only England stands for good; all other things are worthless. Naturally, at one stage, uninitiated Antoinette flings back, "Oh England, England. She called back mockingly." (61) Naive, artless and simple Antoinette will never agree to become a docile subject of Rochester. In fact, she continues to fight the subjugating force till death claims her. The conflict between man and woman for supremacy is eternal. Money gives power and Antoinette is forced to surrender it. Her husband, as Christophine rightly comments, "certainly love money . . . he can't see nothing else." (94) It was a good "bargain" (59) and not love that had made him marry her.

Antoinette has to face Rochester's "Vengeance." (100) Since he feels deceived, he dismantles her identity by taking Amelia, the black servant girl almost in the presence of his legitimate wife. No one condemns him but she is punished for her friendly relationship with Sandi. The tradition of sexual discrimination is prehistoric in nature. The incident alters the equation of love and hate. Once, she had really loved Rochester, but now, "I hate you and before I die I will show you how much I hate you." (121) How she makes true her threat, is history. Rochester's despicable act apparently is quite irrational. His deception has been treated leniently and not adequately and yet, he feels abused. His male chauvinism is badly bruised. This irrational jealousy and anger springs from the unaccustomed defeat of his ego. Christophine the wise judge of human nature, rightly comments: "You want to break her up, because you jealous of her. She is more better than you, she have better blood in her and she don't care for money." (125) These are some of the classic causes of confrontation. To weaken her position, he renames her as Bertha, a common name of mediocre people. This is his revenge. Like her mother, she is driven to madness.

French feminists romanticize Antoinette's madness and their contention is: society is evil and thus her madness represents "a force that is good." She the mad woman articulates "otherness," the "object" becomes the "subject" and she moves from the periphery to the centre.[10] This inversion challenges masculine culture which defines mental health of women in their own terms.[11] Antoinette's feeling of rootlessness is reinforced as she is transplanted again on an alien soil. Rochester fails to break her; she remains quite coherent to us; she becomes anything but passive; reveals her determination to defeat the manipulations of the male gender and chooses her death: "Now at last I know why I was brought here and what I have to do." (155-56) The historic and tragic act articulates her selfhood and alters the norms of "gender reciprocality" that is "the blueprint of all other power relationships and are the models for power relations between generations, socio-economic classes, relations, racial and ethnic groups as well as between imperial powers and colonies."[12] Rochester's sense of gender distinction, designs many plans to colonize Antoinette through isolation, exploitation, disintegration and negation. Under such circumstances conflict is inevitable. Poor Antoinette never gets the chance to learn Christophine's wisdom, "Three children I have. . . . Each one a different father but no husband. I thank my God, I keep my money. I don't give it to no worthless man." (91) Deprived of her money power, Antoinette's feeling of insecurity multiplies. Extremely vulnerable, she tells Rochester, "suppose you took the happiness away from me when I wasn't looking. . . . It makes me afraid." (77) That is exactly what happens to her. Her lack of self-confidence turns her into a natural victim. Christophine very rightly states, 'Woman must have spunks to live in this wicked world,' (84) and initially, she has none. Patricia Meyer Spacks in *Imagining a Self* observes, "A woman fights for her individualism, in her autobiography. It assures existence beyond all possibilities of philosophical denial. Through it comes to term with past or exorcizes it."[13] Antoinette in *Wide Sargasso Sea*, her autobiography more than Rochester's, tries to fight her past and assures her existence through her final act, a form of exorcism. She refuses to be degraded to the level of a beast. Rhys preserves her humanity. Against Bronte's description of Bertha/Antoinette, "a snarling snatching sound almost like a dog quarrelling,"[14] we have Rhys's version also, presented through Grace Poole, "I'll say one thing for her, she hasn't lost her spirit. She is still fierce." (146) Rhys reiterates that Antoinette's spirit is still very much intact. The malevolence of the material world has not been fully triumphant. Rhys compels us to revise the view of the accepted literature by making visible and audible the universal confrontations of minority elements previously ignored. She, in fact, while dealing with the problem, inverts the order and turns the inconsequential into consequential.

II

In her fifth and award-winning novel *Wide Sargasso Sea*, Rhys makes the familiar world of woman and her conflicts transparent for our viewing. But her humane spirit and the wide artistic vision cannot remain circumscribed by gender prejudices. Her novels essentially portray male villainy and her pictures of life could have been questionable if she had restricted herself to female exploitations only. All, male or female, can be abused. Her preference for the suffering female is revealed through her placement of women in the centre and of men in the periphery. Naturally, her portrait of Rochester and his afflictions are not without sympathy. Antoinette is surrounded by a malignant material world but for Rochester, the natural and the tangible world of everyday life is steeped in animosity. Antoinette's condition becomes more poignant because in comparison, she faces a Draconian set up. Rochester himself is a victim of an imperialist system. To preserve his existence he comes to colonize the Creole girl. He himself is the colony of his elder brother and his father. Being isolated, exiled, exploited, ignored and insulted, he suffers. His version in Part Two of the book begins, "It was all over, the *advance and retreat*," (55, my italics) as if the moves of a serious encounter were all over. His struggle for existence had been initiated in England in accordance with the English law that had eroded his position. Being the second son of his father, his right to the ancestral property is completely negated. To survive, he marries Antoinette in a hurry and the entire property of his wife is transferred to his name. He pens a letter to his father:

> The thirty thousand pounds have been paid to me without a question or condition. No provision made for her (that must be seen to). . . . I will never be a disgrace to you or to my dear brother the son you love. No begging letters, no mean requests. None of the furtive shabby manoeuvres of a younger son. I have sold my soul or you have sold it, and after all is it such a bad bargain? (59)

There is no trace of callousness yet; he is still considering about her "provision." His cynical voice gives expression to his latent emotions of sorrow, degradation and frustration. The confrontation becomes serious because, "I did not love her. I was thirsty for her . . . she was a stranger to me, a stranger who did not think or feel as I did." (78) All round him there is nothing but a variation of "hostility." (86) The natural world despite its splendour foreshadows "danger." (87) He is disliked by all the black servants. Christophine is his arch enemy; Amelia the black girl pities him (116); all of them have doubts about his virility. (71) His scream for vengeance turns out to be mere fury of words. He fails to subjugate Antoinette; she continues to meet Sandi, her childhood friend; she destroys his world partially. Repeatedly, she proves that his words are meaningless, "'Justice,' she said, 'I've heard that word. It's a cold word. . . . There is no justice.'" (121) Implicitly, she condemns him for being unjust. Such insinuations are very insulting for an Englishman. In short, her passionate love is transformed into black hatred. He is compared to a "devil" and thought to be very "sly." His conflict with his wife is another version of the tension between man and woman, emotion and reason, innocence and worldly wisdom, natural and the artificial. His money power is defeated by the occult power. Since he is unable to fight the combined powers of two females, Antoinette and Christophine, he uproots one and banishes the other. The use of unfair practice highlights his cornered position. He cannot win. Antoinette refuses to become Bertha; refuses to remain imprisoned through her life and die slowly, unacknowledged. She defies Rochester's patriarchal powers and makes her death very public. The man fails to silence the woman. She constantly intrudes into his speech. Rochester the hunter, ever remains hunted; his status as the under-privileged prevails; his confrontation with society, gender, race, culture, temperament, attitude and ego, continues eternally. Conventionally, masculinity in society is a profound determinant of power but Rochester is never fully empowered to prove his masculinity; he is castrated and branded by conflicts. The male continuum of authority is disrupted, inverted. The tragedy of the novel springs from Rochester's failure to appreciate the 'otherness' of the Jamaican culture, Jamaican race and Jamaican woman. Non-recognition of "otherness" in male or female is the archetypal cause of confrontation.

NOTES

1. Emily Dickinson, "The First Day's Night," *American Poetry and Prose*, ed. Norman Forester (Boston: Houghton Mifflin, 1962), p. 1178.
2. Lucille Clifton, "What the mirror said," *The Woman That I Am*, ed. D. Sayini Madison (New York: St Martin's Press, 1993), p. 58.
3. Gayatri Chakravorty Spivak, "Three Women's Text and a Critique of Imperialism," *Feminism*, ed. Robyn R. Warhol and Diane Price Herndl (New Jersey: Rutgers University Press, 1991), p. 804.
4. *Ibid.*, p. 803.
5. Annis Pratt, *Archetypal Patterns in Woman's Fiction* (Bloomington: Indiana Press, 1981), p. 45.
6. *Ibid.*
7. Michele Wallace, "Variations on Negation," *Reading Black, Reading Feminist, A Critical Anthology*, ed. Henry Louise Gates Jr. (New York: A Meridian Book, 1990), p. 61.
8. Pratt, p. 73.
9. Nancy F. Cott in Introduction to *Root of Bitterness*, qtd. Elaine Showalter, "The Female Tradition," *Feminism*, p. 274.
10. Nina Baym, "The Mad Woman and Her Languages: Why I Don't Do Feminist Literary Theory," *Feminism*, p. 157.
11. Phyllis Chester, *Woman and Madness* (New York: Avon Books, 1973), p. 69.
12. Jean Lipman-Blumen, *Gender Roles and Power* (New Jersey: Prentice Hall, 1984).
13. Patricia Meyer Spacks, *Imagining a Self* (Cambridge: Harvard University Press, 1976), p. 15.
14. Charlotte Bronte, *Jane Eyre* (New York: Signet, 1960), p. 210.
15. Jean Rhys, *Wide Sargasso Sea* (London: Penguin, 1968).

Jean Rhys and the Colonial Experience: *Wide Sargasso Sea*

URBASHI BARAT

> The unity is submarine
> breathing air, the societies were successively amerindian,
> european, creole, the amerindian several; the european
> various; the creole plural
> subsistent plantation maroon
> multilingual multi-ethnic many ancestored
> fragments
> the unity is submarine
> breathing air, our problem is how to study the fragments/whole.
>
> Edward Kamau Brathwaite, "Caribbean Man in Space and Time"

Wide Sargasso Sea[1] is the only one of Jean Rhys's novels to be set in the past and in her native West Indies. All her earlier novels had projected her "bitterly sad, woman's-eye-view of women's lives"[2] against a contemporary urban and European setting; when she broke a long, almost thirty-year-old, silence with *Wide Sargasso Sea*, the shift from present to past, from the Old World to the New, only served to reinforce the impression that for her women, forever "alienated, menaced, at odds with life,"[3] have throughout history and throughout the world been marginalized and victimized. *Wide Sargasso Sea* has thus most often and very profitably been seen as the archetypal woman's novel, in which the bildungsroman structure only serves to emphasize the fact that in a patriarchal society women have no option but to "grow up grotesque"[4] and that her portrayal of "the madwoman in the attic"[5] of *Jane Eyre* is in fact the portrayal of the feminine destination.

In this paper I would like to suggest, however, that our understanding of the novel is enriched if we read it not just as a woman's novel but as an exploration of the colonial experience. As Edward Said points out, the novel form itself in all its manifestations is a product and a mirror of colonialism; indeed, novels are

> the method colonized people use to assert their own identity and the existence of their own history. The main battle in imperialism is over and, of course; but when it came to who owned the land, who had the right to settle and work on it, who kept it going, who won it back, and who now plans its future these issues were reflected, contested, and even for a time decided in narrative.[6]

It is not surprising, therefore, that even the expatriate/repatriated Rhys should use her fiction to explore the relationship between the colonizers and the colonized, the exploiters and the exploited: the major theme of the West Indian novel, with its characteristic search for an identity that is so closely bound to its examination of the historical processes of political and social change, its preoccupation with alienation and expatriation, its concrete geographical localization and its use of childhood and adolescence as a paradigm of the national experience. The novels of George Lamming and Wilson Harris, Andrew Salkey and V.S. Naipaul, Merle Hodge, Jamaica Kincaid and Jean Rhys, different as they are from each other, are all concerned in their own ways with "self-discovery and self-definition, with redefining ancestry, community, and kinship through the restoration of an individual culture devalued by a Eurocentric view of the world."[7] The woman and the colonized in Rhys's work are thus the mirror images of each other—in Margaret Atwood's words, "The positions are the same whether you are a victimized country, a victimized minority group or a victimized individual"[8]—and, as *Wide Sargasso Sea* shows, the exploiter and colonist is ultimately as much the loser as his victim and the colonized. That is why the novel has two voices, two points of view, that of Antoinette Cosway and that of her husband, Mr. Rochester of Charlotte Bronte's novel; its title, with its echoes from Ezra Pound's famous portrayal of the woman's mind, points out that the colonial situation entraps everybody.

At this point it would perhaps be useful to recall Atwood's description of a colony as "a place from which a profit is made, but *not by the people there*" (35-36); money is at the root of colonial society and human relationships, for money is power. All Rhys's novels examine the role of money in shaping people's lives and personalities. Her major characters, almost invariably women, struggle for survival, emotional, moral and economic in a society that is governed by money and in which therefore the colonizer mentality rules supreme; there is thus, for example, the bewildered expatriate in *Quartet*, Marya Zelli, whose marriage to foreigner deprives her of a sense of belonging and pushes her down into a dreary existence of money shortages, hunger and continuous exploitation, or Sasha Jensen of *Good Morning, Midnight*, who must face humiliation and harassment and victimization because she is a woman and poor and West Indies. "Through the power of her analysis," observes Rosalind Miles, "Jean Rhys was one of the few women writers able to make explicit the link between the sex war and the class struggle. To be female is to inhabit, without hope of escape, the lowest class of all in a sexist structure."[9] Throughout her work women live in a nightmare world of the colonized and the dispossessed, exploited and despised, on the fringes of society, the natural prey of the patriarchal male, who shares the colonial belief that it is the moral duty and the right of the colonizer to subjugate and rule over his victim. The colonial experience is most explicitly explored in her one novel to be set in a British colony in the heyday of the British Empire, *Wide Sargasso Sea*.

The opening sentences of the novel immediately establish the reality and the meaning of the colonial world: "They say when trouble comes close ranks, and so the white people did. But we were not in their ranks." (15) The colonial Government in faraway England has just abolished slavery, on which the economy of the colony and the prosperity of the white settlers had depended; it has not, however, paid the colonists the compensation it had promised them. The creoles, all landowners and plantation owners, now have to face sudden financial ruin and betrayal simultaneously, betrayal from those whom they had trusted and to whom they were, ironically, indissolubly linked through race, a common cultural heritage and the shared colonial sense of superiority; added to which there is the undisguised hostility and jealousy of their former slaves, who mock at their poverty and their pitiful attempts to maintain their old colonial airs, calling them "white cockroaches" (20)—that is, despicable and disgusting and unnatural creatures. Old Mr. Luttrell, the narrator-protagonist's neighbour, cannot accept the sudden change, and in despair commits suicide, while his property is left deserted and uncared for. Despair and death are the only realities before the young Antoinette Cosway, left fatherless and neglected like the neighbour's estate; they represent the hidden face of colonialism, in which the colonists become victims of a social structure they have built up themselves. The novel's account of what it means to be a creole—a white West Indian—in a black colony where the blacks are no longer slaves thus throws into prominence the ambiguities and complexities of the colonial situation, imaged especially in the person of Pierre, Antoinette's handicapped brother, the product and hence the victim of a decadent expatriate culture.

Under such conditions people do "close ranks"; but the Cosways do not form a part of the hierarchy of colonial society. Mrs Cosway is a young woman, and beautiful (a woman's physical beauty is invariably feared as a snare in a suspicious and jealous patriarchal structure), and, to boot, she is from Martinique; she is, that is, an outsider from every point of view. Rejected by the other creoles, she is jeered at by the blacks too—"they notice clothes, they know about money," as Antoinette notes in parenthesis, (16) for it is money, and the power it gives, that rules human relationships in the colonial world. The blacks even kill the Cosways's only horse out of sheer malice, and Tia, the little black girl brought into the household to provide company for Antoinette, cheats her of the few coins she has. Tia, in fact, despises Antoinette and her kind because they have become her equals; to gain respect, to be socially acceptable, is to be rich and to look down on the poor and the exploited. As Tia tells Antoinette, "Real white people, they got gold money. They didn't look at us, nobody see them come near us. Old time white people nothing but white nigger now, and black nigger better than white nigger." (21) Both sets of victims, both kinds of colonized people, the erstwhile slaves and the creoles, seem to fall into Atwood's Basic Victim Position One, in which people "are afraid to recognize they are victims . . . and they are forced to account somehow for the disadvantages suffered by the rest of the people in the group by disparaging them." (36) Slowly the Cosways's Eden-like estate turns wild with neglect, with orchids that look like snakes or octopuses, and the smell of dead flowers that pervades the atmosphere: the colonial dream has turned into a nightmare reality.

Antoinette's mother, desperate and lonely, broken by her son's incurable condition, yearning for a past that has vanished so suddenly, has no time for her daughter, treating her "not roughly but calmly, coldly, without a word, as if she had decided once and for all that I was *useless* to her" (17; emphasis added); human relationships here, governed by the cash nexus, are directed solely towards extracting the maximum of profit for the individual, no matter if they destroy others in the process. Mrs. Cosway sees herself as "marooned," (22) abandoned and isolated as on a deserted island (note, therefore, the appropriateness of her description of her condition), living like a "maroon," the fugitive black slaves who lived wild in the mountains of the West Indian islands. Her young daughter, as lonely and deprived, turns to her mother's maid for emotional sustenance, for Christophine, though she was once a slave, is a strong woman—indeed as it turns out, the only strong woman in the novel. The bond between them grows deep and strong, for Christophine is in her own way as much an outsider in Jamaican society as her mistress, and as friendless. The songs that she sings are thus sad ones, of *ubi sunt* and of loneliness, desertion and sorrow, the songs of the life of the outsider, the woman and the colonized.

Christophine is self-sufficient, so much so that she does not even need to meet her son, who lived in nearby Spanish Town; but Mrs Cosway is not. Determined to escape her poverty and her loneliness, she chooses the one way open to most weak women: marriage. Using all the traditional feminine weapons, she sets out to snare a husband, thereby entrenching herself even deeper within the patriarchal enclosure; the colonist longs to be recolonized, that is, not realizing that in attempting to free herself from one kind of misery she is only entering another one, one, moreover, that is a trap of her own making. Even though her husband is no gothic villain but a wealthy, perfectly ordinary, pleasant young Englishman, he is the typical colonial: "so sure of himself, so without a doubt English." (30)

Mr. Mason has come to the West Indies not as exploiter but simply to make money. That is how all colonizers begin, after all, with an understandable greed and an understandable complacency; but they end, inevitably, with death, destruction and despair. This is Mr. Mason's story, as it will be Mr. Rochester's later. In the beginning Mr. Mason and his new wife seem very much in love, and very happy; but the child overhears the cruel comments that indicate that their marriage should be seen in another perspective too: "Dance! He didn't come to the West Indies to dance—he came to make money as they all do. Some of the big estates are going cheap, and one unfortunate's loss is always a clever man's gain." (25) Marriage itself becomes the symbol of the colonial spirit. Even Aunt Cora, whom Mr. Mason does not approve of because she is "an ex-slave-owner who had escaped misery, a flier in the face of Providence," (26) and who thus does not fit into the conventional mould of the traditional female, had not been able to help the Cosways when her husband was alive, for he had been English and had hated the West Indies and West Indians. Aunt Cora is strong only when she is single, as Christophine is.

Mr. Mason's money transforms Coulibri, the Cosway estate. The place is tidied up, and with the new servants, the old ones too come back: "They can *smell* money, somebody said." (26) But in spite of the physical comforts there is a new menace in the air. There are whispers of Christophine practising obeah, and Annette is afraid of the new jealousy and hatred that permeate the atmosphere. Her husband, however, the logical superior male, finds her fears laughable. In the true colonial spirit he patronizes his household, and refuses to take either his wife or his servants seriously. Thus he does not understand why, when as a poor defenceless widow with small children she had not been harmed by the former slaves, she is now so frightened, when she has a rich husband for protection. But physical violence is not the only kind of harm and, as Antoinette points out, in those days they had nothing, so even if they were white "what was there to hate?" (29) Neither does Mr. Mason see why his wife objects to his calling his servants "niggers" when she distrusts them so, nor why, when they are so lazy, she could believe that they can be dangerous and cruel. He shares, that is, the characteristic insensitivity and complacency of the male and the colonial. He even thinks he knows the locals better than the creoles do:

> "Live here most of your life and know nothing about the people. It's astonishing. They are children—they wouldn't hurt a fly."
>
> "Unhappily children do hurt flies," said Aunt Cora. (30)

But in the end it is the women who are proved right. One night they are attacked by the blacks, and their house is set on fire. Though they themselves manage to escape Pierre is fatally injured, and Annette cannot save her parrot, whose wings Mr. Mason had, significantly, clipped, and which therefore, cannot fly to freedom but must be burnt alive; the parrot's fate is thus a reflection of the colonial situation, and presages the protagonist's future and end. Antoinette does not want to leave her old home, and hopes, despite the obvious black hostility, that her old friend Tia might offer her refuge; instead, however, Tia throws a stone at her and injures her. As blood gushes down her face, "we stared at each other, blood on my face, tears on hers. It was as if I saw myself. Like in a looking-glass." (38) Both are victims of colonial forces, though they may belong to different races and different social background.

That fiery night changes their lives for ever. Pierre dies, and Annette goes mad, screaming abuse at her husband, whose obtuseness has brought about the destruction of her world. She has to be confined, whereas her daughter discovers to her horror much later, she is sexually exploited by her keepers. Mr. Mason leaves Jamaica, leaving Antoinette in the safe refuge of a convent, where, cut off from the outside world, she attempts to participate in the values of an artificially secluded world only to discover their irrelevance to her own. Mr. Mason does not forget his stepdaughter, though; he visits her regularly, and gives her presents, and arranges her to meet and marry an Englishman come to the West Indies in search of wealth in the shape of a rich wife. Nothing, evidently, can shake the paternalism of the colonial mind.

The encounters between Mr. Rochester and Antoinette resemble an elaborate charade, for she has had no hand in the decision that they should marry; it has all been fixed by her stepbrother and her husband-to-be, and she has been a puppet in their hands. She makes one attempt to refuse him, but marriage to a rich wife is important to the man, who, besides, "did not relish going back to England in the role of rejected suitor jilted by this Creole girl." (65) Her reluctance is bludgeoned down, and as her new husband looks at the beauty of her mother's estate on their honeymoon he feels that in the last analysis he is the winner: "after all is it such a bad bargain?" (59)—another reminder of the hard reality behind the surface pleasantness of human relationships in a colonial set-up. The woman he has married may be a stranger, an alien, but he is now richer by £30,000; and although it is she who has bought him it is she who is soon emotionally and financially dependent upon him. Their marriage, again, is an image of the colonial experience, which enriches the colonizer but impoverishes and enfeebles the colonized.

Antoinette seems happy, but Rochester sees the sadness in her sleeping face, and recalls the way she had unsuccessfully tried to escape him, both before marriage and after: "she had given way, but coldly, unwillingly, trying to protect herself with silence and a blank face. Poor weapons, and they had not served her will or lasted long. If I have forgotten caution, she has forgotten silence and coldness." (76) For he has been able to manipulate her instincts and emotions to his advantage: "she was as eager for what's called loving as I was—more lost and drowned afterwards." (77) Her new-found happiness is thus inevitably fragile. A letter from someone who calls himself her half-brother tells Rochester of his wife's unfortunate family history, and warns him about her impending madness. The husband immediately accepts Daniel's tale, though its malice is only too evident, and withdraws from her as a punishment, using as his tool her coloured maid Amelie, whose jealousy and dislike of Antoinette is obvious. She even refers to her mistress by that hated phrase of her childhood, white cockroach. If the blacks call the creoles white cockroaches, the English call them white niggers, and, as Antoinette tells Rochester, "So between you I often wonder who I am and where is my country and where do I belong and why was I ever born at all." (85) This, then, is the crux of the colonial experience, the loss of identity. It is not surprising that Rochester decides to call his wife not by her name but by one she hates and cannot identify with, Bertha.

Antoinette is terrified by the change in her husband's attitude towards her. Her old nurse explains that this is what men are like: "If you love them they treat you bad, if you don't love them they after you night and day bothering your soul case out." (91) But Christophine too is shocked by the fact that legally Antoinette's money is now her husband's, and urges her to get at least some of it for herself. It is only when she sees that the girl cannot do so, and is desperate enough to beg her to use obeah to get her husband's love back, even offering her a bribe, that she agrees to try witchcraft. (It may be interesting to note that the witch is the patriarchal image of the self-determined woman, as Pratt suggests. [123]) A cock crows, and Antoinette is reminded of Judas's betrayal; but who is betraying whom? If the bribe she has offered her old servant is a betrayal of their relationship, if she is betraying her husband by arranging for a spell to be cast on him, so does Christophine betray Antoinette by her failure and by her obeah medicine that precipitates her madness. Above all, Mr. Rochester betrays his wife. He has married her with no intention of loving her; he deliberately arouses her erotic instincts only to reject her sexually—indeed, as it turns out later, he is repelled by the intensity of her sexual response (135-36)—and he even indulges in a sexual encounter with the maid she hates just outside her door so that she will come to know of his infidelity and suffer, and not because he is attracted to Amelie. Once his purpose is served, in fact, he pays Amelie off and sends her away; such is the power of money.

Antoinette, pushed over the edge, cries out against the hypocrisy and the cruel self-seeking of the colonial mind. The English had proclaimed their love of justice and their respect for humanity when they had abolished slavery, but, given a chance, they would continue to perpetrate the same injustices on the weak, for they remain the colonizers in spirit and action: "You send the girl away quicker, and with no money or less money, and that's all the difference." (121) The victim, then, remains the victim, regardless of who the colonizer is. Mr. Mason and Rochester are mirror images of each other, as they are of the England which has colonized the world.

Rochester, obviously, is not quite a villain. He too has been used, by his father and his brother, who have urged him into this marriage only so that he be financially independent of them. Besides, there is his colonial/patriarchal conditioning that immediately responds to any challenge to his hegemony. When Christophine begs him to return at least some of his wife's money so that she can live on her own, and perhaps even find happiness elsewhere, he can only hear the word "money" and not the meaning of the appeal: "I thought, of course, that is what the rigmarole is about. I no longer felt dazed, tired, half hypnotized, but alert and wary, ready to defend myself." (130) He will give her neither her money nor any chance to regain any happiness; he will never let her forget her unhappiness, for she is after all his possession, his property, to deal with as he pleases. Christophine exclaims as she sums him up: "You do that for money? But you wicked like Satan self!" (132) This is in fact an indictment of the colonial mentality itself rather than of an individual.

Indeed, if Rochester has been harsh, so has life been harsh to him: "Tied to a lunatic for life—a drunken lying lunatic." (135) His revenge on life is typical of the colonizer's: he takes it out on his wife, because she is a woman, and weak, and his possession. He has been bought with her money, and so, like the pirates of old who murdered and pillaged and destroyed for treasure, he will destroy her after he has used her. (139) He will take her away to England, deny her the sun and the warmth that is her home, and deny her love of any kind too, (136) so that in the end even her hatred is destroyed as her beauty is, and what she is left with is only despair: "A ghost in the grey daylight. Nothing left but hopelessness." (140) Ultimately, therefore, the victor is as much the loser as the victim, for he can feel nothing but hatred: "Above all I hated her. For she belonged to the magic and the loveliness. She had left me thirsty and all my life would be thirst and longing for what I had lost before I found it." (141)

When Rochester returns to England the "gentle, generous, brave" young man has grey in his hair and misery in his eyes, (145) a satanic figure who incarcerates his mad wife in a thick-walled house that shuts out the world. Antoinette is cold and unhappy here, and plans constantly how to persuade her husband to free her. She keeps warm by secret drinking, and when her attendant sleeps she explores her new world, one which she believes is made of cardboard, because her experiences here are so unreal and because she has discovered that "Gold is the idol they worship" here. (154) Somehow she manages to get word through to her stepbrother to take her away, but when he comes to meet her he cannot recognize her, and refuses to "interfere legally" (150) between her and her husband. She tries to kill him then. The law, which was meant to enforce justice and protect the weak, has in fact been turned into the weapon of the oppressor and the exploiter. Thus for example, Rochester lives well on Antoinette's money, but denies her good clothes and the comfort she longs for.

In one of the expeditions through the house one night she suddenly recalls the sunlight and warmth of Aunt Cora's room but she sees the wax candles in the room and is jerked back into her cold and cruel present. She knocks them down—wax is an image of death and of her friendless, death-like condition—and a curtain catches fire. Its warmth and colour delight her; she spreads it all around and runs to the battlements, to see the house on fire behind her and in the red sky her life flashes by. But then comes the voice of the man who hated her, and she runs back to her room. Sitting there, she knows now "why I was brought here and what I have to do." (155-56) She has come to Rochester's house to set it on fire just as the blacks had set fire to Coulibri so many years back. This is the ultimate gesture of defiance that the victim and the colonized can offer: the destruction of the colonizer's home, just as he has devastated theirs.

NOTES

1. *Wide Sargasso Sea* (London: Penguin, 1968).
2. Gilbert Phelps, "The Post-War English Novel," *The New Pelican Guide to English Literature*, ed. Boris Ford, Vol. 8, *The Present* (Harmondsworth: Penguin, 1983), p. 440.
3. Francis Wyndham, Introduction, *Wide Sargasso Sea*, p. 11.
4. Annis Pratt, *Archetypal Patterns in Women's Fiction* (Bloomington: Indiana University Press, 1981), p. 29.
5. Sandra M. Gilbert and Susan Gubar, *The Madwoman in the Attic: The Woman Writer and the Nineteenth-Century Literary Imagination* (N. Haven, Conn.: Yale University Press, 1979).
6. Edward W. Said, Introduction, *Culture and Imperialism* (NY: Knopf, 1993), pp. xii-xiii.
7. Sandra Puchet Paquet, "Caribbean Fiction," *The Columbia History of the American Novel*, p. 588.
8. Margaret Atwood, *Survival: A Thematic Guide to Canadian Literature* (Toronto: Anansi, 1972), p. 36.
9. Rosalind Miles, *The Female Form: Women Writers and the Conquest of the Novel* (London: Routledge and Kegan Paul, 1990), p. 135.

Jean Rhys's *Wide Sargasso Sea*: A Re-Writing of History

VEENA JAIN

"Re-vision—the act of looking back, of seeing with fresh eyes, of entering an old text from a new critical direction—is for us more than a chapter in cultural history: it is an act of survival!"[1]

For Rhys, the act of looking back and revising *Jane Eyre* was an act of pitting two cultures and two genders against one another. It was an act or reliving her childhood, of visiting her birthplace and showing 'the other side' to her twentieth century readers.

In a letter to Selma Vaz Dias, she wrote, "I've read and re-read *Jane Eyre* of course and I am sure that the character must be 'built up.' I wrote you about that. The creole in Charlotte Bronte's novel is a lay-figure-repulsive which does not matter, and not once alive which does. She's necessary to the plot, but always she shrieks, howls, laughs horribly, attacks all the sundry off stage. For me (and for you I hope) she must be right on stage. She must be at least plausible with a past, the reason why Mr. Rochester treats her so abominably and feels justified, the reason he thinks she is mad and why of course she goes mad, even the reason why she tries to set every thing on fire, and eventually succeeds. . . . Take a look at *Jane Eyre*. That unfortunate death of a Creole. I'm fighting mad to write her story."[2]

The story which came out in the shape of her widely acclaimed novel *Wide Sargasso Sea* opened several avenues of interest for critics. Many critics like Dennis Porter, Michael Thorpe and Joyce Carol Oates[3] have treated the novel in relation to Jane Eyre. Others like Marsha Z. Cummins and Nancy R. Harrison[4] have concentrated on its technical felicity. Still others as Kenneth Ramchand, Mary Lou Emery and Nunez Harrel[5] have focused on its West Indian background. Thomas F. Staley[6] has seen *Wide Sargasso Sea* in modern context. I would like to approach the novel from the historical point of view looking at it from three angles:

(a) As a reworking of the colonial past of West Indies.

(b) As recreating the life of mad Mrs. Bertha Rochester which makes the novel a prologue to *Jane Eyre*.

(c) As a novel of alienation, emphasizing the historical uprootedness of its characters. Rhy's linking of history to personal consciousness thus enlarges the panorama of human experience.

The rediscovery of Barth Rochester in *Wide Sargasso Sea* by Jean Rhys paradoxically was also a rediscovery of Jean Rhys herself after a period of thirty years. After the publication of *Wide Sargasso Sea* in 1966 and its wild reception when she was awarded the W.H. Smith Literary award, her earlier works came into focus. As the war broke out her earlier works as *The Quartel, After Leaving Mr. Mackenzie, Voyage in the Dark* and *Good Morning Midnight* which were published between 1927 and 1939 went out of print. In 1957 she was spotted by Selma Vaz Dias who broadcast a dramatized version of her novel *Good Morning Midnight.* Selma encouraged her to write and it took her ten long years of hard work and pain. She had entered the psyche of the creole lunatic. "Eventually I got back to being a Creole lunatic in the 1840s—Quite an effort, sometimes am almost there, sometimes I think I'll stay there." (*Letters*, 156)

Ford Madox Ford had perceived her genius quite early, when in 1927 in an enthusiastic preface to *The Left Bank* he remarked, Jean Rhys had a "terrifying instinct for form and a terrific, an almost lurid passion for stating the case of the underdog."[7] This passion made her interested in characters, whether beast or human being, one could not, at first sight tell. It grovelled, seemingly on all fours, it snatched and growled like some strange wild animals, but it was covered with clothing and a quantity of dark, grizzled hair, wild as mane."[8]

Rhys placed her novel in the West Indies, the islands of Jamaica, the period after the Emancipation Act of 1834. Her central figure, Antoinette, is a product of the conflicting pressures on the white minority by the black Negro community who is suddenly released into power from years of subjugation. Antoinette feels, "So between you I often wonder who I am and where is my country and where do I belong and why was I ever born at all." (102)

The restlessness for her identity is the restlessness of Jean Rhys. Born in 1894, in Dominica (West Indies) one of the windward islands, she was the daughter of a Welsh doctor and a third generation Dominican Creole mother. She came to England when she was sixteen, but could never feel a sense of belongingness in this country. She remained an outcast most of her life travelling and leading a bohemian life in the countries of Europe. "Her sense of being an outsider," feels Linda Bamber, "certainly has roots in her personal history."[9] In her childhood Rhys recalls, "Meta had shown to me a world of fear and distrust, and I am still in that world."[10] She knew that the rejected white creole woman became the "white cockroach" in *Wide Sargasso Sea* who shared the status of the underprivileged and the underclass. Thus rejected by the white world and spurned by the blacks, Antoinette struggles to find her identity in the Caribbean islands.

As a white creole girl, Tia, her negro friend, clearly states her situation: "Old time white people nothing but white nigger now and black nigger better than white nigger." (24)

When Annette, Antoinette's mother, marries Mr. Mason, the rich Englishman from England, to restore her fortune, her house is set on fire and her handicapped son dies. She has to perforce leave Coulibri and with it she leaves a part of herself. Her disintegration begins, she loses a sense of belongingness and as her husband leaves her in the hands of her caretaker negro servants, she goes mad. She becomes a victim of sexual exploitation.

Similarly when Antoinette marries Rochester, again an Englishman from England, not for recovering her fortune, but as an arrangement made by her father and brother (the two powerful male figures who control her life), her sense of belongingness is threatened. Her formative years are shaped by the negro folk songs, dances, vodoo or 'obeah' and the blushful tropical landscape of the Caribbean islands. Wrenching her from her familiar surroundings, Rochester takes her to an alien country among alien people. It is in this context that Rhys places her young, beautiful, sensitive Antoinette lifting her from the third storey of the Attic at Thornfield Hall.

The 'intemperate,' 'unchaste,' middle-aged Bertha is a lonely suffering figure in *Wide Sargasso Sea.*

The West Indian setting is not incidental to the novel; it is its central focus. The West-Indian experience of an expatriate, an alien and the white creole woman links it to the motif of the oppressed, the slave and the female. The dominant forces of suspicion, hatred and fear are revealed in the acts of natives, when Annette's horse dies and their house at Coulibri is set on fire.

Elizabeth Nunez Harrel in her essay "The Paradoxes of Belonging: The White West Indian in Fiction" states the conflict of the white creole woman in relation to history.

In the English speaking Caribbean these women must bear the

> guilt of the horrors of slavery inflicted by their own white ancestors upon the people whose country they call their own. And they must do so in solitude, for England and Europe wishing to obliterate from their memories the part they played in the brutal history of the Caribbean have set them adrift with this guilt. (281)

Rochester is the guilty England and Antoinette must bear the guilt of the horrors perpetrated on the natives. As England's purely mercenary interest in the Antilles cannot foster any hope of reciprocal understanding, similarly Rochester's marriage to Antoinette solely for a rich dowry cannot develop true love and friendship. Rochester's inability to understand Antoinette's feelings and passions is England's failure to comprehend the negro world. Rochester takes his 'plunder' (Antoinette) back to England in both *Jane Eyre* and *Wide Sargasso Sea*. But the difference between Bronte's Rochester and Rhys's Rochester lies in their attitudinal differences and the place they hold in their relationship to their women.

Bronte's Rochester is loved by Jane in spite of his moral lapses as he has some redeeming qualities. The quality of remorse and an ability to give himself are some of his endearing traits that make him acceptable to Jane and to the Victorian hearts. He is the 'Byronic hero' the 'superior male' but with a doubtful past which is reflected in Bartha and Adeile, his former mistress's daughter.

For these moral lapses the Victorian heroine could forgive Rochester. But when Rochester tries to play further deception by making a bigamous proposal, Jane immediately refuses him and "flees temptation." Rochester becomes unacceptable to Jane, not only for his deception but because she realizes that in marrying Rochester, her fate could be like Bertha's. With his class superiority, as his mistress he could have the power to break her. Hence Bronte's Rochester had to be "chastened" and "purged" in a fire at Thornfield before being acceptable to Jane. Jane had to become Rochester's equal in social status as well.

The masterful warm and understanding Rochester of Jane Eyre becomes the hard-hearted cruel oppressor in Rhys's second part of *Wide Sargasso Sea*. He becomes the narrator himself. Hence, though a little more honest than his Brontean prototype, he also becomes, what Mona Fayad says, "the omnipotent God like creator of Bertha's narrative text." Rhys does not allow any sympathy for him from her twentieth century readers.

Rochester comes to the West Indies to make a fortune by marrying a rich heiress like his counterpart in *Jane Eyre*. Unable to fathom the mysteries of nature and disconcerted by the overpowering edenic yet wild setting of the islands, "the orchids threatening like an octopus tentacles bare of leaves hanging from a twisted root." (19) Rochester attributes this wildness to Antoinette. He begins associating her with wildness, sensuality and primitive passions. Faced with primitive passions of his innermost self, an entrance into the inner recesses of being, Rochester begins to feel the threat of Antoinette's world overpowering him. Their blissful honeymooning days at Granbois soon end when Daniel Cosway the self claimed brother of Antoinette and the Iago-like figure intensifies Rochester's mistrust and fear in his letter.

Daniel's letter is an important document which lays bars the hidden feelings in Rochester. It gives him the excuse to brand Antoinette as a slave and rename her 'Bertha.' It gives him the excuse to denounce her sexuality and consider her an unworthy Victorian English gentlewoman. "She'll moan and cry and give herself as no sane woman would or could." (165) Antoinette's desperation for his love takes her to Christophine, her negro nurse. Christophine mixes a drink for Rochester. After making love to her, he feels a repulsion for Antoinette and swears that she has poisoned him. It is actually the revulsion of Antoinette's power over him, over his passions. Out of hatred, fear and desperation and a strong desire to hurt Antoinette, he makes love to Amelie, the slave girl in the next room. Rhys could not forgive Rochester for this unfeeling act. She explains Rochester's behaviour in a letter to Diana Anthill.

> The 'love' drink on obeah night merely releases all his misery, jealousy and ferocity that has been piling up, in Mr. R. for so long. He pretends to think he's been poisoned, that's only to pile up again everything against her and so excuse his cruelty. He justifies it that way (it's often done). I do not think it justifies him at all. I do not think it explains him a bit. (*Letters*, 269)

Antoinette begins breaking up. When finally Christophine asks Rochester to set Antoinette free, by giving her half her money so that she could live her own life, Rochester is filled with a deep jealousy and decides to take Antoinette with him to England to make her a prisoner in the attic at Thornfield. He himself feels justified in indulging in licentious affairs, but denies human contact and warmth to her. He has lost the capacity for remorse.

The result of her imprisonment is seen in the final act where the two novels are linked together. Antoinette turns into Bertha, a bundle of violence and passions and begins to live in a world of memories and dreams. She attacks Mason, sets fire to Rochester's clothes and then to the house. Rhys explains her madness through these incidents and justifies her actions. In her mind, reality and dream are mixed up. Dreams for the Rhys heroine are an escape from the harsh cruelties of this world. She survives through these dreams and hallucinations. Time becomes relational in the heroine's mind, and Rhys in this way links the past and the present. When Tia, her childhood friend, beckons, she signifies feeling, remorse and an affinity with her childhood world; of the blacks, of her mother and Aunt Cora. Antoinette makes the final triumphant jump and finds release from her prison. In her last act, she defies Rochester—her oppressor and victimizer. Bertha of Rhys is a victim and the Bertha of Bronte is a victimizer.

Bronte could find "an escape into wholeness" for her heroine. The same optimism could not be shared by the author of *Wide Sargasso Sea*. Sexuality was a potent force to be shunned and avoided in the Victorian ethical norms. Jane, who has a rich cultural background of religion, ethics and heritage, possesses a strong morality to control her feelings. Her instinct for self-preservation saves her from sexual exploitation. She is passionate but with a strong sense of self-control. In the famous Gypsy-scene in *Jane Eyre*, she deftly sidetracks the overtures of Rochester. Paradoxically, it is the Victorian heroine who finds ways of self-fulfilment in a male-dominated society.

Rhys's Antoinette and Rochester cannot hope for a union in the colonial setting. Antoinette as a white creole girl in Indies has no culture or heritage to fall back on. Religion gives a brief respite. Sexuality is openly experienced and also discussed by Rhys, whereas the references to sexuality are veiled in *Jane Eyre*.

Gilbert and Gubar in their brilliant analysis of the 'doubles' in *Mad Woman in the Attic* even go to the extent of considering Bertha Rochester as the 'veiled' sexual self of Jane. Rhys brings the problem of sexual repression out into the open. Antoinette's madness is the result of her sexual castration and human contact. Jane[11] accepts Rochester's double standards. Antoinette retaliates by involving herself with Saudi. Nevertheless, Antoinette becomes a victim of sexual exploitation and in the absence of sustaining values, moral or psychological, she is set adrift in the unbridgeable gulf of *Wide Sargasso Sea*. Antoinette becomes a symbol of displaced personality, of social and cultural exile. In her portrayal of individual consciousness, Rhys resembles James Joyce, Ernest Hemingway and Dorothy Richardson. Rhys's raw material from Bronte's novel transforms it into a modern experience of insecurity, alienation and despair and the Emancipation Act functions as the background.

NOTES

1. Elizabeth R. Bear, "The Sisterhood of Jane Eyre and Antoinette Cosway," *The Voyage in Fictions of Female Development*, ed. Elizabeth Longland, Marianne Hirsch and Elizabeth Abel (Hanover and London: University Press of New England, 1983), p. 131.
2. *Jean Rhys*: *Letters 1931-66*, ed. Francis Wyndham and Diana Melley (Harmondsworth: Penguin, 1985), p. 156.
3. Dennis Porter, "Of Heroines and Victims, Jean Rhys and Jane Eyre," *The Massachusetts Review*, 17, 3 (Autumn 1976), pp. 540-77; Michael Thorpe, "The Other Side: *Wide Sargasso Sea* and *Jane Eyre*," *Ariel*, 8, 3, July 1977), pp. 99-100; Joyce Carol Oates, "Romance and Anti-Romance: From Bronte's *Jane Eyre* to Rhys's *Wide Sargasso Sea*," *Virginia Quaterly Review* (Winter 1985), 61, pp. 44-58.
4. Marsha Z. Cummins, "Point of View in the Novels of Jean Rhys: The Effect of a Double Focus," *World Literature Written in English*, 24, 2 (1984), pp. 359-73. Nand R. Harrison, "Jean Rhys and the Novel as Women's Text" (Chapel Hill and London: University of North California, 1988), p. 136. Mona Fayad in her article "Unquiet Ghosts: The Struggle for Representation in Jean Rhys's *Wide Sargasso Sea*," *Modern Fiction Studies* (Feminism and Modern Fiction), Autumn 1988, 4, pp. 437-52, traces Antoinette's search for identity through narrative strategies.
5. Kenneth Ramchand, *The West Indian Novel and Its Background* (London: Faber and Faber, 1970); Mary Lou Emery, "The Politics of Form: Jean Rhys' Social Vision in *Voyage in the Dark* and *Wide Sargasso Sea*," *Twentieth Century Literature*, Vol. 28 (Spring 1982), pp. 418-29. Elizabeth Nunez Harrel, "The Paradoxes of Belonging: The White West Indian Women in Fiction," *Modern Fiction Studies* (Summer 1985), 3, 2, p. 281.
6. Thomas F. Staley, *Jean Rhys: A Critical Study* (Austin: University of Texas Press, 1979), p. 116.
7. Francis Wyndham in introduction to *Wide Sargasso Sea* (London and New York: W.W. Norton, 1982), p. 5.
8. Charlotte Bronte, *Jane Eyre* (1847; Delhi: Peacock, 1994), p. 295.
9. Linda Bamber, "Jean Rhys," *Partisan Review*, Vol. 49, 1982, p. 30.
10. Jean Rhys, *Smile Please*: *An Unfinished Autobiography,* ed. Diana Anthill (London: Andre Deustch, 1979), p. 32.
11. Sandra M. Gilbert and Susan Gubar, *The Madwoman in the Attic: The Woman Writer and the Nineteenth Century Literary Imagination* (New Haven: Yale University Press, 1979).

Counterpointing the "Mammy" and the "Da": A Case Study of Dilsey in William Faulkner's *The Sound and the Fury* and Christophine in Jean Rhys's *Wide Sargasso Sea*

RAMA KUNDU

The present paper proposes comparison of the treatment of the black woman servant figure in the American and the Caribbean contexts respectively with particular focus on the character of Dilsey in Faulkner's *The Sound and the Fury* (1929)[1] and of Christophine in Jean Rhys's *Wide Sargasso Sea* (1966).[2] Undeniably the two belong to two different chronotopes (as also do their writers); they are divided by the 'wide Sargasso Sea'—the great geo-political cultural divide. And although originally ancestors of both had been shipped over from Africa as slaves, in course of time they had imbibed newer and divergent ethno-cultural ways and life-patterns owing to their different continuum. However, certain points of comparison persist.

Faulkner had described *The Sound and the Fury* as the tragedy of two lost women, Caddy and Quentin, the mother and the daughter.[3] In this turbulent tragedy of passion and rebellion, confusion and chaos, Dilsey provides the only point of stability. She also proves a succour to the mother and later to the lonely helpless daughter. *Wide Sargasso Sea* is a sad tale of a creole girl of the Carib islands who had been married by a metropolitan British, robbed of her money and then systematically broken and finally deported to England to the attic of the country mansion of Rochester. It is actually Charlotte Bronte's *Jany Eyre* rewritten from the angle of Rochester's mad wife from Jamaica, who gets a voice here, a past, and an identity. As a child Antoinette had seen her mother turn mad at the shock of her little brother's death in estate-fire, then left by her second husband in the hands of paid people who sexually exploited the helpless woman. This terrible knowledge had undermined Antoinette psychically, so that later her calculating husband found it so easy to "break" her. It is a story of violence and dislocation, of racism-imperialism-androcentrism working hand in hand to perpetrate the tragedy of two lost women. And both the mother and the daughter, in their brief sad transit through this life get consistent affection, understanding and support from only one person; she is Christophine, Antoinette's 'Da' (nurse).

Both Christophine and Dilsey hail from ex-slave communities which had once been forcibly uprooted from their native place to serve alien white masters in alien lands; and though slaves no more in the continuum of the two novels, they remain servants nevertheless, and women servants, who had known the double ignominy of racism and sexism. As women of a marginalized group in their respective societies, these black servants were necessarily subjected to the double burden of bearing-rearing-homemaking for her own family as well as looking after the master's children and household. The life they had to encounter was, at its best, to say the least, difficult. What is interesting is to see how they negotiated with this life, and emerged as women of strength and dignity who could offer a counterpoint/solution to the problems of identity/selfhood—not only to the black but also to the white women of their respective milieu. Both anticipate, though in different ways, the New Woman of a later era.

Dilsey represents the Southern black woman of America—an emergent generation of blacks, still smothered by memories of slavery and yet in full possession of the self-esteem that helps to hold one's head high. In spite of the abolition of slavery, they are still little more than slaves, riddled by poverty and ignorance. But Dilsey stages a triumph above her narrowing circumstances through sheer strength of character and no external assistance.

In contrast to Dilsey, Christophine had herself been a slave once; she had gone through the s/exploitation of the slave-market as a commodity/labourer; then given away as wedding gift by her last master to his newly-wed second wife. But even after the abolition of slavery in the island she stayed on with the ex-master's family, by then quickly getting pauperised as the master died, the former servants refused to work, and the young beautiful wife, helplessly tethered to the place with two children, faced starvation. When thus deserted by all, it was only Christophine who came to the succour and helped them to survive through these hard times by means of her own personal influence among the blacks of the locality. Moreover, she had been a mother-surrogate to Antoinette (the name given to Rochester's first wife in Jean Rhys's novel) in her lonely childhood, a most sympathetic and understanding nurse or 'da.' She had remained loyal to the child through ups and downs, when the estate was burnt down, the mother Annette turned mad, the parents died; later when she grew up and got married, Christophine again came to serve the couple in the honeymoon house at Granbois. Soon afterwards, Antoinette started breaking down as her British husband began to show his hatred of the creole wife, and had servant girls in bed with a thin partition wall keeping her off. In her anguish she could turn only to Christophine—who was blacker than anyone and smelt of all the black women of her childhood—for comfort and support. Again, it was Christophine alone who stood up in defence of her '*doudou,*' though ineffectively but courageously. She had also given Antoinette a piece of practical advice—to pack up and go away from her husband since women must have "spunks" in order to survive in this hard world; she gave her own example: she had three sons, each by a different father, but she allowed "no thief husband to steal" her money. Antoinette had failed to act according to the advice and suffered miserably in consequence. But when finally she set fire to Rochester's house/her prison, she cried out only to Christophine for help. Though Christophine was miles away by that time, if at all alive, she helped her as it were by raising a wall of fire.

Perhaps because this is a novel written by a woman from essentially a woman's standpoint, the relationship between Antoinette and Christophine attains a most satisfying and enriching level of emotion and understanding. At the end Antoinette realizes that as a creole girl she does not belong to the colonist's milieu, but rather her true identity lies with the oppressed women of her own island, for whom Christophine stands as a symbol of assurance and confidence. As Laura Niesen de Abruna observes: "She demonstrates that bonding is possible for white Creole women and African-Caribbean women if the women can bracket the sexism, racism, and imperialism that are thrust upon them."[4]

This kind of awareness may not be found in *The Sound and the Fury* which is written by a male writer and in a different social context. But even here Dilsey emerges as a remarkable figure carrying significances beyond the immediate continuum of the text as counterpoint to a number of racist paradigms.

The portrait of Dilsey in Faulkner's most well-known novel has drawn the readers' attention. Though apparently Dilsey is no major character, nor is she involved in 'the sound and the fury' that occupies the main personae, yet she leaves a lasting impression on the reader. This was intended by the author as is evident from his apportioning the last section of the novel to Dilsey. Thus Cleanth Brooks, even while dismissing Irving Howe's claim about Faulkner's continuous moral growth in his depiction of the Negro,[5] yet concedes that Dilsey is "one of Faulkner's most sympathetic Negro characters, surely 'conceived in warmth' and 'developed in depth.'" (385) Of course this encomium does not suffice for the black feminist critics of our times. Barbara Christian's is a typical instance of this rejection of the 'mammy' myth, one of the stereotypes of black women as perceived by the white writers. She includes Dilsey too as part of this conventional pattern which epitomises the ambiguity of the white male's response to the black woman: "the way the guilty and the powerful always delight in looking obliquely at their guilt."[6] Christian is no less ironical in her summing up of the 'mammy' myth—the black female figure in Southern white literature,—the fat, nurturing, religious, kind, strong, enduring woman who is unable to do harm, and is of an all-giving nature. Thus she would angrily point her finger at the limitedness of white perception in this respect: "Who is a Southern black woman? To a white man, those words might connote a mammy, a good-looking wench, or Dilsey, as it did to Faulkner." (33)

It is but expected that as a model of Christian resignation and endurance, Dilsey may cease to appeal to the present-day reader, who has been taught to dismiss such values as the 'poor's opium'; or the exploiter's shrewd devices to keep the mill going. But Dilsey may still be considered in historical terms if not as a moral archetype or model. Christian's exasperation with the 'mammy' myth is understandable. But is Dilsey that simple, or to be that summarily dismissed? Does Dilsey epitomize abject surrender to the prevailing system or rather the beginning of an assertion of the New Woman—self-sufficient, self-conscious—who should be from the most underprivileged and exploited section of the society; a self-assurance that would get increasingly pronounced in the subsequent decades of American history as well as global history.

It is rather unlikely of course that Faulkner intended to present a case either for the women or the Negro through Dilsey. Faulkner was never known for any pronounced feminist sympathies, and he had other types of Negroes to offer; even within this book Luster provides an example. It is more likely that Dilsey was imagined by Faulkner as an individual rather than as a stereotype. And what kind of individual is she? Apparently she is just any/every 'mammy,'—the kind, harmless, humble, serving creature. But that Faulkner intended her to be more than that is evident from the very patterning of the book. Dilsey is foregrounded in the last and only omnisciently narrated section (generally denominated by critics as 'Dilsey's section') that follows and sets in perspective the preceding disjointed fragments of separate interior monologues. It is also in this section that Dilsey, the poor old black woman, a real 'have not,' emerges as the most impressive 'counterpoint' to all the other 'points' represented by various members of the Compson family—old and young, decadent and confused alike.

Faulkner's critical attitude to all the other characters, irrespective of their colour or position, is obvious. But for Dilsey he reserves an unreserved respect. She is not once treated with disapproval or ridicule. No posture of kind condescension of a superior may be traced in Faulkner's treatment of the character.

Dilsey is one of Faulkner's noble Negroes. She is noble not because she is Negro but because of her very nature. She has been made to function in a difficult situation which is also typical of the mammy's world. She has held up her head in a world that would have rather knocked her down. She has to find a way of coping with a very hard life. She achieves this simply by being herself/what she is. Brooks finely sums up this way of her with reference to her relationship with Jason—the most difficult, mean and demeaning person in the text: "She forces Jason Compson to fear and respect her though she is armed with little more than a dedication so evident that Jason, in spite of himself, is overawed."[7] She is so sure of herself that she is not afraid of Jason who does not fear God or the laws, and shows the courage to protest against Jason's treatment of Quentin.

Not that Dilsey gets a recognition or appreciation of what she does for others. It is she alone who responds most adequately and affectionately to Benjy's helpless dependence, while Benjy's own mother almost grudges this attention. Apparently what Dilsey does for Benjy is out of pure self-motivation and not in obedience to any stricture from the employer. Even the small girl Quentin, whom Dilsey tries to mother is callous and harsh to her. Anyway, Quentin has been made cruel by a loveless home, and she despises both her uncles. But when the occasion arises, it is to Dilsey alone that she appeals for protection against the cruelty of the adults.

Mrs. Compson, who suggests a parody of the Southern white lady image—incompetent, ill-tempered, unable to cope with the small and big problems of life—provides a surface to reflect Dilsey's positive attributes by contrast. Dilsey is what Mr. Compson is not. Barbara Christian defines the Southern lady image—"the respectable lady, the desired concept of woman in the society" as "not only sexist and racist, [but] . . also classist." (2) Faulkner, however, upholds the other woman of the lower "class" instead in comparison with the "lady." True, Dilsey is not analyzed in the Toni Morrison way, that is, in terms of the relationship between class, race, gender. Nevertheless, she emerges as the focus. Thus, not only the other characters but even the "lady" too would instinctively turn to Dilsey for physical and mental comfort. As she needs Dilsey's help to allay her physical chilliness, so she needs her in the moment of mental unease and spiritual confusion following Quentin's disappearance. Dilsey hands over the Bible to her which she does not open. This detail has been usually considered by critics as an ironical touch. But this may also be seen in another way. Dilsey's very act of handing over the Bible may be emblematic of an extension of confidence, a gesture of some deeper assurance, which may soothe even the ever-fretful Mrs. Compson in her spiritual chaos.

Again, Dilsey provides the counterpoint at a climactic moment in the novel; when Jason goes along on his frustrating search for Quentin and her money, Dilsey goes to the church and has her ecstatic vision of fulfilment. Unlike the fury of Jason, the dullness of Benjy, the confusion of Quentin (male) and Caddy, the chaos of Quentin (female) and Mrs. Compson, Dilsey proves to be a point, and the only one, of stability. It has not been an easy attainment. She had to bleed and sweat all the way, one may assume, to reach this position; the careful description of her physical appearance at the opening of the last section shows how a woman has been scarred, scathed and furrowed by life, eaten away/exhausted by the many claims of life. The "collapsed face" bears the expression at once "fatalistic" and that of a child's "astonished disappointment." Yet she carries on painfully, slowly but steadily with her head held high.

Not that Faulkner casts Dilsey on the typical soft-sweet model of the conventional 'mammy.' She has an element of toughness which makes her disregard unjust demands from her employer, or leaves her indifferent to the shallow snobbery of "trash white folks" on the way to church. Neither does she indulge in any illusions regarding the black. She knows that her own son Luster, the "nigger boy" has "got jes as much Compson devilment" in him. This rare insight and clarity is the gift of her toughness which has carried her through a long ordeal in which she had no capital but her physical energy to invest, and that was used abused s/exploited by the white employer as well as the black male at home.

Dilsey's much-emphasized and sometimes derided religiosity may also be seen in this light. Most conventional readers and critics are impressed by Dilsey's simple faith in contrast to Mrs. Compson's lack of belief.[8] The angry young women since the 60s might find Dilsey disagreeably (and conveniently for the system) addicted to the 'poor's opium.' However, it may not be far-fetched to see her religiosity from another perspective. The ecstatic vision at the church has been grabbed by critics as unmistakable evidence of her humble Christianity, her surrender to the values of suffering and endurance; but this may also be seen in relation to her own life with its crosses and nails and thorns, its lashes and disappointments; life-long suffering has given her a philosophical poise, so that she can identify with the suffering god. Religion only helps her to make sense of her painful long ordeal in her own way. Her own life has been crucifixed onto exacting daily duties over the years; there has been no respite, consideration, concession. Yet she has attained the release of resurrection/transcendence through sheer strength and self-discipline; having conducted her own life with dignity and poise, with fatalistic stoicism in spite of so many disappointments she is at last at peace with herself and the world. Caddy and Quentin had also suffered in their own way: they too had been subjected to the humiliation and cruelty of an insensitive male-dominated society. They too had bled, but unlike Dilsey, failed to find transcendence. "I've seed de first en de last" reads like the choric wisdom of an old matriarch who has made sense of events through suffering.

It is because of this hard-earned wisdom that Dilsey can stand as an epitome of order amidst pervasive chaos and confusion, by uniting work, order, tradition, nature, god. This order is further reflected in her sense of time. Perrin Lowrey notes the brothers' defective sense of time.[9] Indeed each of them fails to make sense of time, i.e. Benjy is not conscious of it at all; Quentin is puzzled and afraid; Jason is mechanically obsessed. Only Dilsey can derive the right time from the incorrect clock and work out her schedule accordingly. This adds an extra dimension to her perception of the 'beginning and the ending,' i.e., eternity as perceived in terms of human consciousness. Thus it is Dilsey who appears as the only "integrated" person;[10] and in spite of her being just a servant by status can unify, and sustain at least to some extent, the Compson household.

Critics like Isadore Traschen have preferred to perceive Dilsey in the light of "instinctive motherliness"—a myth revived by the negritude movement: "She is the Great Mother who feeds, warms, and cares for everyone. As such, she is natural, not sentimental . . . grounded in her faith and her self as the Mother she is sustained by a kind of well-being that finds miraculous expression in the fact that she sings. . . . Certainly nothing more clearly indicates her power of transcendence." (465)

However, Dilsey's worksong is no mindless cheerfulness. It springs from profundity, from a stoic mastery over personal sadness and trouble, and may fall in line with the typical rhythm of worksongs by black women[11]—just as her appearance—though neat and trim—still bears traces of fatigue, long-suffering, the sadness of a wasted life, and the ruins ravaged by time and experience. That this has not embittered her only underscores her extraordinary strength and vitality.

Indeed, by relating the woman's power of transcendence to her 'motherliness' negritude also attempts to impose a role and gender expectation on the black woman by creating the idealized image/assumption about the African woman as Mother Earth. Faulkner, however, does not appear to have intended Dilsey to be a role model, either as the 'great mother' or as the submissive, soft-sweet 'mammy.' Rather she emerges just as a remarkable individual—an old woman who has lost physical strength and charm, who has no material property, power, or social status, and who has still solved her own identity-problem, and has emerged as a self-assured, self-contained, self-sufficient individual who may be considered by 'the second sex' all over the world with admiration, as an early anticipation of the emerging 'New Woman' of our times who can stand on her own—alone—in the face of the heaviest odds.

Dilsey and Christophine thus represent the marginalized and oppressed victims of racism/sexism/imperialism in two countries, who prove—by means of their dignity, poise and courage—what a woman and an underdog with no power/status/possession could still achieve, and thus emerge as model and inspiration for oppressed women anywhere in the world, who would be in search of an identity.

NOTES

1. William Faulkner, *The Sound and the Fury* (1929; rpt. New Delhi: O.U.P., 1981).
2. Jeans Rhys, *Wide Sargasso Sea* (London: Oliver and Boyd, 1961), p. 33.
3. Michael Millgate, *Faulkner* (London: Oliver and Boyd, 1961), p. 33
4. L.N. de Abruna, "Twentieth-Century Women Writers from the English-speaking Caribbean," *Modern Fiction Studies*, 34:1 (1986).
5. Irving Howe, *William Faulkner* (N.Y.: Vantage Books, 1962).
6. B. Christian, *Black Feminist Criticism* (N.Y.: Pergamon Press, 1985), p. 3.
7. C. Brooks, *William Faulkner* (1963; U.S.A.: Yale University Press, 1976), p. 357.
8. *Ibid.*, p. 7.

9. P. Lowrey, "Concepts of Time in *The Sound and the Fury*," R.S. Downes, ed., *English Institute Essays* (N.Y.: Columbia University Press, 1952).
10. I. Traschen, "The Tragic Form of *The Sound and the Fury,*" *Recent Studies of American Literature*, ed. P.C. Kar and D. Ramkrishna (Hyderabad: ASRC, 1985), p. 464.
11. "Almost always the substances of the worksongs about or by women are sifted through the cry of hard times . . . (these) shape the songs and give even the gayest song an undertone of plaintiveness." Christian, p. 7.

"Make me a captive, Lord, and I shall be free": Ironic West Indian Dilemma in George Lamming's *In the Castle of My Skin*

ROOPALI SIRCAR

George Lamming's first novel *In the Castle of My Skin*[1] published in 1953 by Longman and critically acclaimed, is a successful tale of West Indian reality. Set in the Barbados of the nineteen thirties and forties, the story is for most parts narrated by a young boy whose growth to manhood corresponds with the gradual disintegration of the social ethos in which he grows up. But this is more than just a novel of nostalgia and disillusion. It is as Ngugi Wa Thiong'o argues "a study of colonial revolt." The boy 'G' acutely experiences the non-existence of ties, and his inquisitiveness on his ninth birthday regarding father and relations, hints at an exodus, an aspect of West Indian life, that touches all classes of society and all races.

Home was always *there*, never *here*, and the call proved irresistible to generations. Cultural and economic pressure made the average West Indian long with intensity to emigrate. "My birth began with an almost total absence of family relations" (12) heightens the boy's isolation and his "My father only fathered the idea of me" (11) is a pain that is also the historical reality of the people of these islands. The African, the Indian and all those millions of people who have tasted the bitter fruit of colonization were able to reject its cultural dimension because they were fortunate to have a historical identity, a cultural past, and a language of their own. While the others were colonized, the West Indian was enslaved, and in the process of enslavement the West Indian was uprooted geographically and deprived of his roots and his personality and his cultural identity. Forced by stringent laws of the colonizers, the West Indian was forced to abandon any semblance of his culture.

The West Indian novel has been especially rich in accounts of childhood and adolescence, tracing the individual's journey to consciousness and his struggle to understand himself and the world he lives in. This journey to consciousness is not simple at all. In *In the Castle of My Skin*, the narrator's childlike consciousness grapples with this inexplicable sense of exile, and in the opening chapter Lamming lets the boy describe the state of his mind in the twilight zone between daylight and darkness. "It made no difference whether it was noon or night" because incessant rain which submerges his ninth birthday is filled with "enormous phantoms with eyes of fire and crowned with bulls's horns stalking through the dark." (13) Closing one's eyes ostrich-like drove them away only to have them appear soon. "Hovering over my head in a jeering silence. . . ." This somnambulism and terror of the child's experience is of "Thirty Thousand" men and women in the village in "a remote corner of a small British Colony, the oldest and the latest adulterated . . . Barbados or Little England as it was called in The Local School Texts." (25) Here in this feudal colonial village, *ruled by* Mr. Creighton the Landlord, whose house on top of the hill overlooks the village, it was an accepted fact that if "The Landlord was safe. The village was safe."

How this inexplicable connection came to be made is never questioned by the villagers themselves. It is much later in chapter five when the threat of losing one's land penetrates the haze and fog of colonized minds that they understand that "For reasons which were different" the land had got into the blood of the Englishman too. (98) "They called it Little England with the pride of the villager who thought the name carried with it a certain honourable distinction." (99) Only the shoemaker found "something suspect" in the Englishman's attachment. It was then for the first time the shoemaker "started to think of Little England as a part of some gigantic Thing called Colonial." (99)

George Lamming explains in his essay "The West Indian People" that the West Indian stunned by the horrors of the Middle passage, deliberately discouraged by slave laws from preserving more than fragments of his own culture, was ripe to be seduced into accepting as his own a value system profoundly opposed to his need and totally alien to his tradition and race.

Between the landlord and the villagers were the village overseers. Interestingly they were villagers themselves who were granted special favours. "These favours turned them fierce, aggressive, and strict." They had to be, they rationalized, because the villagers, their own folk were low-down nigger people "who were jealous of their own people who had done well for themselves." This "tense" relationship between the overseer and the villagers made them look at each other as enemies. Ironically there's no conflict between the landlord and the villagers.

This image of one's own people, in this case the villager as the enemy had "become a myth which like rumour drifted far beyond the village." (26) The better educated, those in responsible government posts, were also affected by this image of the enemy which "had its origin in a layer from which many had sprung and through accidents of time and experience forgotten." (26) Lamming stresses through the young narrator, the incredible and frustrating situation of the enemy being "My people." The overseer's and the Civil Servants' language had created a myth which had "eaten through their consciousness like moths through the pages of ageing documents. (27)

The images are dark, foggy, phantom like, full of potential horror and terror, of black night and decay. A surrealistic picture emerges "at the street corners the gas lamps winked within their netted cages, and the light leaking past the frosty domes, fell dully on the water . . . the moon . . . remote and ineffectual." (14)

For the West Indian the world which lies about him from his childhood is filtered through a set of alien images, actively fostered by an educational system which renders it unreal and fictional. The cultural patterns imported from England to the West Indies and carefully fostered to supplant any existing African, Indian or Asian patterns were designed to perpetuate a status quo in which the 'native' was taught to despise himself and to see his advancement in terms of the successful imitation of his English masters. The more successful he became in this endeavour, the more he was alienated from his own people and the more dependent he became on the English ruling class who retained the reality of power. The upward limit of his own social mobility was clearly defined to include only the trappings of power, to create on "Overseer' class. For a writer like George Lamming the new post-Independence rulers are only the final representatives of this class of middlemen.

This alienation was deliberately fostered by an educational system designed to maintain and reinforce the colonial status quo. With implicit irony but touched with the brilliance of the child-narrator's perception of the school function celebrating "Empire Day" and "The Queen's Birthday" exposes the tie at the heart of the colonial educational myth, that nothing happened in the West Indies.

History and achievement were English, poetry was Wordsworthian, beauty and nature were English, and human endeavour and pride happened elsewhere. The school in *In the Castle of My Skin* is a literal extension of the slave ship: "There were nine squads comprising about a thousand boys. The squads were packed close, and seen from the school porch the spectacle was that of an enormous ship whose charge had been packed in boxes and set on deck." (36) It is ironic cruelty that this ship load of individuals believe they are going to make history.

Fourth Boy: We are going to make history. I always want to make history.
Second Boy: Me, too. I read all those who been making history, William the conqueror and Richard an' all those. (48)

The boys desire to "make history by Foster Fence" has implicit ironic overtones—They have been taught the history of Sussex and Yorkshire but know nothing of the island they live in or of their own people's past. Even slavery which has shaped the West Indian reality is a mythic event for these children who have no direct experience of slavery. "Slavery was thousands of years before . . . probably it never happened." (58) The overcrowded suffocating metaphor of "Everywhere the red and the white and the blue" of the Union Jack flying its "message" is reinforced by "the colours though three in number had by constant repetition produced something vast and terrible, a kind of pressure or presence of which everyone was a part." (36)

A close analysis of the passage yields the insidious manner in which the colonizer gripped the minds of the West Indians, who, although no longer slaves like their forefathers are so totally in the grip of the colonial masters who, though small in number, had through constant repetition of their superiority, created an aura that was a constant reminder of their omnipotence and omniscience. Woven into this acceptance of the white man's superiority is the conviction of religious sanction. The young narrator and his friends in trying to grasp the myth of slavery overlap the stories of the Empire with that of the Garden of Eden. In doing so they expose, as Lamming intends to do, the sanctification by Christian grace of Imperialism and colonialism. All this points in the direction of subservience and acceptance, because the Christian view of man—"Make me a captive, Lord, and I shall be free," fits in perfectly with the colonial scheme. "The garden is God's own garden and the empire is God's only empire. They work together for us . . . when you are a slave of the empire and the garden at the same time, you can be free to belong to both." (71)

The contradictions are painfully apparent and the children's confused minds unwillingly unravel it. The apathy of the villager whose world is imaged by Lamming in semi-darkness, where vendors sell black pudding, where dogs and human beings copulate in the shadow of trees and "leaking moonlight" and life "oozes" "thick and congested" is contrasted with the excitement of the children as they "scramble wildly, flashing the fine narrow blades," created out of pins. Touched in this act is the seed of revolution:

Three—Thirteen—Thirty Boys.
Three—Thirteen—Thirty Knives. (31)

So many more than the three colours, red, blue and white in the Union Jack and in the Queen's bloomers.

Like the child in the Emperor's New Clothes whose innocence lends him the courage to publicly expose the King's vanity, the children in Lamming's novel are symbolic of those who can and will protest vehemently. Reviewing the beating their mate gets from the master, they express anger. "It aint fair in the sight of God or the Devil." But they have a solution. "By Christ stone him, stone him. I say stone him" because as they declare: "He's an advantage-taker" but "whenever you meet them, here or in heaven there's a way to deal with them." It is easy because "Stones are free—free—free—free." (47) The young boys despite their sense of righteous anger also know this would be a big incident because the school teacher has power and authority vested in him second hand by the invisible "Empire." "Stones don't cost money,"—this is George Lamming's message to his apathetic people who live in fear of power and authority.

There is a shift in the narrative when the first person boy narrator yields to the dialogue between Pa and Ma: "Everyone called them Pa and Ma. They were the oldest couple in the village." (14) Pa and Ma give us a glimpse of a world that is dimly recollected but all the same it is the reality of the West Indian's African roots. The old couple and the children are at two opposing poles, but conversely the old people belong to the *innocent past* and the children to the *experienced present*. Ma has sympathy for the Landlord and is pained by the disrespect that is being expressed. She distrusts violent changes and the future is to be feared for its dark unpredictability. Pa on the other hand welcomes the new dream: "If Mr. Creighton an' all the Creightons from time past can own it, there aint no reason why we mustn't." This, Ngugi Wa Thiong'o calls "A revolutionary thought: What it calls for is a total overhaul of all relations hitherto governing the islands—the colonial plantocracy." Mr. Slime is a grasping exploitative 'native' who unwillingly gives his people a measure of self-respect. They are afraid but not apathetic any longer and the possibilities mesmerize them.

Christian values legitimize colonial authority in the novel, and spiritually emasculate a whole community. When the villagers reject Creighton's domination, it is preceded by a rejection of religion and Christian teachings, calling it "Tomfoolery—o' joke about an old man goin' born again." (136).

Ironically Mr. Slime becomes a new Moses for his people. The strike and its amplifications are reported by Lamming in short staccato sentences. "There was a kind of horror in the air . . . that was clear." (193) The strike and the riots force Crieghton to sell out to the 'Penny Bank' and leave. It is the lawyers, the teachers, the doctors and the MLAs, the emergent national bourgeoisie who buy up all land, dispossessing all those who for years had eked out their existence on the land. The shoemaker's wail expresses all the surprise and pain with which the simple village folk have been confronted. Their dispossession in historical terms is a second exile. Pa's going away to the Alms House symbolizes the crisis. Creighton and the peasants break free of their feudal relationship, but the peasants are now the hordes of urban labour. "At one level nothing happens in the village. On another level things change in the village irrevocably. For the boy narrator of the novel adolescence and maturity has taken the place of childhood. He accepts this change as inevitable but the villagers continue to be bewildered by the suddenness of the events. Pa tells G: "I don't know. A man makes a promise an' a man change an' the man makes the promise ain't the same said man who change, an' I don't know who got the right to judge. Why we change or whether he should have changed at all. I don't know." (303)

It is the narrator's boyhood friend Trumper who has been to America and has seen the plight of negroes there, who recognises a solidarity with the oppressed in his own village. "Their suffering teach them what we here wont even know, the Race. Our people." (246) Condemning in no uncertain words the kinds of Mr. Slime, Trumper angrily expresses his feelings and that of all the villagers: "nothin' he do surprises me." (296) Trumper promises to "fight for the rights of the negroes" at the cost of his life. The end of the novel sees the traditional roles destroyed and everybody is dispossessed in many different ways.

George Lamming in his "Critical Insight into Shakespeare's *Tempest*" has expressed the necessity for Caliban in a dialogue with Prospero to re-invest and redefine their relationship. Because if Caliban must become a man, Prospero must cease being a myth of a superman. In *In the Castle of My Skin,* George Lamming demythologizes Prospero and allows Caliban to grow out of a stultifying relationship, because unlike V.S. Naipaul's West Indies which is only a "transitional land" where "nothing was created," Lamming's West Indies is seen through the eyes of Caliban, not Prospero, and in doing so he fulfills the children's desire- to "make History" and free the 'enslaved' mind from the prison of the colour of his "skin."

George Lamming's *Of Age and Innocence*: A Critique

VINEY KIRPAL

The West Indian novel is characterized by a robustness and vigour that is very attractive to the Indian reader. It expresses an energy and vitality that is the distinguishing feature of all community-oriented, "traditional" societies. It also is the product of shared historical forces. George Lamming, V.S. Naipaul and Wilson Harris continue to be its foremost practitioners. Lamming, whose very first novel, *In the Castle of My Skin* (1953), bagged for its author a clutch of awards, has written five other novels to date: *The Emigrants* (1954), *Of Age and Innocence* (1958), *Season of Adventure* (1960), *Water with Berries* (1973), and *Natives of My Person* (1972). All his novels are as carefully crafted as his masterly first novel. However, existing criticism has not done equal justice to all of them.

The novel that I wish to discuss and which in my view has not received the attention it deserved is Lamming's third novel, *Of Age and Innocence*.[1] Prevailing criticism on the work has been general in nature.[2] No particular effort has been made to undertake a full length analysis of the book. The novel merits a detailed appreciation and the present article hopes to fulfil this need to some extent. Chronologically, *Of Age and Innocence* is Lamming's third novel but thematically it begins where *In the Castle of My Skin* leaves off—that is, with the West Indies on the brink of freedom from the repressive colonial regime.

Of Age and Innocence, set in the 1940s and 50s, depicts the West Indian (San Cristobal in the novel) struggle for independence, which had just begun on the island. The movement, in its initial phases, fails to gather momentum because of racial differences. Then, Isaac Shephard, a native of Negro origin, returns to the island after a lengthy stay in England and raises the slogan of a basic West Indian identity which goes beyond narrow communal loyalties and underlines the racial diversity on the islands. The slogan unites the people against the colonial forces on the island. Shephard joins Aly Singh's Indian Freedom Party and gets it renamed as the Peoples' Communal Movement. It is led by Singh (an Indian), Lee (a retired Chinese Schoolmaster turned merchant) and Shephard himself (a Negro).

The People's Communal Movement symbolizes the theme of multi-racial unity. Its membership is open to West Indians of all races and communities. The national independence movement then gathers strength and Shephard becomes famous overnight. Who is this man, everybody on the island is soon asking? Is he a mad man, as some people insinuate? Or, a savior as he himself claims? His character is drawn without idealization or simplification. Shephard, the son of a preacher, becomes the people's revered leader and messiah.[3] His personal charisma and the magic of his philosophy of a common West Indian identity having worked to make his movement a truly peoples' movement.[4] As Thief (the character in the book who represents the common man's viewpoint) aptly remarks to his friend Rockery, the fisherman: "An twus a special moment strike the night before San Cristobal declare him Lord o' the day. You hold my word, Rockey, that Shephard won't happen again, but San Cristobal goin' grow from his grave as it rise from the water that wet his breathing." (355) The impact of the movement is also felt by the colonial administration so that people like Crabbe, the Police Commissioner, feel threatened and try to break it through ruthless measures. For example, Crabbe employs Baboo—ironically, an Indian native—to spy on Shephard. Crabbe even draws up a plan to have Shephard murdered which would cripple the liberation movement, depriving it of a powerful leader. All these are indications that the movement led by Shephard, Lee and Singh had become a force on the island.

Returning to San Cristobal on the same flight as Shephard after twenty years in England is Mark, a writer, also a native. He had once the ambition to write the biography of a three-fingered pirate, a legendary figure from the eighteenth century. But he gives up the idea when he sees how easily any public figure—Shephard in this case—can become a legend while the truth—that, Shephard for example whom he has known from childhood is a megalomaniac—becomes inaudible in the loud noise of artificial public adulation.

Coming to San Cristobal for no particular reason, he gets briefly involved with Shephard's movement. In his first speech at Shephard's pre-election rally at Sabina Park, he defines nationalism as more than anti-colonialism and multi-racial unity. He sees it as the ability to grow emotional roots in one's country by returning to one's own traditions and by trying to see their creative relevance to contemporary times and challenges. He demonstrates this in his re-telling of the legend of the

Tribe Boys and the Warrior Ants. His purpose is to show to the people that the Tribe Boys, despite their military defeat at the hands of the Bandit Kings, had freedom of spirit which they asserted by preferring suicide to enslavement.[5] This was the spirit which was lacking in the West Indians today as a consequence of a long colonial domination. They had to reacquire this spirit if they wished to win freedom from the colonizer. Mark urges the native to "decolonize" himself:

> Freedom is not a habit which may be overcome, nor is it a fashion which changes with opinion. It is an instinct; it is a nerver. And the spirit which gives life meaning revolts when that instinct is threatened. . . . The freedom which you sing is not freedom for San Cristobal only. . . . You are only servants of spirit which possesses all men . . . and when you rejoice in the knowledge of your own freedom . . . you are rejoicing on behalf of all men. The legend of the Tribe Boys is being enacted again in the history of this movement for freedom. (173)

The legend of the Tribe Boys as interpreted by Mark, provides the people for the first time with the notion of a decolonized psyche. Later the model way of the Tribe Boys inspires the native boys Bob, Lee and Singh with a method of protesting against the unjust award of the sentence of death of Lee and Singh who are falsely accused of starting the fire at the mental hospital during the electricians' strike. The three boys decide to commit suicide just as the Tribe Boys had done many centuries ago to protest against this decision of colonial law. Having taken this decision, the boys experience a sudden liberation of the spirit exactly in the manner of their ancestors:

> "Tomorrow is the trial," said Bob.
> "Tomorrow an' may be till a next tomorrow it last," Singh said.
> "But hardly more," said Bob, "tomorrow an' a next tomorrow."
> The curfew rang, ordering every street to be empty. But they would not stir. They sat in silence beside the grave. And the sound reached them again, irrelevant as the noise of the sea, an ordinary part of the night, like the howl of a dog shut out. The law could not now enter their feeling. (412-13)

The myth of the Tribe Boys becomes relevant to contemporary West Indies. It re-creates the meaning of a "decolonized" spirit so that the illiterate people can understand the concept itself; it provides the boys with a strategy for action drawn from their own history and value system.[6]

In evoking tradition for its relevance and value, Mark is not idealizing the whole of West Indian tradition but only that which he considers relevant to contemporary times, that which represents the presence of the past. Ma Shephard—Shephard's seventy-year-old mother—very much like the old woman in Raja Rao's *Kanthapura*—represents tradition in its negative as well as positive aspects. Ma Shephard is an allegorical character without ceasing to be flesh and blood. She is the repository of all the legends and myths of San Cristobal and the island's younger generation—in particular, the boys of the secret Society—have acquired their knowledge of tradition from her. (63-64)

But she is also the tradition that the boys shun towards the end of the book. On a literal level, Ma doesn't understand the boys's rejection of her and is hurt and puzzled by it. (40) Yet in rejecting her now, the boys are rejecting a tradition which is effete, which calls for blind faith in religion and custom, rejecting free inquiry. (Ma Shephard testifies against Singh in the mental hospital grounds and had discovered a lighter with Singh's initial in a bag she had found on the grounds.) The tradition that the boys retain and turn to, to find their living ideals, is the creative tradition that Mark had spoken of with vitality and value, with faith, hope, dignity and self-respect.

Closely linked with the role of tradition in the modern West Indies is the conflict between Age and Innocence—that is, "Age that apprehends" and "Innocence which can only see."[7] The novel draws its title from it. In the novel, the conflict is represented as the conflict of the two generations—the generation of the three native boys and Rowley Crabbe (Police Commissioner Crabbe's son)—members of the secret Society[8] and their fathers. The boys feel impatient with the ways of their fathers, though the author ironically also suggests that they derived their status and identity from those of their parents. (Bob is the only one whose father is not in the movement and this hurts him and makes him sometimes feel insecure and diffident). The boys's Society begins with contempt for the movement which their fathers had led. They assert their superiority:

> "San Cristobal goin' look like what we doin' now" said Singh, "an' we'll be the first to start what the big ones always talking."
>
> "My father say they goin' keep San Cristobal," said Lee, "like how we have the Society, but he don't know 'bout the Society, the way we three different an' still alike."
>
> "The talk 'bout the future like a war," said Singh, "how the fu-

> ture goin' come only with the struggle."
>
> "An' we have the future already," said Lee, "'cause we make a little Society for three, an' we see how it work."
>
> "Tis 'cause they live so long before," said Bob, "that the future look hard to reach. But we reach already." (118-20)

However, it is clear that the secret Society is a satire on the immaturity and naivete of those who fail to see that political and social change is serious business, calling for sacrifice, dedication and endurance. Not that the boys do not have a glimpse of the difficulties and complexities of achieving national integration. On the day they spend in the woods to celebrate the inclusion of Rowley in their Society they play the game "Penny for your thoughts," and it becomes obvious to them that each of them has a secret that he cannot divulge to the other members though they have vowed to have no secrets from one another. Their contempt for the failure of their fathers to achieve national unity is exposed. Again, in another scene, the author depicts the boys idly drawn to a row of ants in the wood, monotonously carrying food to the anthill. They interpret this as a journey to success, failing to realize, as the author points out, that the ants were travelling "in a drama which made obstacle and endurance, equal, infinite." (124) However this realization comes to them only towards the end of the book—when Shephard is murdered and his "assailants" are helped to escape. Martial law is declared and every one is afraid. Their own fathers are falsely implicated in crimes they haven't committed so that they can be done away with. The truth dawns on them that political struggle is not easy, that existing power groups will resort to authoritarian or foul means to suppress such struggles. Thus the political consciousness of the boys develops. Their growth is not the same as that of the boys in *In the Castle of My Skin*. They represent the growing consciousness of the people rather than boys growing up to become adults. In a spirit of supreme sacrifice they decide to commit suicide to protest against the injustice to their father. The book concludes with all of them standing for a consciousness awakened to the reality of the country's problems. (We recall Mark's vision of the birth of an animal-consciousness.) The boys now grown mature symbolize the hope which began in age. Baboo's murder of Shephard so that Singh, an Indian like himself, may head the new government represents only a temporary regression into the past of narrow communal loyalties. The collective decision of the boys to die, if necessary, to protest against the colonizers's suppression of the movement is an affirmation of the national integration that Shephard had envisaged. (58)

An interesting feature of the novel is the artistic re-creation of a colonial consciousness in the characterization of Mark and Shephard. In Mark—sensitive, lonely, diffident—this consciousness is seen in a continual "disinclination of feeling." Except once—at Sabina Park when he briefly recovers his identity—he is never able to overcome his diffidence. The death of Marcia (Mark's girl friend) in the fire at the mental hospital leaves him broken and he returns to his earlier state of emotional disintegration. In Shephard, the colonized psyche manifests itself in the obsessive fear of "the eye of the other." (112-13) The fear had begun in England with his isolation as a colonial with a black skin.[9] This isolation is re-created in the description of Shephard on the plane to San Cristobal:

> The enormous black skull which had been wagging from side to side like a clock's dull tongue rose gradually, showing its heavy thick neck, and the ample shoulders that sloped abruptly into arms.
>
> The man turned slowly, ignoring his neighbours, his hands falling stolidly down his sides, and his massive ears twitching under the naked dome of skull. He stood heavy and still, staring vacantly over the heads of those who immediately confronted him. His presence made the air thick with confusion . . . his face, like a lost piece of night carving its image upon the afternoon, was the face of fugitive who had meandered through all weathers to a season of insanity. A red range coaxed his eyes from their sockets, and the words churned his passion to a fury which now separated him from the memory of himself. Some animal of the air, more fantastic than beasts or birds of the familiar earth, inhabited his brain and romped with the words which had made subversion among his senses. (48-52)

These descriptions are presented through the consciousness of the white passengers on the plane. (Mark, for instance, doesn't find Shephard strange to look at.) Their responses depict their revulsion from and fear of the monstrous, the animal—a stereotype of the coloured man[10] that exists only in their own imagination. In order to overcome the shame he feels instinctively at this "animal view" of him, Shephard attacks his tormentors to force them to really look at him and to savour their fear. To free one's consciousness, Frantz Fanon says, a reversal of roles from the prosecuted to the prosecutor is required at least for a while.[11] Shephard is able to achieve this and liberate his consciousness. But Mark is not aggressive. He remains therefore colonized.

Although the theme of the novel is essentially political, community life is evoked with feeling and authenticity as for example in the scene at the beach when the boats race in from sea.[12]

> A huge crowd waited on the shore, watching the slow, turbulent traffic of animals between the ship and the boats. They could see the men through the casual drift of smoke, leaning over their boats in a swift and desperate conflict with the ropes and the sea. Each man found his beast, latching the ropes to his boat, and the oars slapped the water in a slow propulsion away from the ship. For a while the animals were completely covered with foam. The boats pulled them forward, and their heads surfaced. Two of the boats waited ahead until the others came into line, and then they started their journey towards the shore.
>
> They came nine at a time, and the crowd shouted their impatience, arguing about the skill of the oarsmen. They were beginning to anticipate the order of these arrivals, wondering which boat would make the first landing, and who would be the first to release the animal from the stern and race across the sand to the market stall. The betting had begun, and it seemed for a while a very difficult crossing. (74)

The same feeling of communal togetherness is evoked again in the scene where the people gather to offer propitiatory gifts to the sea, an important West Indian rite:

> The crowd had travelled with their gifts to propitiate the thirst of the sea. The sand received their weight from the abrupt boundary of the weed that rambled inland under the trees to the slipping edge of the sea, and their voices journeyed in a grave echo across the water. There were children everywhere, eager and credulous as they listened to the story of their island.
>
> "You turn in your gift?"
>
> "Yes, Ma, I give it up."
>
> "An' with a good heart, Ma."
>
> "Time an' the water will make your reward with mercy." (63)

It is difficult to capture community life without using community speech rhythms. Communal speech rhythms are characterized by reverberation, repetition of some phrases and words, and by the dialectical mode of question and answer. All these patterns are to be found even in so casually chosen a passage as the one cited immediately above, and evoke the oral narrative manner that distinguishes the literature of community-oriented societies from that of individual-oriented societies:

> "You *turn in your gift*?"
> "Yes Ma, *I give it up*."
> "An' *with a good heart you give it?*"
> "*With a good heart*, Ma." (Emphasis mine)

In the more stylistically sophisticated sections of the novel, the sense of "collective improvisation" as in New Orleans Jazz music[13] seems to pervade. For instance, in the scene where the three native boys of the secret Society retell the legend of the Tribe Boys to Penelope and Marcia with a synchronization that originates only in music and in community life. (In fact, one of the reasons why music is basic to a close-knit communal way of life is that the quality of harmony and consonance is common to both.) An extract from this section would give us some idea. The connective "an'" ("and") used iteratively enhances this sense of unity, orchestration and harmony because of the impression of cyclical endlessness and continuity that it generates:

> Marcia nodded as she put the cigarette in her mouth, and when she lowered her head, and Penelope scratched the match, the boys decided that it was the moment to begin.
>
> "'Twas like in that time when the world known only nature an' noise."
>
> "Bird noise and wind," said Singh. "An' plain animal talk" Bob continued. "An' the fish dancin' wild an' makin' faces at the bottom o' the ocean, an' only the sun get permission to say the time, an' the moon only making plan to decide the size o' the sea, or makin' fun at some mountains which couldn't climb no more, an' sometimes collapse if a new tide turn upside down, and shape up the sand. Like such a time it was for San Cristobal, long, long before human interference."
>
> "Like in Genesis," Lee said.
>
> "As in the 'beginning,'" said Bob, "'before sense start to make separation betwixt some things an' some things."
>
> "An' food was free," said Singh, "'cause there was no han' to hide what it take."
>
> "Except for the animals who fight an' fail" said Lee. "Except for them," said Bob. "But Lan' didn't belong to nobody, an' the

law, you feel, was only nature authorisin'."

"Or refusin' to interfere," said Lee.

"So we say," Bob continued, "that San Cristobal set up a good example like the world before men make arrangement."

"Or refusin' to interfere," said Lee.

"So we say," Bob continued, "that San Cristobal set up a good example like the world before men make arrangement."

They paused as though they wanted to make sure of the women's attention. (95)

Besides employing prominent features of oral narrative and indigenous music rhythms, the novel also brings out the dignity, and aptness of the local idiom to express the native sensibility. A rather successful attempt is made in the conversation between Rockey, the unlettered fisherman (the fisherman, in Lamming's books,[13] always represents the truest inhabitant of the sea-surrounded West Indies) and the educated clerk (who is subtly ridiculed for having grown away from the vigorous native culture and idiom because of his education). The episode appears on p. 340 of the book:

> Witness (Rockey): ". . . An' what you call the night in question was, I recollect, no bed o' roses at Paradise Point. It was a complete blackout of light for the night, and it take a *reg'lar piss-to-win'ward* to say the settin' out for a swim on that sea."
>
> There is a brief interruption while the Clerk says for some of clarification of the term *piss-to-win'ward.* It means simply a foolish man, one has observed in the witness's example, making water with his organ held up to the wind, so that the urine was returned in his face, . . .

Finally, perhaps the most striking quality of Lamming's fiction is its sensuousness. In an interview, Lamming has stated that he writes "very much with the ear, very much an aural and visual prose."[14] Indeed, that is the impression that this novel also makes—that Lamming writes prose with a poet's ear and eye. His descriptions are rich, sensuous and vivid. Indeed, in this passage, which describes a lizard caught under a tree branch in the woods, the terror and the helplessness of the reptile are caught in a close-up in words that could match the skills of a photographer or a painter. The lizard remains no mere object in the general landscape but a creature with feelings to be regarded in its own right:

> He [Rowley] rubbed his eyes and looked more closely at the lizard, fat and green as young grass with a yellow tuft of throat hanging like a fried yolk under its head. The eyes were the size of peas, restless and black with fear. The lizard was caught a little above the base of the tail. Its body stretched and swelled like rubber on either side of the bramble. Now and again the head lunged forward in an effort to escape, and the throat widened and trembled, until the lizard tired and the head leaned wearily down to rest on the bramble. The mouth was open and the tongue showed like a disc of spit, frozen red and hanging at the edge of the breathing lip. The feet shrank visibly over the bramble, and the tail started to change colour. The lizard was going to die unless someone separated the sticks of bramble and made way for it. (142)

NOTES

1. George Lamming, *Of Age and Innocence* (London: Michael Joseph, 1958).
2. Here are two examples of available criticism on *Of Age and Innocence*. V.S. Naipaul in *New Statesman* (December 6, 1958, p. 827) writes: "Mr. Lamming is only thirty. He is one of the finest prose-writers of his generation. Purely as a work of fantasy *Of Age and Innocence* is really quite remarkable. It fails through its sheer unreadability. Mr. Lamming should be warned by this that his best subject, as in *In the Castle of My Skin* and the first 50 pages of this novel is himself." Gareth Griffiths in *A Double Exile: African and West Indian Writing Between Two Cultures* (London: Marion Boyars, 1978, p. 138) opines: "*Of Age and Innocence* is a successful attempt to disentangle some of the main issues confronting West Indian society and to try and define the nature and cost of a decision to alter it. . . . In the reactions of all groups to the issues posed Lamming provides a very strong case against the racially based solutions to the West Indian problem. . . . If the problem is founded in the history of their past interactions the solution can be found there too."
3. Like Slime in *In the Castle of My Skin*, Shephard was probably just an ambitious opportunist, who, had he lived on, may have proved himself to be one within a short while. Yet the most positive aspect of his leadership was that it initiated a noteworthy change in the consciousness of the masses.
4. Instances of the people's new awareness of their rights and the need to unite against the colonizers are the strike of the electricians and the creation by the shopkeepers of an artificial oil shortage to compel the white to

meet the strikers' demands. In another instance, the employees of the mental hospital suddenly strike work and take out a silent protest march, going round and round the building.

5. The legend of the Tribe Boys is a true story of West Indian heroism. It occurs in at least two novels of Lamming. A group of forty Carib Indians on Grenada after a pitched battle against the French in which many of their men are killed, committed suicide rather than be conquered, by jumping off a cliff onto the rocks below. Derek Walcott also narrates this story in *Another Life* (London: Jonathan Cape, 1973, p. 70) as an example of native heroism as against European heroic exploits. Cited in John Thieme, "Narrative Modes in West Indian Literature" in *A Sense of Place*, ed. Britta Olinder (Goteborg, 1984), p. 144.
6. For example Mark's statement that "The legend of the Tribe Boys is being enacted again in the history of this Movement for freedom," (p. 173) reminds of Rao's depiction in *Kanthapura* of the Indian freedom movement as a re-enactment of the liberation of Sita by Rama from the clutches of Ravana—as narrated in *The Ramayana*.
7. George Lamming, *The Pleasures of Exile* (London: Michael Joseph, 1960), p. 103.
8. The secret society had been formed merely in sport at first to mimic the political concerns of the larger movement. But as the boys live through the national events, the objectives of the society also become serious.
9. Compare M.K. Gandhi's experiences in South Africa recorded in *An Autobiography or the Story of My Experiments with Truth*, trans. Mahadev Desai (Ahmedabad: Navjivan Publishing House, 1945), pp. 134-84.
10. "[The colonizer] dehumanizes the native, or to speak plainly [he] turns him into an animal. In fact, the terms the settler uses when he mentions the natives are zoological terms." Frantz Fanon, *The Wretched of the Earth*, trans. Constance Farrington (New York: Grove Press, 1966), p. 34.
11. Fanon quoting and elaborating on the slogan, "The last shall be first and the first last," makes this point. *Ibid.*, p. 30.
12. One recalls the boat race among the fishermen in *Chemeen*: "The boats were heading home, dancing on the waters. . . . Karuthamma and her mother argued as to which was their boat, but they soon identified it as the one in the end, speeding like a bird, skipping from the crest of one wave to another . . . the approach of the boats was like a grand procession." Thakazhi S. Pillai, *Chemeen*, trans. Narayan Menon (Bombay: Jaico, 1971), p. 52.
13. *Brother Man* then reveals certain rhythmic thematic and structural features which justify I think my comparing it to music. Its specific relationship to New Orleans Jazz comes with its peculiar sense of union and unity; its

contrasting 'duets' its improvisation and correspondences and above all, its pervading *sense of community* (its collective improvisation)." E. Brathwaite, "Roger Mais's *Brother Man* as Jazz Novel," *Critics on Caribbean Literature*, ed. E. Baugh (London: George Allen and Unwin, 1978), p. 110.

14. R. Sanders and Jan Munro, "A Conversation with the West Indian Writer George Lamming," *Caribbean Quarterly*, XVII, 3-4, November 1970, p. 78.

Satire and Structure in Naipaul and Narayan

N. RAMA DEVI

The unpredictable nature of Naipaul as a man makes it difficult to place him or identify him with any one particular tradition. He was born and to some extent brought up in Trinidad. His grandfather had come from Bihar to Trinidad as an indentured labourer and had settled in Trinidad. Naipaul was educated in England. His belated visit to India created a cultural shock. The sceptical notions that he entertained about Trinidad made it impossible for him to call it his own. Trinidad to him is an unimportant, uncreative and cynical society devoid of achievement and history. About Trinidad he says: "A peasant-minded, money-minded community, spiritually static because cut off from its roots, its religion reduced to rites without philosophy, set in a materialist colonial society: a combination of historical accidents and national temperament has turned the Trinidad Indian into the complete colonial, even more philistine than the white."[1] Everyone including an Indian is bound to exist there as an oddity as it encouraged only eccentricity. And being a society without traditions, everyone finds it easier to be an oddity. He has also admitted that the Americans do not accept him because he was too British and the English do not want him because he was too foreign. Further as Anthony Boxill points out, "One cannot place Naipaul in the tradition of European culture because he lacks the optimism of writers who come from rooted societies."[2]

Hence it might be plausible to place him in the tradition of Indian literature by virtue of Indian names, customs and cultural ideas, that proliferate in his works. And given the similarities, in such aspects as the use of English language in a careful and dexterous manner along with occasional regional (Trinidadian and Tamil respectively) locutions, the use of certain traditional rituals and motifs, presentation of the consequences of a twisted use and exploitation of legacy and 'degree' or hierarchy, Naipaul can be placed by the side of R.K. Narayan.

Since both Naipaul and Narayan are writing about heritage and legacies which have been degraded by the distorted use of these key concepts by unscrupulous people, satire becomes their indispensable novelistic tool. The novel, which is a representation of reality, takes nothing that is ideal. Furthermore, as both Naipaul and Narayan are intent on giving a social comment on life, they cannot present the ideal. Satire and irony are the only tools which they can use. Narayan's irony is mild and comic whereas irony becomes rather bitter in the hands of Naipaul which can be attributed to the traumatic encounters he had, and the cultural shock he experienced on his first visit to India. His bafflement at the distorted use of certain verses of the most sacred treatise of the Hinuds, *The Gita*, becomes evident through his words in *An Area of Darkness*:

> The prompting is universal, but the Indian practice is purely of India. "And do thy duty, even if it be humble, rather than another's even if it be great. To die in one's duty is life: to live in another is death." This is the *Gita*, preaching degree fifteen hundred years before Shakespeare's Ulysses, preaching it today. And the man who makes the dingy bed in the hotel room will be affronted if he is asked to sweep the gritty floor. The clerk will not bring you a glass of water even if you faint. The architecture student will consider it a degradation to make drawings, to be a mere draughtsman. And Ramnath, the stenographer, so designated on the triangular block of wood that stands on the desk, will refuse to type out what he has taken down in short-hand.[3]

What we encounter in the citation is an attempt on the part of certain selfish people to amend, to redefine the concept of 'degree' (that should exist for the welfare of polity) to suit their own selfish needs. It brings to the surface an ironic reversal of the situation, i.e., instead of heritage or legacy defining the needs of the people, what we find is, the needs define and interpret the legacy. Instead of practising the Gandhian ideal of "Means justify the ends," the people are practising the Machiavellian ideal, "Ends justify the means." The 'degree' or hierarchy that ought to exist for the sake of polity is being put to all sorts of distorted use by the people. It is this tendency that has become the bane of our country, bringing about the collapse of societal relationships. This concept has been treated very well by both Naipaul and Narayan in their novels.

For convenience sake, let us take Narayan's *The Financial Expert* and Naipaul's *The Mystic Masseur* into consideration.

In *The Financial Expert*, the narrative proceeds from a single point of view, that of Margayya. The narrative opens with a semantic exploration of the protagonist's name, Margayya, which means "one who shows the way," the way out to those in financial trouble. Margayya's capacity to make nice distinctions between money, riches, wealth, and fortune suggests that he makes a good use of his wits through which he shows the peasants an easy way to draw unlimited loans from the co-operative bank, without committing themselves to repay the loans until the bank authorities put an end to his activities. He then wants to propitiate goddess Lakshmi not for any kind of spiritual fulfilment but to earn money. Then he becomes the owner of a pornographic manuscript called *Bed Life* at first and then *Domestic Harmony* through which he acquires a lot of money. He then begins to hoard more and more money gathered from his clients. But even he miscalculates the significance of *Domestic Harmony*. Earlier he had taken all the care to avoid any kind of undesirable influence of the book on his son, Balu. But when Balu and his wife shift to their new house, Dr. Pal, the author of the book visits them and influences Balu to put the aesthetic of *Domestic Harmony* into practice. An irate Margayya beats Dr. Pal for corrupting his son. As an act of revenge Dr. Pal spreads rumours about Margayya's insolvency and incites his customers to withdraw their deposits along with interest from Margayya's bank. Thus Margayya's fortune vanishes overnight. And he prepares to start again as a petty operator under the banyan tree.

The Mystic Masseur, on the other hand, is about an Indian, Ganesh Ramsumair, who begins his career as a secondary school teacher. But being inept, he quits the job and survives mainly due to the oil royalties inherited after his father's opportune death. He then becomes a writer and writes an absurd book, *101 Questions and Answers on the Hindu Religion*, published at his own expense and which no one buys. He then becomes a masseur. But he achieves success only when he becomes a 'mystic,' dresses in traditional Indian robes and attends to Trinidad's spiritual problems. After some time, he manages to cure a black child, though by a mere combination of commonsense and fakery. His reputation spreads throughout the island. His brilliant success as a mystic helps him to become a successful author at first, then a politician, and then an M.L.C. Being an opportunist he soon changes his name to G.R. Muir and from a rebel he becomes a government supporter. He is awarded an M.B.E. and sent abroad by the British government to defend their colonial policy.

As we see, both Margayya and Ganesh of two novels interpret the *Gita* in a distorted way and use the rituals—the worship of Goddess Lakshmi not for spiritual exaltation but for the fulfilment of their urge for money. When the ritual fails to furnish what they seek, they do not mind going to the extent of adopting other methods, quite contrary to what the rituals preach, just to get what they want. It is at this juncture that irony comes into play in the form of consequences of the riches. The consequenecs ironically are beyond the grasp of the characters.

The similarities between Narayan and Naipaul come to surface once we compare Margayya with Ganesh. "Each rises from poverty and obscurity to a certain prominence in his community. Their rise is associated with books in spite of their incredible naivete about the world of books."[4] When they are forced to deal with the printers, we find both of them playing pretence in a similar way:

> "Look, how much you know about this thing?"
> "Printing?"
> Ganesh smiled, "I study it a little bit."
> "What point you want it to be in?"
> Ganesh didn't know what to say.
> "Eight, ten, eleven, twelve, or what?" Basdeo sounded impatient.
> Ganesh was thinking rapidly about the cost.
> He said firmly, "Eight go do me.'"[5]

We find Margayya doing almost the same thing.

> Margayya true to his principles did not wish to show his ignorance.
> Hal asked: "Shall we print on demy or octavo?"
> What was demy and what octavo? What strange terms were these: to what universe did they belong? . . . He said grandly: "Each had its own advantage, it's for you to decide; you are a technical man."
> Lal said: "You see, demy will give us greater area."
> Margayya was hearing the word for the first time in his life.[6]

The similarities between these two scenes suggest that both the authors are making similar remarks about the role books play in an illiterate society.

Regarding the differences between these two authors who use irony and satire as the chief means to reflect the follies and weaknesses of the society, their treatment and personal attitudes, and vision are different. While Narayan's satire is rather comic and wild, Naipaul's is an intense and bitter one. Narayan merely visualizes his characters through the comic irony with no strong intention to change them, probably he wants others who follow their destinies to overcome their fates. As George Woodcock points out, "Narayan never condemns men because they are not better than they are: he merely shows how the evil they manifest may in true comic manner be diverted."[7] Naipaul, on the other hand, satirizes the follies of the people and the society very severely. He wants the society and situations to be ideal and totally different from what they are in actuality. His bitterness and mercilessness may be the result of his failure to find fulfilment and roots in society he has been searching for. It is the traumatic experiences that he countered when he came to the land of his ancestors which might have made him react with a kind of pessimism.

The difference in the endings of the two stories, *The Financial Expert* and *The Mystic Masseur*, in spite of the similarity in their themes and characters, may be attributed to the difference in the outlook of the two authors on the legacy they have inherited. While Naipaul bears the legacy as an overwhelming burden, Narayan bears it as a cross. While Naipaul wants to repudiate the burden in strong terms to suggest the inadequacies of the legacy, Narayan likes to come to terms with it with the help of comic irony as reflected in the ending of *The Financial Expert*, Margayya coming back to square one. Naipaul, on the other hand, seeks refuge in bitter satire as could be seen in the epilogue of *The Mystic Masseur*, i.e., Ganesh becoming G.R. Muir, Esq., M.B.E., and sent abroad by the British government to defend their colonial policy. Thus the more intense the satire, the more glaring appears the inadequacy of the legacy.

NOTES

1. V.S. Naipaul, *The Middle Passage* (England: Penguin, 1969), p. 89.
2. Anthony Boxill, "Mr. Biswas, Mr. Polly and the Problem of V.S. Naipaul's Sources," *Ariel*, 8, No. 3 (July 1977), p. 136.
3. V.S. Naipaul, *An Area of Darkness* (England: Penguin, 1970), pp. 47-48.
4. Anthony Boxill, p. 137.
5. V.S. Naipaul, *The Mystic Masseur* (England: Penguin, 1982), p. 36.
6. R.K. Narayan, *The Financial Expert* (Mysore: Indian Thought Publications, 1979), p. 83.
7. George Woodcock, "The Great Commonwealth Novelists, R.K. Narayan and V.S. Naipaul," *The Sewanee Review*, 87 (1979), p. 23.

"Disorder within, Disorder without": Naipaul's Delineation of the Dilemma of the Fractured Indian Consciousness

R.S. PATHAK

Writing about Commonwealth literature, Ravenscroft opined that it implied "a monolithic oversimplification that is hardly justified by fact, that being written in English is only the superficial similarity shared by a number of national literatures in English, many of which, as in India and partly of Africa, are sub-divisions of multi-lingual literatures."[1] This view represents typical British thinking about Commonwealth literature. It must be emphasized that Commonwealth literature is now a reality which cannot be ignored. Despite tremendous diversity and divergence, this literature is characterized by a certain "colonial consciousness,"[2] and is the product of a well-known fact of history, i.e. English education, English literature and English institutions, which caused an intellectual ferment in the Commonwealth countries enabling their writers to assert their national identity and to give befitting expressions to their distinct creative urges and aspirations. As Patrick White observes in *Voss*, "common forms are continually breaking into brilliant shapes. If we will explore them."

The "colonial consciousness" finds a powerful expression in the writings of V.S. Naipaul. There were writers before him who contributed to the range and variety of the West Indian literature, but very few of them enjoyed Naipaul's reputation outside the West Indies. His powerful mastery over the language and vision helped him add new dimensions to the "astonishing achievement"[3] of the West Indian novel. An important feature of his fictional world is his delineation of the Indian immigrant's dilemma, his problems and plights, in the fast-changing Caribbean world. Coulthard has specified the following common characteristics, which shaped the creative sensibility of writers like Naipaul and was responsible for their grappling of the national ethos:

The historical background in all the islands has followed the same

> pattern: discovery and conquest by the Spaniards; extermination of the native Indian populations and their replacement by slave-labour from Africa; the introduction of sugar and the world of the sugar estate, both during and after slavery; and independence at varying dates (Haiti first in 1804, with Jamaica and Trinidad gaining their independence as late as 1962). All the islands have known the common experience of colonialism, exploitation, poverty and economic frustration. In all the islands racial discrimination has been a problem, and racial resentments and complexes continue to be an important factor. The last twenty-five years have seen the growth of a middle class in all the islands, living largely on borrowed values (either American, British or French), and an intelligentsia seeking urgently a spiritual and cultural orientation of its own.[4]

The West Indian novel is the creation of a society which descended from European landlords, traders and functionaries, African slaves and indentured Indians. A hybrid society like the Caribbean has to face innumerable challenges in finding out itself after a prolonged subjection and cultural deprivation. The literature of the region tries to voice aspirations and yearnings, problems and plights of an emergent nation. It pulsates with a vast amount of felt life and the power "to suggest in concrete terms the menace and comfort of discovering origins."[5] George Lamming, himself a major West Indian novelist, points out three important events in the history of the Caribbean islands: "The first event is the discovery. . . . The next event is the abolition of slavery and the arrival of the East—India and China—in the Caribbean Sea. . . . the third important event . . . is the discovery of the novel by West Indians as a way of investigating and projecting the inner experience of the West Indian community."[6] The West Indian novel articulates in a powerful way the complex sensibility of the people and their disillusioned experience and riddling uncertainties.

Naipaul excels in presenting the indentured Indian immigrant's predicament in the West Indian context. All his troubles originated from an unfortunate coincidence in the political history of the world. When slavery was abolished in 1833, let us remember the facts, the planters needed cheap labour. The shiploads of Indian labourers were transported to many parts of the world, including the Caribbean. Hugh Tinker writes: "They arrived as coolies, and in many people's eyes they are itinerant coolies still. For slavery is both a system and an attitude of mind. Both the system and the attitude are still with us."[7] Tinker also cites Lord Russell's announcement of 15 February 1840, according to which the transfer of labourers from British India to these places was highly improper precisely because it might "lead to a dreadful loss of life on the one hand, or on the other, to a new system of slavery." (v) The act of uprooting Indian peasants, most of whom had not travelled beyond the narrow confines of their villages, were bound to have devastating consequences. These Indians, despite their poverty and social ills, possessed an extraordinary sense of continuity of tradition and undisrupted community life, both of which were the very first casualities in the new environment. Their economic exploitation and cultural disorientaion inflicted lacerating wounds in their psyche, rendering them orphan and destitute.

The Indian society constitutes a sizeable proportion of the total population. It is made up of the indentured slaves's descendents, whose world and world-view have been ruthlessly fragmented more than once and who have lost, consequently, a sense of the wholeness of existence. They are doomed to face a cultural vacuum as also various human and natural hostilities. Writing about this society, Naipaul observes:

> A peasant-minded, money-minded community, spiritually cut off from its roots, its religion reduced to rites without philosophy set in a materialistic colonial society: a combination of historical accidents and national temperaments has turned the Trinidad Indian into a complete colonial, even more philistine than the white.[8]

Naipaul's novels—especially the novels of the first two phases—explore the failures, futility, isolation, dispossession, rootlessness and valuelessness of this unanchored community. Though the cultural crisis of the West Indian immigrant has also been treated by writers like Samuel Selvon, Wilson Harris and Shiva Naipaul, and poets like Derek Walcott, Hendricks and Mervyn Morris, V.S. Naipaul's is probably the most detailed and illuminating analysis of it. Most of his works aim at defining "the setting, the historical time, [and] the racial and social complexities of the people concerned."[9]

Naipaul regards the novel as "a form of social inquiry" rather than "an opportunity for autobiography and boasting."[10] His own fiction is both a creative interpretation of past and a criticism of the contemporary life. It emerges as an authentic account of the agony and the pride, the trials and tribulations of his people. Both the Negro and the Indian suffered dislocation, but the fate of the latter is pathetically tragic; his experiences have been far more bewildering and his problems of adjustment far more acute. Distinguishing between the attitudes of the two immigrant communities, Naipaul remarks in *The Middle Passage*:

> Much of the West Indian Negro's drive arises out of his desire to define his position in the world. The Indian, with no such problem, is content with his narrow loyalties. . . . Indian politicians have created Indian racialism out of an harmless egoism. Negro racialism is more complex. It is an overdue assertion of dignity; it has elements of bitterness; it has something of the urban mob requiring to be satisfied with bread and circuses. It has profound intellectual promptings as well, in the realisation that the Negro problem lies not simply in the attitude of others to the Negro, but in the Negro's attitude to himself. It is as yet confused, for the Negro, while rejecting the guilt imposed on him by the white man, is not able to shake off the prejudices he has inherited from the white man. (83)

One may not accept Naipaul's neat distinction, but the problems of Indian immigrants are no myth but reality. The task of giving a really faithful picture of them was not easy. It was further complicated by the fact the Caribbean society underwent uprootings more than once. As Naipaul reminds us in his *Autobiography*:

> So there was a migration from India to be considered, a migration from within the British Empire. There was my Hindu family, with its fading memories of India; there was India herself. And there was Trinidad, with its past of slavery, its mixed population, its racial antagonisms and its changing political life; once part of Venezuela and the Spanish empire, now English-speaking, with the American base and an open-air cinema at the end of Bogart's street. (45)

Naipaul assumed the responsibility of delineating as honestly as possible the dilemma of the Indian immigrant's fractured consciousness, resulting from factors like transplantation, exploitation, rootlessness, and so on. George Steiner is of the view that "the modernist movement can be seen as a strategy of permanent exile."[11] He places Nabokov, Burgess and Beckett at the centre of this movement. Meenakshi Mukherjee, however, feels that some Commonwealth writers like Naipaul should also be taken to belong to the same category, for "their apprehension of reality has been affected by the experience of more than one country and conditioned by exposure to more than one culture."[12] It would be worthwhile to analyse Naipaul's delineation of the predicament of Indian immigrants and their descendents in the Caribbean islands.

II

Naipaul's early novels—*The Mystic Masseur* (1957), *The Suffrage of Elvira* (1958) and *Miguel Street* (1959)—evoke the life of a tradition-ridden, decadent society based almost entirely upon the degrading and demoralizing facts of colonialism. It is a world without "scientists, engineers, soldiers or poets." The people, by and large, lack cultural ties with their heritage. As is clear from the novel *Miguel Street*, the past in this society is generally non-existent, "a thing without a name." The street represents the deprived and captivating world of its inhabitants. It is also symbolic of the confusion of life, the chaos of values and the lack of guiding norms in the community. Things, as the novelist sums up, are "crazily mixed up" here. The state of affairs is aptly suggested in the novel. The stray mongrel dog is a befitting symbol of the life people lead.

The Mystic Masseur presents the picture of the West Indian society, its crisis and challenges, in a more systematic way. As M.K. Naik points out, "Naipaul's main aim in *The Mystic Masseur* seems to be to exploit the comic absurdity in the lives of the transplanted Indians in the West Indians."[13] The novel charters the progress of Ganesh Ramsumair, the central character in the novel, and his relationships with others with clarity and irony. He is in the beginning an unknown schoolmaster but becomes later a masseur, a mystic and an MLC. Eventually he rises to such dizzy heights of eminence that the British rulers of the island make him an MBE.

Ganesh has all along been leading the life of sham and pretensions. When he goes to join the "town College," carefully dressed in a Khaki suit and topee, he and his father "knew they looked important." (19)[14] At the college, Ganesh is so much ashamed of his Indian name that he circulates the story that he was actually called Ganesh. Ganesh's behaviour in the course of the story and social observances affecting him have been presented in such a way that the novelist is able to put his finger on the weak points of the society and its customs. For example, at the time of his initiation into Brahminhood, Ganesh is given a saffron bundle and is called upon to go to Benaras as rituals demand:

They shaved his head, gave him a saffron bundle and said, "All

> right, off you go now. Go to Benaras and study."
>
> He took the staff and began walking away briskly from Fourways. As arranged, Dookhie, the shopkeeper, ran after him, crying a little and begging in English, "No boy, don't go away to Benaras to study." (21)

This type of behaviour speaks voluminously about a degenerate society which clings to ceremonies and observances inherited from their ancestors but never bothers to know their deeper significance. Even marriage, a very personal affair, is treated in it as 'pre-ordained' (46); eligible bachelors are ear-marked and trapped as prospective husbands for marriageable daughters, and then 'it was all right.' (35) Wife-beating has a social sanction here, as would be evident from the following episode which took place on the day after Ganesh's marriage and may be taken to provide an apt prelude to his married life:

> Leela continued to cry and Ganesh loosened his leather belt and beat her. She cried out, "Oh God! Oh God! He go kill me today self!"
>
> It was their first beating, a formal affair done without anger on Ganesh's part or resentment on Leela's and although it formed no part of the marriage ceremony itself, it meant much to both of them. It meant that they had grown up and become independent. Ganesh had become a man; Leela a wife as privileged as any other big woman. Now she too would have tales to tell of her husband's beatings; and when she went home she would be able to look sad and sullen as every woman should. The moment was precious. (55)

Another equally interesting aspect of Ganesh's character is his Anglomania. What hastens him on is his meeting with Mr. Stewart. The enthusiastic Englishman claims to be a Kashmiri Hindu, dresses like an Indian mendicant, and lost in his rosy vision of Hinduism, makes Ganesh a mystic. "You must write your thoughts," says he. "They may help other people. You know, I felt all along that I was going to meet someone like you." (41) Ganesh reciprocates their relationship by dedicating his autobiography to "Lord Stewart of Chichester/Friend and counsellor/Of many years." (42) We will easily appreciate the absurdity of the whole issue if we remember that Ganesh had met the Englishman only twice over a period of few days. The novelist tells us that Ganesh's autobiography, "variously described as a spiritual thriller and a metaphysical whodunit had a considerable success of esteem in Central America and the Caribbean." (14)

Ganesh's early career as a masseur is a failure. The narrator describes his futile attempts to work a miraculous cure on his foot and comments: "He began mumbling a Hindi couplet over me. . . . If I had been sharper I would have paid more attention to that, for it showed, I am convinced, the incipient mystical leanings of the main." (16) Ganesh's passion for reading, however, establishes his reputation as a scholar. His ambition to write fructifies in the production of a slender book on Hinduism. His campaign of self-advertisement, his self-description as 'Ganesh, Mystic' and the great drama of his first cure make him a miracle-performer. "The wide world has not learnt of Ganesh's early struggles, and Trinidad resents this." (14) A shrewd planning brings about the commercial success of the Fuente Grove establishment of the Mystic Masseur, although "there was no hint of a fountain anywhere; no hint even of water." (12) The novelist has revealed Ganesh's literary pretensions, too. He is sick of self-love and is given to tall talking. "How much book I buy last week, Leela?" asked Ganesh, to which his wife replied: "Only three man. . . . But they was big big books. Six to seven inches altogether." (15) His book *What God Told Me* is followed by a treatise on constipation, and we are told that "because *Profitable Evacuation* was published during the war its title was misunderstood." (165) Given these facts, it is not surprising that 'Pundit Ganesh Ramsumair, B.A., Mystic' became, finally, a loyalist and a pillar of the Establishment and promptly changed his name into 'G. Ramsay Muir.'

III

Another novel that deserves consideration is *The Suffrage of Elvira*. Despite its rather flippant tone, the novel is a sincere study of the functioning of the most promising political system in the developing world. Naipaul seems to have been particularly happy with the work. He once remarked in an interview: "I would like to be frivolous again. I would love to write another *Suffrage of Elvira*."[15] The novel interests us primarily as an examination of the working of democracy in a world where it has no sanction in tradition. While commenting upon the democratic set up in India, Naipaul once said: "Formal politics answered less and less, became more and more formal; towards the end it had the demeanour of a parlour game, and became an affair of head-counting and floor-crossing."[16] The conditions in Trinidad do not seem to be significantly different.

The novel records the experiences of Surajpat Harbans. Who was contesting election from Elvira in the Naparoni county—"the smallest, most isolated and most neglected of the nine counties of Trinidad." (9) Democracy was 'a brand-new thing' in Trinidad, which is described as 'a creeping nation,' (25) and it presupposed elections. Harbans had to square Chittaranjan, the 'aloof and stiff' goldsmith, (13) to get the Hindu votes, and the tailor Baksh, with 'the squat built of the labourer' and having no resemblance with a leader, (16) for the Muslim votes. He had also to woo the Negro votes away from his rival Preacher who kept on 'waking about quiet quiet and brisk brisk from house to house.' (19) Harbans managed to win the election after spending exorbitantly on petrol and rum vouchers, posters and banners, a loudspeaker van, and so on. But this was 'the first and last election' he was to fight. (169) What sins he had committed, he asked, to deserve this fate by getting himself 'in this big big mess in . . . old old age!' (146) "Elvira, Elvira," he said, summing up his experiences, "Elvira, you is a bitch" and "he came to Elvira no more." (206) The novelist ironically comments: "And so democracy took root in Elvira." (193)

The novelist seems to be fully cognizant of the pitfalls of a nascent democracy. A couple of illustrations will suffice. The astute goldsmith is of the view that "People *like* to know that they could get a man to do little things for them every now and then." (153) Personal favours are claimed as a matter of right even if that meant violation of certain crucial democratic principles. The unpredictable appearance and all the more sudden disappearance of political parties just on the eve of the election day is another feature of such countries. Regarding the status of the Party for Progress and Unity, we are informed: "The party had been founded two months before the parade; it died two days after it. It won one seat out of twelve; ten of the candidates lost their deposits; the president and the funds disappeared." (162) Such practices do not augur well for a country and its political system.

It has been aptly said that people get the government they deserve. The public interaction is of a crucial importance in democracy, "the government of the people, for the people and by the people." The shoddiness of the political system in Trinidad, as depicted in *The Suffrage of Elvira*, would become clearer if we have a look at its pillars and prime movers. Harbans was more worried about the loss of the Muslim votes than "about the loss of honour of his prospective daughter-in-law." (129) Chittaranjan, "the great controller of votes," was in reality "a lonely man," "a sad humiliated man," who wore at home, after his election visits, "his torn khaki trousers, patched shirt and sabots." (137-38)

This duplicity characterizes Dhaniram's conduct also:

> That day Dhaniram was not being a pundit. He was in his other, more substantial role as the owner of one-fifth of a tractor. No dhoti and sacred thread; but khaki trousers, yellow sports shirt, brown felt hat and brown patent leather shoes. (128)

And this is what is worth knowing about Mahadeo, 'a devout Hindu': "He did his *puja* every morning and evening. In all his prayers now, and through all the ritual, the *arti* and bell-ringing and conch-blowing—which seemed in the most discovering way to have nothing to do with what went on in Elvira." (164) Democracy cannot be hoped to function and survive in an atmosphere like this with people like Harbans, Dhaniram, Chittaranjan and Mahadeo. It is interesting to note that even ordinary people like Mrs. Baksh had no illusions about it:

> Mrs. Baksh didn't like it at all. "Nobody ain't listening to me," she said. "Everybody just washing their foot and jumping in this democracy business. But I promising you, for all the sweet it begin sweet, it going to end damn sour." (40)

She kept on harping her fears again and again: "I been telling him [Baksh] . . . a hundred times if I tell him one time, that this election begin sweet sweet for everybody, but the same sweetness going to turn sour sour in the end." (120) According to Dhaniram, "This democracy is a damn funny thing." (130) To Teacher Francis, "this universal suffrage nonsense" is "just another British trick to demoralize people" of "a good friendly place." (85) Even the attitude of Rampiari's husband, "a truculent lout," is not without its relevance. He decided to vote for nobody: "he didn't believe in this new politics business, politicians were all crooks, and nobody was going to do anything for him anyway." (77-78) Harbans's own experiences as a politician led him to conclude: "This democracy is a strange thing. It does make the great poor and the poor great." (156) Whatever be the reasons, the democratic set up in such places does not seem to serve a really useful purpose either to the benefit of people or their representatives or to the advantage of social and cultural institutions.

Although politics and electioneering constitute the central theme of the novel, they are not the sole concern of the novelist. He presents scenes dealing with family misunderstandings, neighbourly quarrels, breaches of etiquette, lovers' meetings, peeping-toms and other incidents, which refuse to be integrally related to the main political theme. They shed, however, a significant light on the ways and manners of the people. Elvira is "a funny world." (149) We are pointedly reminded that it is virtually "a wilderness." (86) The culture of the place is a hybrid culture, if it can be called culture. "Things were crazily mixed up in Elvira." (66) No one would expect a well established set of values in such a chaotic condition. There isn't any place in it for "educative nonsense." (76) Obedience and respect were rejected as of very little consequence: "Some people in Elvira don't know their elders and betters." (75) People, in general, were unenlightened and orthodox, and had profound belief in *obeah* and magic, *jharay* and "spiritual fumigation." (80) "Nearly everybody else in Elvira had some experience of the supernatural." (72) People have little time or inclination for better things in life. What comes to them easiest is the aping of the western modes.

In one of his non-fiction books, Naipaul writes of such a character: "'I am craze for foreign,' Mrs. Mahindra said, 'Just craze for foreign.'"[17] The Indian community in Trinidad also suffers from a craze for 'foreign' things and values. According to Naipaul, this mimicry is both more and less than 'a colonial mimicry.' "Yesterday the mimicry was Moghul; tomorrow it might be Russian or American; today it is English." This mimicry has resulted in unfortunate schizophrenia; it is 'like fantasy': "It is as if an entire society has fallen for a casual confidence trickster." (60-61) The *Suffrage of Elvira* presents quite a few characters of this type. The rumseller Ramlogan "was lavish with the Canadian Healing Oil . . . the only thing Ramlogan didn't do with Canadian Healing Oil was drink it." (105) Harichand "liked sporting the American raincoat," which he had acquired "at enormous cost": "He was the only man in Elvira who possessed a raincoat." (110) Nelly Chittaranjan had her greatest wish fulfilled when "she went to London and joined the Regent Street Polytechnic. She went to all the dances and enjoyed them." (207) The D.M.O. "hadn't forgotten his association with England and continued to wear a Harris tweed jacket, despite the heat." (171) Finally, the Trinidad Flim Board were making a documentary film for a Colonial Office, "the script of which was to be written, poetically, in London, by a minor British poet." (180) This state of affairs is symptomatic of cultural bankruptcy of a nation.

IV

The Mimic Men (1976) is a more substantial novel than the earlier novels. The narrative is in the form of the dramatized reminiscences of an exiled politican. It presents, incidentally, a detached understanding of a violated, colonial society. The novel explores "the ways in which the conscious individual in a given society establishes modes of mediation between himself and his experience."[18] In a mixed society like the West Indian, an individual faces multiple problems of adjustment. Farrukh Dhondy, reviewing Naipaul's *In a Free State*, remarks:

> We demand of an artist, especially a writer, that he have his finger on the pulse of the essential creation of his time, more today than ever before. The sustenance that Naipaul drew from the English literary tradition is now inadequate and starves his vision. . . . Naipaul's characters are all emergents from a transient planetary age of mimic men.[19]

The mimic men have an attitude which is in conformity with that of the empire builders. They look down upon common people and try to keep themselves aloof from their company. Their elitist mode renders them alienated from their society. Naipaul's novel, however, seems to suggest that they are what they are because of extenuating circumstances of chance and environment. Ralph Singh, the protagonist, says: "I wish to avoid satire. . . . It is that the situation satirises itself, turns satire inside out, takes satire to the point where it touches pathos if not tragedy." (250) *The Mimic Men* is an interesting study of the interplay of people and circumstances and of the revaluation of their attitudes and values.

Ralph Singh is residing in a modest hotel on the outskirts of London, which he has known as a student and a celebrity. He is in early middle age now and, after a life of opulence and after a failed marriage to an Englishwoman, is leading the life of a colonial politician in exile from the island where he was born. The narrator records his reminiscences with perfect candour and sincerity. "These are the political memoirs," however; they are "a more than autobiographical work, the exposition of the malaise of our times pointed and illuminated by personal experience." (10) The narrator feels that writing will do good to him because "for all its initial distortion, [it] clarifies, and even becomes a process of life." (301) He confides:

> It was my hope to give expression of the restlessness, the deep disorder, which the great explorations, the overthrow in three continents of established social organizations, the unnatural belonging together of peoples who could achieve fulfilment only within the security of their own societies and the landscapes hymned by their

> ancestors, it was my hope to give partial expression to the restlessness which this great upheaval has brought about. (38)

The subject of the novel is thus more than politics, marriage or race. It is nothing less than 'a vision of disorder'—'placelessness' and breakdown of human relationships in the world of the 'mimic men.'

The narrator fails to perceive any definite pattern in his life. It is an aimless wandering from frivolity and lack of judgement to irrelevance and intrusion to inevitable failure. "From play-acting to disorder: it is the pattern." (20) His marriage and the political career are viewed by him as parenthetical acts—"aberrations, whimsical, [and] arbitrary acts." (219) All his other acts were misjudged and he is branded as "a racialist and a radical, a dangerous man, a troublemaker." (267) Overwhelmed by the formlessness of his experiences and their irrelevance to the setting, he wished "to make a fresh, clean start." (292, 141) But all his efforts were thwarted. He "had nowhere to go." (91) And he could not pretend even to himself "to be part of a community or to be putting down roots." (13) A hopeless spectator of his misery, he was always haunted by the "feeling or drift and helplessness, the nightmare." (61) He regarded himself as "an outsider" and was always oppressed by insecurity and a feeling of waste. He felt as if he was hanging between two worlds—"a world without end and a world without point" and that "there was no middle way." This kind of life has a devastating effect upon the psyche. "It sets us apart; it distorts us; it separates us from the self we recognize and to which we remain close." (73) Nevertheless, what tormented him even more was the fear of losing his identity, "the threat of other people's lives": "Not the panic of being lost or lonely; the panic of ceasing to feel myself as a whole person." (33)

Commenting upon Malgonkar's novel *The Princes*, Naipaul draws attention to "the Indian withdrawal and denial," which, according to him, "is part of the confusion of Indian Anglo-Indian."[20] This "withdrawal, denial, [and] confusion of values" is the lot of all colonial people. And Ralph Singh is no exception. Withdrawal "had been a part of [his] fantasy, part of [his] urge to escape shipwreck." (173) His ambivalence and jumpiness only aggravated his disappointment. He thought of "this life as the life of the maimed." (296) How can a man feel happy who is obsessed with "this absurd disorder" and the "sense of captivity" and of "placelessness!" (184) He can express occasionally "the negative frenzy of a deep violation which could lead to further frenzy alone." (245) This attitude denies even a creative feeling or revolt. The person begins to suffer from schizophrenia and is perpetually at war with himself and the world. "Until at last an undeclared state of war existed between the others" and Ralph. (79) He loses his sense of reality and possesses "the fear of the man who feels the veils coming down one by one." (85) We may safely assume that Ralph's predicament is the predicament of all rootless colonials like him. In the novel he speaks not as an individual but as a representative of his people.

During the course of the narrative, there are in the novel some revealing comments on the people, their society and race. Placed against their background, Ralph's problems acquire a tangible shape and his experiences become the microcosm of the plight of his people. The people of the island of Isabella, we are told, have "their feeling for the stylish, [and] their tolerance, of what they felt to be absurd." (26) The narrator asks: "They had lost their sense of their self-esteem?" (46) So long as they remain in the island, their life is the life of perpetual self-deception and hypocrisy. "We began in bluff," writes Ralph. "We continued in bluff." (249) Those who try to get out of this rut have a greater danger to face. They go out, like Sally, and get absorbed in "the contamination of the wider world." (197) Nirad Chaudhari calls India "the continent of Circe." Naipaul also imagines a similar power operating upon the West Indies, turning them into misfits: "Those of us who came to it lost some of our solidity; we were trapped into fixed, flat postures. And, in this growing dissociation between ourselves and the city in which we walked . . . and then the personality divided bewilderingly into compartments." (32-33)

Naipaul presents a lurid picture of the West Indian society. It is a society hopelessly disorganized and torn asunder by its conflicting loyalties. Though it is a small world, its issues are "more complex" than in any normally civilized society; here "everyone's motives remain unclear" and these "motives and alliances shifted rapidly." (261) The narrator describes it as "a haphazard, disordered and mixed society," (66) a small community with its "upper element crisscrossed with marriages, inbred already." (192) He further observes:

> We were trapped in our situation. Each attempt at the establishing of a personal security prepared the way for further disorder. . . . But on power and the consolidation of passing power we wasted our energies, until the bigger truth came: that in a society like ours, fragmented, inorganic, no link between man and the landscape, a society not held together by common interests, there was no true internal source of power, and that no power was real which did not come from the outside. Such was the

> controlled chaos we had, with such enthusiasm, brought upon ourselves.(256)

The West Indian's dilemma is not sorted out by redeeming graces of what Naipaul calls 'the racial sense,' the absence of which he holds responsible for the present-day India's problems. "The racial sense is alien to Indians," says he. "they do not see themselves as belonging to an Indian race; the words have no meaning. Historically, this absence of cohesiveness has been the calamity of India."[21] His words are more applicable to the West Indian context. He writes of Indians: "These people are all helpless, disadvantaged, easily unbalanced; the civilization they have inherited has long gone sour; living instinctive lives, crippled by rules . . . they make up a society without a head." (109) *The Mimic Men* presents the West Indians as "a melodramatic race," (62) which has to encounter "its own racial contradictions." (78) They always lead the life of mental and physical violence, (234-35) and this life can hardly be conducive for any creative work. Ralph reminiscences:

> I had ceased to feel I could form part and . . . we had all managed to withdraw [from] . . . this fragmented world. . . . I belonged to a small community which in this part of the world was doomed. We were an intermediate race, the genes passive, capable of disappearing in two generations into any of the three races of men. . . . I visualized it as existing within a walled, impregnable field. (68)

He looked upon himself as a "late intruder, the picturesque Asiatic." (93) Because of various pressures and immigrations "the Caribs had been absorbed and had simply ceased to be," remaining aliens in their own "little bastard world." (146) Deschampsneufs, who knew various people intimately, describes the Orients as "the long-visioned types" who "give up too easily." (205) This fact would account for aimlessness and impracticality of Indians portrayed by Naipaul.

In Naipaul's novels, the physical and cultural setting acquires a significant role. It is not merely a lifeless background against which human beings act and react; it is a potential means of shaping their destiny and character. It is but natural that uprooted persons regard it of little consequence, this "ambiguous New World background" of theirs. (101) "We had converted our island into one big secret," says Ralph. "We denied the landscape and the people we could see out of open doors and windows." (114) Migrations and immigrations make these people's existence even more precarious. They are reduced to "faceless men." (287)

". . . departure is departure," we are told. "It fractures; the bone has to be set anew each time." (215) This "switching back and forth between one world and another, one set of relationship and another" only deprives these people of the sense of place. (185) The contact with the larger world and industrialization provide no solution to their problems. In countries with a hybrid civilization, industrial revolution hardly means more than "a process of filling imported tubes and tins with various imported substances." (258) Under these conditions, the people lose all sense of belongingness with their world. Their values, like their articles, are imported from outside:

> We, here on our island, handling books printed in this world, and using its goods, had been abandoned and forgotten. We pretended to be real, to be learning, to be preparing ourselves for life, we mimic men of the New World, one unknown corner of it, with all its reminders of the corruption that came so quickly to the new. (175)

The severing of bonds with the physical world around one is a sure sign of rootlessness. Ralph is right when he observes: "You know, you are born in a place and you grow up there. You get to know the trees and plants. You will never know any other trees and plants like that." (204) The intimate relationship with nature and its objects shapes the personality of a sensible man. It gives him boundless confidence and resourcefulness. The snapping of bonds, on the contrary, with the cultural and physical background will have a ruinous effect. It can lead to conditions which may make a civilization fall like an uprooted big tree: "A tree in the park groaned in a series of accelerating snaps and then slowly collapsed, rocking to rest on its branches. It was a great tree, one of those with a history. Its leaves were green and shining wet, its shallow, lateral roots shaggy with earth." (182) This is, precisely, the fate reserved for all 'mimic men,' who, like the Indian immigrants in the West Indies, have to lead a life of double standards. The cultural chaos of the island of Isabella is representative of the cultural anarchy affecting the whole of the people, and their predicament in this respect is not 'unique.' (230) This can happen to any people who have undergone a prolonged crisis of rootlessness!

V

The Indian immigrant's dilemma has been delineated even in more realistic way in *A House for Mr. Biswas* (1961), which has been claimed by critics to be Naipaul's most important work. Though written at the age of twenty-nine, the novel presents the problems and plights of a whole people. It is "conceived and executed in the great tradition of the humanist novel, and is as subtle and comprehensive an analysis of the colonial experience as anything in imaginative literature."[22] It is the character of Mohun Biswas against his background that imparts the striking success to the novel. Mr. Biswas's complex and insightful story is the story of the community he belongs to. The novel is said to have a direct bearing on the important modern problem of the "crisis of identity."[23]

The "crisis" originates from the excruciating historical experience of slavery of various kinds. The novel explores the consciousness of the people who constitute a destitute culture and "carry about them the mark, in their attitudes and sensibilities and convictions, of the slave, the unnecessary man."[24] Mr. Biswas is an 'unnecessary man' *par excellence*, and is pitted against the Tulsi family and its establishment. The Hanuman House symbolizes the conventional Hindu world abounding in rituals, vagaries, superstitions and hypocrisies. Significantly enough, it is referred to as "an alien white fortress":

> Among the tumbledown timber-and-corrugated-iron building in the High Street at Arwacas, Hanuman House stood like an alien white fortress. The concrete walls looked as thick as they were, and when the narrow doors of the Tulsi store on the ground floor were closed the House became bulky, impregnable and blank. The sidewalls were windowless and on the upper two floors the windows were mere slits in the facade. The balustrade which hedged the flat roof was crowned with a concrete statue of the benevolent monkey-god Hanuman. From the ground the white washed features could scarcely be distinguished and were, if anything, slightly sinister, for dust had settled on projections and the effect was that of a face lit up from below. (80-81)

The Hanuman House is teeming with almost innumerable slaves subjected to inhuman bondage. The condition of these old men squatting on sacks on the ground and "pulling at clay cheelums that glowed red and smelled of ganja and burnt sacking," is really pathetic. Although it was not cold, "many had scarves over their heads and around their necks," which "made them look foreign":

> They could not speak English and were not interested in the land where they lived; it was a place where they had come for a short

> time and stayed longer than they expected. They continually talked of going back to India, but when the opportunity came, many refused, afraid of the unknown, afraid to leave the familiar temporariness. And every evening they came to the arcade of the solid, friendly house, smoked, told stories, and continued to talk of India. (193)

The Tulsi establishment is governed by the cunning colonizer Mrs. Tulsi and her terrorizing slave master Seth, both of whom are insensitive to the creative aspects of the Hindu culture as also of the individual urges and aspirations. The hypocrisy and mercenary outlook of the Tulsi antagonizes Mr. Biswas, for to accept the Hanuman House and its rule would be to have the soul of a servant and to acquiesce to slavery. He struggles hard to free himself from the suffocating, disintegrating, tradition-ridden world, though his fight looks like an ordinary man's obscure struggle against overwhelming odds. He revolts against the whole system, though he cannot defy authority openly. Throughout his life he tries to seek and assert his own independent identity. Asked by Tulsi's son-in-law Govind to give up sign painting, Mr. Biswaś replies: "Give up sign-painting? And my Independence? No, boy My motto is: Paddle your own canoe." (107) Sign-painting may be a futile-looking act of no importance, but to Mr. Biswas it is a way of preserving his independence and identity. This very urge finds its complete manifestation in his keenness to acquire a house of his own.

It would be interesting to recall how passionately Mr. Biswas attends to various details of house-building:

> Materials came that afternoon. The erapaud pillars looked rough, they were not altogether round or altogether straight. But Mr. Biswas delighted in the new scantlings and the new nails that came in several wrappings of newspaper. He took up handful of nails and let them fall again. The sound pleased him. "Did not know nails was so heavy," he said.
>
> "Gallery, drawing-room, bedroom, bedroom," Mr. Biswas said, hopping over the stairs. "Gallery, bedroom, bedroom, drawing-room." (254)

The process of acquiring a house "on the face of the earth" becomes more exciting than the actual ownership of it. The house assumes a greater importance than the people:

> But bigger than them all was the house, his house. How terrible it would have been at this time, to be without it: to have died among the Tulsies. Amid the squalor of that large, disintegrating and indifferent family, to have left Shama and the children among them, in one room; worse, to have lived without even attempting to lay claim to one's portion of the earth, to have lived and died as one had been born, unnecessary and unaccommodated. (13-14)

Even for Mr. Biswas's children the house was to provide an ordered world, which was never granted to their father: "Soon it seemed to the children that they had never lived anywhere but in the tall square house in Sikkim Street. From now on their lives will be ordered, their memories coherent. The mind, while it is sound, is merciful. . . . Events will be telescoped and forgotten." (381) It was hoped that in this changed environment the children would get an opportunity to discover themselves culturally and spiritually.

The vision of the house sustains Mr. Biswas through all these years of dismal decadence. It epitomizes his inner faith (and this is what his name stands for) and all his 'stupendous' achievements and satisfaction: "It gave Mr. Biswas some satisfaction that in the circumstances Shama did not run straight off to her mother to beg for help. Ten years before that would have been her first thought. Now she tried to comfort Mr. Biswas and devised plans of her own." (7)

The building of the house, however, was not an easy job. It consumed all his energy and resources. His several efforts at it resulted only in failure. The novelist hints at this possibility through Mr. Biswas's frustrated efforts to plant a garden: "the rose trees grew straggly and hard" and "The lily-pond collapsed again and the lily-roots brown and shaggy out of the thick, muddy water." (376) It is nothing but irony of circumstances that Mr. Biswas's new position poses certain new challenges which he is unable to face. He turns ultimately, to the Hanuman House for security. When the house in Greenvale gets burnt, "An immense relief had come upon Mr. Biswas. The anxiety, the fear, the anguish which had kept his mind humming and his body taut now ebbed away. He could feel it ebbing; it was a physical sensation; it left him weak and very weary." (301)

Mr. Biswas's persistent desire to understand life and to assert his identity in a chaotic world was thwarted. Persons like him cannot be allowed the luxury of stability and identity! It may be noted that he himself is not unaware of his ambivalent position. He tells his son: "I am just somebody. Nobody at all. I am just a man you know." This is, obviously, the fate of men like Mr. Biswas, who are historically displaced and have the misfortune of living in a derelict land. Society offers very little possibilities to each one of them, and he has therefore no option but "to balance his personal inadequacies against the contradictions of existence itself."[25]

Mr. Biswas's vicissitudes lend a deeper perspective to colonial experiences. He is denied the satisfaction of seeing his aspirations and dreams come true. It is interesting to note that Mr. Biswas's eagerness to have a house of his own has an element of self-revelation about it. Naipaul lived in the beginning in the "big house" owned by his mother's mother in Chaguanas. "It was built in the North Indian style. It had balustraded roof terraces, and the main terrace was decorated at either end with a statue of a rampant lion." He was bound to become a "nonentity" in this atmosphere. He remembers: "Growing up within the extended family, knowing nothing else, or looking at everything else from the outside, I had no social sense . . . and as a result . . . I couldn't enter worlds that were not like mine." Naipaul's last two years in the 'big house' were 'close to a nightmare.' By the time his father managed to buy a house of his own in 1946, when Naipaul was 14, it was already a little late. "By that time my childhood was over and I was fully made," adds Naipaul.[26] His experiences in this respect are thus not different from those of Mr. Biswas. The problems of the latter, however, are the problems of the entire West Indian society.

VI

Naipaul has thus presented in his novels the predicament of Indian immigrants to the West Indies and their descendants. His treatment of the issue is exhaustive and can be found in most of his novels. His approach to the problems in the early novels is unidirectional but it comes to acquire a complex turn in his mature novels. His views may look biased and neatly sophisticated. But nobody can doubt the genuineness of his intentions and sincerity of his vision, and the picture that he portrays rings true at all essential points. It is a half-made society with its mixture of cultures. The novelist is a member of this society which he denounces vehemently at times, and he writes about it with an insider's knowledge. "Disorder within, disorder without," he complains in his autobiography, and this is not so much true of his own life as that of his countrymen. He is acutely conscious of the severe limitations under which he and his people had to work:

> In England I was also a colonial. Out of the stresses. . . . My very particularity—which was the subject sitting on my shoulder—had been encumbering me.
>
> The English or French writer of my age had grown up in a world that was more or less explained. He wrote against a background of knowledge. I couldn't be a writer in the same way, because to be a colonial, as I was, was to be spared knowledge. It was to live in an intellectually restricted world; it was to accept those restrictions.[27]

That precisely is the problem of all right-thinking, original writers belonging to the half-made societies of the postcolonial world. In his *In a Free State* Naipaul confesses that he "felt exposed and futile." Mr. Biswas's son Anand also had the feeling of being "led to inadequacies, to self-awareness and a lasting loneliness." (413) The "perpetual ostracism" render one incapable of any meaningful achievement, including the quest for identity. On revisiting the Caribbean, the novelist wrote: "How can the history of this West Indian futility be written? . . . The history of the islands can never be satisfactorily told. Brutality is not the only difficulty. History is built around achievement and creation—and nothing was created in the West Indies." In this sterile atmosphere the writer has an onerous responsibility to fulfil. He further remarks: "Living in a borrowed culture, the West Indian more than most, needs writers to tell him who he is and where he stands. Here the West Indian writers have failed."[28] The degenerate social set up can produce only characters like Ganesh Ramsumair, Ralph Singh and Mohun Biswas. Naipaul has nevertheless made commendable efforts to put up "a resistance to annihilation" against all odds, "in the face of shapelessness."[29] He has been able to go a long way to diagnosing ills of the contemporary society, even if the remedy suggested by him may not be always effective.

George Lamming and others took Naipaul to task "for not paying sufficient attention . . . to non-Indian groups."[30] The delineation of the indentured Indian consumed, for obvious reasons, Naipaul's primary interest. Explaining his position, he himself remarks:

> The confrontation of different communities . . . was the fundamental West Indian experience. . . . But to see the attenuation of the culture of my childhood as the result of a dramatic confrontation of opposed worlds would be to distort the reality. To me the worlds were juxtaposed and mutually exclusive.

He was always guided by his zeal to portray the contemporary reality. In his book *An Area of Darkness*, he took Indians to task for ignoring reality. He seems to be somewhat obsessed with the reality of the West Indian life. He once described India as "the featureless area of darkness." (38) This featurelessness characterized the West Indian life and characters before Naipaul's appearance on the scene. He tried to give a specific character to it, and then "In Trinidad to be an Indian was to be distinctive; difference was each man's attribute." (46) He made use of his powers to create images of reality of colonial experience out of the featureless men and women. This is his major contribution to our understanding of the predicament of the modern man.

The Indians of Trinidad, as shown in Naipaul's novels, are a decadent group. Rootless and alienated, they live in a world of cultural confusion. Their lives and interests are petty and trivial. The men make strenuous efforts to earn money or indulge in political squabbling; the women gossip and comment when they are not busy match-making. To these people, the outer and inner worlds have "physical separateness"; they do not "coexist." (60) Theirs is a mixed culture. Janus-faced, they look to distant India for their religion and to their white neighbours for their manners and modes of a civilized living. Their ambitions and yearnings are, by and large, those of the semi-literate people doomed to reside in a corrupt society. Most of them suffer from a shocking lack of awareness of their plight. The novelist has exposed their smugness, pseudo-European pretensions and hypocritical standards. He has taken special pains to delineate in great details the colonial world of the West Indies, their hybrid culture and the Indians's struggle to seek and affirm their identity. Identity, to him, is "related to a set of beliefs and rituals, a knowledge of the gods, a code, an entire civilization." It is a "discovery" and holds "the key to a whole world of belief and feeling."[31] The quest for one's identity is of great value, and its frustration or failure, a colossal misfortune.

The setting of Naipaul's novels is incapable of producing really creative characters. It is peopled with persons like Ganeshes, Ralphs and Biswases. It has been remarked: "Naipaul's areas of darkness are hopelessly mythridated vortices of being, from which no purgatorial awareness emerges and no resonance of human motion is generated. The solemn mimicry of his characterisation touches no chord of life."[32] It may be remembered, however, that it was none of the novelist's intentions to create 'heroic' characters. A colonial society suffering from and acute sense of lethal dispossession and disinheritance very rarely does that. On a superficial look, his characters may look like crude distortions or "eccentrics." Naipaul once told that his characters were really based on men and women fostered by the society:

> Trinidadians are more recognizably "characters" than people in England. Only a man's eccentricities can get him attention. It might also be that in a society without tradition, without patterns, every man finds it easier "to be himself." Whatever the reason, this determination of people to be themselves, to cherish their eccentricities, to reveal themselves at once, makes them easy material for the writer.[33]

Naipaul's characters evoke the life of the Caribbean people. Their shortcomings originate from the novelist's particular point of view and his vision. Critics have drawn our attention to "a certain quirk in Naipaul's sensibility" and a "mind flinching from the horror staining so much human life."[34] It is also felt that "a certain etiolated vision and desiccated spirit dominate" his works.[35] The real danger of this situation is said to lie in the fact that Naipaul may be "in the process of washing his hand of smelly humanity and therefore of the novel too."[36] These fears seem to be mostly baseless. It is the novelist's ironical point of view that necessitates the presentation of facts in a slightly abnormal way. In an interview with Derek Walcott, Naipaul said in 1965: "I am not a satirist. Satire comes out of a tremendous optimism. One simply does not indulge in satire while one is awaiting death. Satire is a type of anger. Irony and comedy, I think, come out of a sense of acceptance."[37] In another interview with Robert Lowell, he, again, expresses his preference for what he calls "true satire." By "true satire" he seems to mean the wider, understanding ironic vision, which, he says, "grows out of the largest vision . . . that 'all embracing Christ-like' vision."[38] All distortions and eccentricities result from this ironic mode of apprehension. The impression that he leaves seems to be the one that the novelist purposely strives at. He has done what he could do to give a much-needed jolt to complacent sensibility, as has been done, in a different context, by Nirad Chaudhuri, whom he remembers as a competent writer "beating his own way out of the thicket of Indian attitudes."[39]

In his delineation of human problems Naipaul is under a profound indebtedness to Conrad. The protagonist in *The Mimic Men* claims to have been "stirred by Lord Jim," which presents the experiences of "the solitary Negro among an alien petty people." (180) Naipaul frankly admits a lot of Conrad's influence in *The Return of Eva Peron*: "I found that 60 years before, Conrad had been everywhere before me. Not as a man with a cause, but as a man offering, as in *Nostromo* a vision of the world's half-made societies as places which continuously made and unmade themselves."[40] It is worth noting that the very title of Naipaul's first work on India reminds one of Conrad's *Heart of Darkness*.[41] Conrad's novel is also the inspiration for *A Bend in the River*. "What is the meaning?" asks Marlow in Conrad's novel. (57) Are human beings merely "sluggish beetles crawling on the floor of a lofty portico?" (50) or, "lunatics . . . capering on the iron deck" dashing against a "great wall . . . piled up, crested, ready to topple over?" (42-43) He tried to penetrate "deeper and deeper into the heart of darkness" (50) and came to realize that "His very existence was an unsoluble problem. His very existence was improbable, inexplicable, and altogether bewildering. He was an insoluble problem. It was inconceivable how he had existed, how he had succeeded in getting so far, how he had managed to remain—why he did not instantly disappear." (78) Naipaul attempted to probe into the profound human question with particular reference to the destiny of the Indian indentured labourer in the West Indian set up, and the results are not unsatisfactory. Despite all his limitations, the picture that he paints is plausible and candid.

NOTES

1. *The Journal of Commonwealth Literature*, 13/3 (April 1979).
2. S.K. Desai, "History against History: Commonwealth and Colonial Consciousness," *The Literary Criterion*, 16/4 (1981), pp. 34-43.
3. William Walsh, *Commonwealth Literature* (OUP, 1973), p. 51.
4. G.R. Coulthard, *Caribbean Literature: An Anthology* (London, 1996), pp. 10-11.
5. Kenneth Ramchand, *The West Indian Novel and its Background* (London, 1970), p. 62.
6. *The Pleasures of Exile* (London, 1960), pp. 36-37.
7. *A New Slavery* (OUP, 1974), p. 383.
8. *The Middle Passage* (London, 1962), p. 89.
9. Cited from pre-publication excerpts of V.S. Naipaul's *Autobiography* given in *Gentleman*, February 1984, p. 43.
10. *India: A Wounded Civilization* (London, 1997), pp. 18-19.
11. *Extraterritorial* (Penguin, 1969), p. 26.
12. "Inside Outsider" in C.D. Narasimhaiah, ed., *Awakened Conscience: Studies in Commonwealth Literature* (New Delhi, 1978), p. 86.

13. "Irony as Stance and Vision: A Comparative Study of V.S. Naipaul's *The Mystic Masseur* and R.K. Narayan's *The Guide*," *The Journal of Indian Writing in English*, 6/1 (January 1978), pp. 1-2.
14. The following editions of Naipaul's novels have been used: *The Mystic Masseur* (Penguin, 1964), *The Suffrage of Elvira* (Penguin, 1969), *The Mimic Men* (London: Andre Deutsch, 1967), *A House for Mr. Biswas* (Penguin, 1969).
15. Interview with David Bates, *The London Sunday Times Supplement* (26 May 1963), p. 13.
16. *India: A Wounded Civilization*, p. 167.
17. *An Area of Darkness* (London, 1964), p. 90.
18. Walsh, *Commonwealth Literature*, p. 60.
19. *Economic and Political Weekly*, 6/52 (25 December 1971).
20. *An Area of Darkness*, pp. 71, 66.
21. *India: A Wounded Civilization*, p. 154.
22. Francis Wyndham, *The Listener* (7 October 1971), p. 1.
23. C.N. Srinath, "Crisis of Identity: Assertion and Withdrawal in Naipaul and Arun Joshi," *The Literary Criterion*, 14/1 (1979), p. 33.
24. William Walsh, *A Manifold Voice* (London, 1970), p. 71.
25. Landeg White, *V.S. Naipaul: A Critical Introduction* (London, 1975), p. 92.
26. *Autobiography*, in *Gentleman* (February 1984), pp. 46-49.
27. *Ibid.*, p. 45.
28. *The Middle Passage*, pp. 29-73.
29. Patrick White, *The Living and the Dead* (London, 1962), p. 20.
30. *An Area of Darkness*, p. 37.
31. *India: A Wounded Civilization,* pp. 70-71.
32. D.V.K. Raghavacharyulu, "Naipaul and Narayan: The Sense of Life," in Narasimhaiah, p. 218.
33. "The Regional Barrier," *TLS* (15 August 1958), p. xxxvii.
34. Walsh, *Commonwealth Literature*, p. 60.
35. Satendra Nandan, "The Immigrant Indian Experience in Literature: Trinidad and Fiji," in Narasimhaiah, p. 356.
36. D.J. Enright, Review of *In a Free State* in W. Walsh, *Commonwealth Literature*, p. 339.
37. *Trinidad Sunday Guardian Magazine* (6 August 1967), p. 8.
38. *20th Century* (Winter 1964), p. 18.
39. *India: A Wounded Civilization*, p. 139.
40. Qtd. by Iqbal Masud in *Gentleman* (February 1984), p. 50.
41. Joseph Conrad, *Heart of Darkness* (Penguin, 1973).

V.S. Naipaul and the New Narrative Technique of the Non-Fiction Novel

A.J. KHAN

V.S. Naipaul has made his mark as a very impressive writer with economy of expression and sharpness of perception, chiefly in the new literary form known as non-fiction. In fact, it is through this new genre that the novelist/narrator has been able to adopt an altogether new technique and express his ideas in a startling and arresting way. V.S. Naipaul is among the few postcolonial writers who have emerged as the most prominent and successful exponents of this new technique of narration. In recording the impression of his travels to various countries, he has shown such skill both in his use of language and form that he has come to be known as a superlative traveller who misses nothing worth the record in a narrative which is beautifully written and almost impossible to put down.

Before one proceeds to highlight the remarkable features of Naipaul's skill of narration, it is imperative to consider the essential features of this new technique in order to distinguish it from the traditional fiction. One of the first and foremost features of this technique is that, while standing close to the art of a journalist and yet differing fundamentally from his method, the writer of this form makes use of an altogether new mode of expression which enables him to occupy a privileged position and write in the first person while cutting away sharply from the usually known literary forms like autobiography, travelogue, travel fiction, confessional and journalistic writing. The writer may be called the unacknowledged journalist who expresses his ideas and thoughts on a given situation in the society or country.

An outstanding feature of this technique is what may be called the expression of the filtered truth. The writer describes things in a seemingly journalistic manner but his statements have a touch of universal truth, which gives a deep philosophical touch to the entire work.

Another important feature of the non-fiction novel is its dependence on the recreation of memory. While narrating his experience the writer links them to wider visions and experiences. While the writer is recreating, the names of places and persons throw up other associated names. His knowledge is drawn from a deep reservoir, as opposed to the kind of data-recovery a reporter may depend on for packaging and dissemination.

This technique has been used by some powerful post-colonial writers like the Danish writer Isak Dinesen, the African writer E. Amadi, two West Indian writers, Shiva Naipaul and V.S. Naipaul, and an India-born emigrant Bharati Mukherjee and Canadian writer Clark Blaise.

The lone artist among the writers of the third world countries who has explored this new form very successfully in his literary works is V.S. Naipaul. Born of Hindu parents, he has swept the Western world by his novels and other literary works. His works like *The Middle Passage* (1962), *An Area of Darkness* (1964), *The Loss of El Dorado* (1973), *The Overcrowded Barracoon* (1976), *India: A Wounded Civilization* (1977), *Among the Believers* (1981), *India: A Million Mutinies Now* (1990) record the experience of his travel in various countries. The highly poetic and imaginative mind of the artist pulls all the strings together with his art of centrifugal technique and piles memory upon memory and experience upon experience, transforming the whole record of his experiences and facts into a highly literary work of art.

While using all the features of this technique of non-fiction in all his non-fiction novels, Naipaul uses a few more devices and makes this technique all the more brilliant and a powerful mode of communication. One such device is his treatment of history. Salman Rushdie has treated history in his novels *Shame* and *Midnight's Children* in such a way as to bring the past in close juxtaposition to the present. He uses history to recreate the past for the review of the present which serves to throw light on the similarity or difference of attitude of the people towards an identical situation.

Commenting on Naipaul's use of the historical problems, Subramani rightly observes: "It is true that in Naipaul's novels personal and historical problems are closely linked. Speaking of his method, Naipaul has said that he creates the socio-historical condition and the characters are subjected to its needs. This is why he insists that a knowledge of the West Indian background is necessary for understanding of his fiction. No discussion of his works can ignore the historical dimension, which is inseparable from the philosophical and artistic dimensions. Thus there is an organic connection between Ralph Singh's mimicry of the black man's basis of inferiority, and the historical basis of his existence. Man's homelessness is not an external fate: Naipaul attributes it to concrete historical circumstances. Naipaul often finds the plots for his novels in history, and the dramatic actions flow from the conflict between character and historical circumstances."[1] Subramani also points out how Naipaul connects the history of the colonial experience with his personal history in two of his important non-fiction novels.

Naipaul successfully brings the past close to the present by connecting different events of history which occurred at different points of time chiefly on the basis of their identical impact and effect. While narrating the history of the Sikhs, Naipaul connects the following events revealing his novel treatment of history:

> Events which can be dated and analyzed, and placed at a proper distance from the present, can also at some stage begin to appear far away; can fade. Myths are fresh; they never lose their force. Though at Malerkotla in 1762 the Sikhs were massacred by an invading Afghan army, in Malerkotla in 1947, the time of the partition of India and the population exchange between India and Pakistan—the flight of Muslims to Pakistan, and Sikhs and Hindus from Pakistan in Malerkotla in 1947, because of that Afghan nobleman who laid down gold sovereigns over the cremation site of the two sons of the 10th Guru, no Muslim was harmed. In the 1960s the Sikh political party, the Akali Dal, nominated the Nawab of Malerkotla as their candidate, and he got the Sikh vote in three elections.[2]

Besides, Naipaul has such tremendous power of telescoping historical events as to throw open a big span of time through a very limited use of words as may be seen in the following passage in which he sums up the changes that have occurred within six months in the world:

> Karachi, Pakistan, six months later. Many things had happened in those six months; the Muslim world had been on the bail. The American embassy in Tehran had been seized by Iranian students and more than fifty embassy staff held as hostages. There had been a seige and gun battle in the mosque at Mecca, hinting at underground movements in the kingdom of Saudi Arabia. The Russians had invaded Afghanistan.
>
> In Pakistan itself there had been changes. In August and September there had been talk of elections. Those elections had been cancelled; martial law had been tightened; the newspapers were censored; there were public whippings.[3]

Naipaul resurrects history when he connects two different events in different parts of the world to focus a similar situation as a result of which he appears to add some veracity to what may be called myth and legend in history. "In the Sikh catalogue of the torments and martyrdoms of its founding Gurus, the bricking up alive of the two sons of the 10th Guru has a special place. The story—with its echoes of king John and Richard III—has some of the quality of myth." (382)

One of the most striking features of his narrative technique is the art of reiterating an event or a situation or an experience in order to focus his point of view. This is chiefly to be seen in *India: A Million Mutinies Now* in which he repeatedly refers to his visit to India in 1962. The writer goes over and over what he has stated before, like a spider spinning itself into its own web projecting the dual childhood emotions which first set him out of India:

i) The India I had gone to in 1962 was like a different country.
ii) The India I had gone to in 1962 had been like a place far away, a place like a long journey.
iii) I had not seen that kind of private wealth in 1962.
iv) I had not seen anyone like that on the boating steps in 1962.
v) In 1962 there had been nine rooms in the hotel. (490-97)

Besides, Naipaul has a fine skill of quoting a journalist to support his own reporting while transforming facts into fiction. Thus in *The Middle Passage,* while describing the plight of slavery in Surinam, he quotes another writer and journalist Stedman to illustrate his own idea of slavery in this island:

> Yet one needs a strong stomach to read Stedman today. The Surinam he describes is like one vast concentration camp, with the difference that visitors were welcome to look round and make notes and sketches. The slave-owner had less on his conscience than the concentration camp commandant: the world was divided into black and white, Christian and heathen. White might conceivably be expected to show some scruples in his relations with black; but the Christian had no such inhibition in his relations with the heathen. In fairness to the Dutch, however, the earlier quotations should be given whole: 'It is felt as a terror to menace a Negro with selling him to a Dutchman. The Dutchman, however, has a terror in reverse, and threatens to sell his slave to a free negro.'[4]

Naipaul's narrative technique comes to acquire greater meaning and significance when Naipaul, the journalist, comments on Indian journalists with regard to their defective reporting. This diversion adds a new dimension to his travel writing.

One of the important features of the non-fiction novel is the filtered truth that the writer attempts to present. Instead of stating bare facts, the artist makes a deep probe into the heart of things based on truth. This may be seen in his analysis of the Indian concept of illusions with which Naipaul closes the book:

> The world is illusion, the Hindus say. We talk of despair, but true despair lies too deep for formulation. It was only now, as my experience of India defined itself more properly against my own homelessness, that I saw how close in the past year I had been to the total Indian negation, how much it had become the basis of thought and feeling. And already, with this awareness, in a world where illusion could only be a concept and not something felt in the bones, it was slipping away from me. I felt it as something true which I could never adequately express and never seize again. (266-67)

Another important and peculiar feature of the narrative technique of the non-fiction novel has been described by the term bricolage. This term distinguishes an engineer from the bricoleur; like a bricoleur, Naipaul appears most refractory; he does not use a limited set of instruments like an engineer. On the contrary he uses all kinds of materials. While describing a thing he bases his narration on the circumstances that tend to be centrifugal rather than centripetal. While talking of the Hindu concept of Drama, he dives into an unsystematic, 'almost haphazard way of thinking,' that leads him to other works of art throwing light on the subject of discussion.

Thus we see that Naipaul has made spectacular achievement in this field with his various aesthetic devices of transforming facts into fiction. Eminent writers before Naipaul have certainly attempted this, but Naipaul remains a unique artist in the sense that, while remaining close to the art of travel writing, he ultimately emerges a very successful artist of the non-fiction novels. Just as in the hands of Lytton Strachey, biography tends to be the art of fiction, so with Naipaul, travel-writing tends to be the art of fiction. This is chiefly owing to the unique narrative technique, the peculiar features of style and the centrifugal associations and their candour in the recreation of memory that enable him to achieve great perfection in this art. Thus, while describing a historical monument like Pandavas' fort, he enriches this picture with as much historical allusions as with artistic and literary touches in consequence of which the final picture becomes more artistic than mere factual. It is this art that transforms all his travel writings into great non-fiction novels.

NOTES

1. Subramani, "The Historical Consciousness in V.S. Naipaul," *Commonwealth Quarterly*, 1979, pp.18-19.
2. V.S. Naipaul, *India: A Million Mutinies Now* (London: Munerve, 1990), p. 462.
3. V.S. Naipaul, *An Area of Darkness* (New York: Vintage, 1981), p. 364.
4. V.S. Naipaul, *The Middle Passage* (London: Andre Deutsch, 1982), p. 203.

India Theirs and Mine: V.S. Naipaul's *An Area of Darkness*

I.K. MASIH

My first response on reading V.S Naipaul's *An Area of Darkness* was that here was a gifted writer with the dexterity of a magician to forge fact and fiction together. It was only during my stay in England and Ireland in 1980-81 that I could fully experience and appreciate an expatriate's feelings and attitudes. In the citation for the Bennet Award 1980 it was said, "He has risen to the challenge of a great subject—the wreckage of empire and the emergence of the third world—and out of it has created a fictional world that is now as much a part of the permanent geography of the imagination as Dickens's London or Faulkner's Yoknapatawpha county."[1]

There is no doubt that he stands free from the "ideological cant" of the age and has a "sharp clarity" of social vision. My only difference with Naipaul is that his centre is tilted. Robert Martin Adams writes that his centre has always been "the anomalous, grotesque and tragic, of half-formed provincial societies, trying to adapt themselves to formulas made elsewhere, anxiously shifting roles and images to fill the vacancy within."[2] My point is that the vacancy within Naipaul cannot be filled either by shifting roles or creating fresh images. It is composite experience which he lacks because of his birth in Trinidad where he was of a coloured minority within a black majority province of a white empire. Reconciliation is difficult, almost impossible for him. It is largely because of his "cosmopolitan rationalism"[3] that he manages his way in the "treacherous waters" of lost identity, broken images.

Nissim Ezekiel, who feels alienated from his Bombay world, agrees with Naipaul and shares his disgust. But I don't agree with his idea of India either. "Mr. Naipaul's conclusion is negative. 'Shiva has ceased to dance.' It would be too facile to say that he may dance again."[4] For me Shiva has not ceased to dance. The cosmic dance has never ceased for millions of Indians. Grossness, if exaggerated, does look appalling. Ezekiel, like Naipaul, in spite of his love for India is sceptical. He writes, "Culture doesn't consist only of literature, and philosophy and art, and it is certainly not acquired by adhering to the beliefs of the past and conforming to its institutional demands."[5]

Well, Naipaul has a right to see us as we are—defecating in the streets, craving for foreign things, being sloppy and dirty in our poverty. It seems he forgets that he himself is a Dube whom he despises. The picture which he presents is true but the basic fact is missed that he himself is the chip of the same block. The cosmopolitan Hindu society of modern India has its roots in the soil because of which even I, a Christian, an alien in many ways, feel at home and chip of the same block. The whole problem with Naipaul is that he looks at India through Western kaleidoscope which takes myriad unreal shapes when aimed at lighted areas. His vision remains limited to the possible patterns inside and he is tragically deprived of a genuine and real view of Indian life outside the narrow view-pipe.

P.C. David is right in saying, "The darkness of Naipaul is the darkness of his own situation born out of a romantic reverie which cannot stand the glare of the day."[6] He commits the basic mistake of looking at East through Western eyes, naturally the whole perspective appears wrongly aligned. This attitude of Naipaul surprises Adams too who writes, "Naipaul never lets us forget how curious a role the European West plays in the spiritual life of these semi-developed countries—as instigator and flatterer, as horrible example to be shunned and glittering example to be imitated, as authenticator of one's own mediocrity and artifice." (474) In *An Area of Darkness*, obviously, Naipaul has become a victim of the dilemma mentioned above. Why use the Western criteria in determining India to be an area of light or darkness? Naipaul's view of India is biased though it must be added that it is not cynical as in Nirad Chaudhuri's *The Continent of Circe*. Though there is no venom in his attack, it betrays shock of recognition—similar to Gulliver's discovery that he was after all a despised 'Yahoo.' I wish Naipaul could identify himself with the dirt, squalor and poverty of India. I wish he had taken a mouthful of food at his ancestor's house which might have helped him out of his predicamental trauma on finding his fairy land crumble before his eyes. This requires a little more elaboration.

Naipaul's account of India in *An Area of Darkness* is his sincere attempt to come to terms with the problem of identity. He is a victim of what Gareth Griffiths calls, "a double exile." He adds: "The African was colonized, the West Indian was enslaved. In the process of enslavement the West Indian was deprived of his personality, as well as his roots and cultural identity."[7] The grandfather of Naipaul in leaving India left behind a certain way of life—a culture. In Trinidad these indentured labourers were exposed to cultural patterns imported from England. The generations grew up in this foster culture—even the educational system was geared to produce 'overseers.' The natives, Chinese and Asians, were taught to despise themselves, for advancement in life meant imitation of their white masters. Thus for a people, for whom Cromwell was more real than the disgrace and erosion of their own beliefs, the sense of history and achievement got jumbled up. For them India was a mythical land—a dream world. As Michael Anthony has very rightly shown, a Trinidadian learnt to be blinded by his own inheritance. The three hundred years of enslavement and studied annihilation of a sense of past and heritage has left them rootless. When Naipaul went to England, he discovered that he was rootless—neither he had a personal sense of identity, nor an Indian link, nor even a British. His chartered journey to England via the colonial enslavement in Trinidad has left him cut off from his Hindu heritage. An enslaved man has no religion—not even a Brahmin. This has been the dilemma of a Caribbean writer for he has seen his past collapsing and the possibility of a new set of culture pattern appears bleak. His world is a divided world. A new culture which should have emerged has failed to take roots. For Naipaul pretences will not do; that is why "there is nothing left but flight and denial."[8] It is in this mood of flight and denial that he approached the land of his grandfather. But he remained like Mr. Biswas who in spite of his Brahminical presence, money and a place as a Tulsi son-in-law remained only a labourer's son herded back to a crowded, shabby room. Thus Biswas answers to the query of his son Anand, "Who are you?" with a candour—"I am just somebody. Nobody at all. I am just a man you know."[9] And Shiva Naipaul's predicament is that "he has been unable to accept what he has discovered."[10]

His home-coming had been an assault on his European-styled sensibility. He failed to find unluckily thousands of Gold Teeths and in spite of his one year stay it remained an unreal country—"out in the void."[11] His annoyance with the legacy of British empire—the red tapism of the Bombay Customs is not very significant. For him "Real Brahmin" label is more real than the vast expanse of India—"the featureless area of darkness which was India." (35) He had hoped India to be a resting place for his troubled realisation that England after all was not the centre of his world. But within a week he found out that he was an alien. "I was faceless. I might sink without a trace into that Indian crowd. I had been made by Trinidad and England: recognition of difference was necessary to me." (43) In his failure to accept the fact that he was no different from an Indian student staying in Europe too long lies his ordeal. Why does difference matter so much to him? Griffiths writes: "Naipaul's desperate attempt to be accepted as a special society of one, unique and above the conflict, inevitably fails." (98) And it is this failure because of which he sharply reacts against India which he saw. Compassion and pity are mere magic words. And the need to offer alms to the beggars is not perverted Indian attitude towards poverty. Naturally he fails to understand the finer feelings involved in the Premchand story. He will not see the fact that poverty is no excuse for charity but an inherent character of Indian way of life. In spite of his preparedness to understand alien Indian culture, all that he sees is—"I had seen Indian villages: the narrow broken lanes with green slime in the gutters, the choked back-to-back mud houses, the jumble of filth and food and animals and people, the baby in the dust, swollen-bellied, black with flies but wearing its good-luck amulet. I had seen the starved child defecating at the roadside while the mangy dog waited to eat the excrement." (45) He builds up a disgusting picture of the land of his ancestors forgetting to appreciate the fact that in spite of the assault of the British for hundreds of years Indians have not broken down. They still have a sense of belonging whereas his counterparts in the West have collapsed under the burden of progress. The mimicry of British which he discovers is an exception and not the rule. The Indian Army officer may look English but it is often mere appearance. He too in spite of his stiff collar and direct link with the Anglo-India of clubs and sahibs has his roots in the poverty and squalor from which the writer shrinks. Similarly if he thinks that churchgoers are only Anglo-Indians following an alien faith in a grotesque manner, he is absolutely wrong. After all Christianity came to India centuries back when the Western world was not even aware of it. This mimicry, as he calls all this, is his 'fantasy.'

I do not link myself with the traditional or institutionalized Hindu myths. I grew up an Indian and Christian. And I am not bothered by the fact whether several generations back we were Hindus or Muslims. For I have experienced the same blood flowing in my arteries which enriches my other fellow Indians with the consciousness of thousands of years. Thus in spite of my alien (?) faith I am a fulfilled Indian. And I am proud of the fact. I gladly gave up chances of, perhaps, better life in Australia and was pained to see mimicry, Naipaul-style, in Britian among the Asians. No, no, this will not do. I am proud to be an Indian for it gives me a relevance—a meaning in a maze of meaninglessness. Shiva is still dancing and I feel the beat of each step in my heart.

It is not Indian but the British who are gloating over the memory of the Raj. And it didn't need a Paul Scott to chart it in his *Raj Quartets*. The keen interest of British in TV serials on Indian themes is one such demonstration of their Indian link and interest. It is too facile to say that British did not learn anything from us. The love-hate relationship is too well-grounded now to debate the issue. Some curry, some mahogany and an India Festival are not the end—it is finding a connection with the Indian soul—and respecting it.

My main objections are to his attempt at corroding the soul of India in his 'Fantasy and Ruins.' As pointed out earlier Naipaul arrived in India as if he was visiting another British colony expecting it to be similar to his island of adoption. Trinidad had no population before 1800 A.D. and the British were interested only in the sugar it yielded. For fulfilment of this goal they indentured labourers from India, China and Africa. Therefore, they left behind no history, no monuments on which these expatriates could lean upon. This resulted in their having no culture besides an imitation of British culture from which they were separated not only by colour but by the fact that they were slaves. In India, on the other hand, the relationship was fundamentally different. When the British arrived in India, it already had an ancient culture. A culture about which Naipaul himself agrees quoting Albert Camus that "Indians are incapable of rebellion as they have a tradition which is sacred. Through the centuries their every problem has been taken care of. This feature of Indian culture is unique and basically opposed to Western concept of rebellion. This is the reason why "Hindu India met conquerors half-way and had always been able to absorb them." (209) A point which he makes at length does not hold to analysis, that is, "The country had been pillaged before. But continuity had been maintained. With the British continuity was broken." (208) In spite of the fact that the "British refused to be absorbed in India," (211) as Moghuls and others had done earlier, the British came half-way to meet Indian culture. If one goes minutely through the first freedom struggle (1857) it is evident that the British respected Indians for their valour and spiritual attainments. The latter always left them dazed but they realized that here they were in for an experience. They confronted in India, for the first time, a culture different from theirs but at the same time rich. Naipaul as an outsider never realizes what the British meant to Indians and what we did to them. Rammohun Roy and Aurobindo Ghosh were not representing Indian degeneration and decay as the writer asserts but they were trying to electrify the ancient culture with the new light of reason from the West. This is the continuity because of which temples exist amidst the giant steel factories. "Indian schizophrenia" (213) as Naipaul ludicrously calls our civilization and culture, which he failed to understand, require no fantasy to sustain them. We have a tradition, a heritage to keep us going even when the West has tried to annihilate us economically. Shiva's dance of life and death appear to him futile and erotic sculptures represent mere painful sex. He misses the reality, the inner meaning of the beginning and end meeting at a point. To me these sculptures and carvings are an embodiment of the spiritual craving in physical terms. But all that Naipaul could see was the child defecating and the mangy dog eating it. The passion which he misses is not physical. He claims that Indians live on the memory of the past, the ruins. But only those who have a past worth remembering can live on it. To say that "the Taj Mahal is exquisite. Transported slab by slab to the United States and re-erected, it might be wholly admirable." (206) As artist Naipaul should know better. No work of art or architecture has its meaning in isolation and out of context. It is the receding Yamuna, the red fort on the horizon, the dirt and the dust, and the poverty around it which gives a meaning to this "despot's monument to his wife." Similarly he does not succeed in making a point that Indians are surviving on a dream-world of ruins when he mentions the Kurukshetra temple. Krishna teaching Arjuna in the chariot represented in marble appears "less than Bazar art" to him. He concludes: "That chariot will never move." (207) For him all attempts at finding a growing and progressing India is abortive—"Shiva has ceased to dance." (217)

East cannot be West. Neither can India, though his grandfather came from Uttar Pradesh, provide him a sense of belonging. Naipaul's basic mistake is that he takes the shrub for the woods. Shiva has not ceased to dance. The continuity, which is a living past, bestows on us strength to cope with the New World Order. Naipaul could not meet the fairy-like people. And he fails to accept the real flesh-and-blood people—defecating, quarrelling, living—he met. Naipaul is rootless. He remains an outsider, unable to connect his self with the past "Indian confusion." Even for me, a Christian, the chariot is not static and horses are ready to leap in spite of the fact that he considers our civilization to be wounded and decaying.

The problem with modern India is that too many forces are operating on us. Even Nehru dreamt of an industrialized Rhine built in a year or two. The bureaucracy is still a legacy of the Empire. And the people, used for centuries to the ways of the despotic rulers, have not adjusted fully to the ever-changing rhythm of democracy. With its past and multitudes, India is a different country. It cannot be simply an industrial modern state nor can it arrange its life into a systematized soulless rational pattern. For it has the wisdom of the centuries to give every move its meanting and relevance. And it is because of this that in spite of change of religion by my forefathers I am still an Indian culturally and spiritually. Naipaul has lost his identity, and I have my sympathies with him. He is too caste-conscious and egoistic to appreciate and understand the rhythms of Shiva's cosmic dance and Krishna's eternal sermon. No, Shiva has not ceased to dance. India lives on the beats of Shiva's cosmic dance. It may be a land of darkness for Naipaul, for me it is an area of light and it will remain so.

NOTES

1. "The Bennet Award, 1980," *The Hudson Review*, XXXIII (Autumn 1980), p. 321.
2. Robert Martin Adams, "V.S. Naipaul," *The Hudson Review*, XXXIII (Autumn 1980), p. 474.
3. *Ibid.*, p. 475.
4. Nissim Ezekiel, "Naipaul's India and Mine," *New Writings in India*, ed. Adil Jussawalla (Harmondsworth: Penguin, 1977), p. 90.
5. *Ibid.*
6. P.C. David, "Between Two Stools: Naipaul's *An Area of Darkness*," *Alien Voice*, ed. A.K. Srivastava (Lucknow: Print House, 1981), p. 230.
7. Gareth Griffiths, *A Double Exile* (London: Marion Boyars, 1978), p. 79.
8. *Ibid.*, p. 124.
9. V.S. Naipaul, *A House for Mr. Biswas* (Harmondsworth: Penguin, 1969), p. 279.
10. Griffiths, p. 129.
11. V.S. Naipaul, *An Area of Darkness* (Harmondsworth: Penguin, 1977), p. 27.

Changing Indian Critical Response to V.S. Naipaul's *An Area of Darkness*

T.S. BORATE

In the last week of December 1988, V.S. Naipaul was in Bombay, his first visit to this country in nine years. His twentieth book *A Turn in the South* has been serialized in the prestigious American magazine *The New Yorker* prior to being published. It is about the southern part of the USA and to research it and get a "feel" of the subject he spent six months in the southern states of the USA. A newspaper columnist[1] says that "perhaps that is what he might end up doing in India" once again. The columnist also feels that "something of great literary value will come out of it." He does not, further, forget to remind us that Naipaul "makes literary waves wherever he is" and that his "*An Area of Darkness* got so many in this country hot under the collar." Another columnist writing in another newspaper humorously describes Naipaul's discomfiture amidst the prostitutes of Bombay's infamous Kamathipura area and jocularly adds that "what Mr. Naipaul thinks of this particular area of darkness should make interesting reading."[2] These recent newspaper write-ups, in spite of being rather light-hearted, indicate an important thing about India-Naipaul relationship. They remind us once again of the impact that *An Area of Darkness*, published exactly a quarter century ago, had made on us. Based on his homecoming during his Indian sojourn of 1962-63, "*An Area of Darkness* portrayed the contemporary Indian milieu so unflatteringly that it provoked waves of protest throughout India."[3] The Indian critical response to both of Naipaul's books on India (the second one being *India: A Wounded Civilization*, 1977) spread over the last twenty-five years, make interesting reading. This paper aims at examining the Indian critical response to *An Area of Darkness*, with a view to suggesting why and how it need to be further adequately modulated so that the critical darkness that still occasionally surrounds the book disappears, allowing the book to illumine the whole of the Naipaul canon.

The task is extremely difficult for it had been impossible to collect and study everything that has been said in India about the book during the last twenty-five years. Naturally, only those articles that are often cited in critical writings, and are easily available, have been analyzed in the next few pages. An attempt is also made to show how the graph of the Indian critical response to the book rises from outright condemnation and rejection to somewhat hesitant and yet whole-hearted appreciation and acceptance of the book as the years pass and as Naipaul reaches greater and greater heights as an international writer.

The most notable early attack on *An Area of Darkness* came from C.D. Narasimhaiah, one of India's most distinguished of literary critics. While considering D.J. Enright and Jill Hugh-Jones's earlier reviews of *An Area of Darkness* "as notable exceptions" to have come from foreign critics, he bitterly castigates John Wain, V.S. Pritchett and a *TLS* reviewer as ill-informed (of India). He is also disturbed to find an important (unnamed) Indian critic extending a warm welcome to the book. Of the two earliest reviews he absolves calling them "notable exceptions," Jill Hugh-Jones's comes fairly close to what Narasimhaiah has to say about the book. But D.J. Enright's review, which undoubtedly shares a few of Narasimhaiah's later observations, has a predominant tilt in the opposite direction. Unlike Narasimhaiah's, it is formalist in tone and approach. To Enright "the book is strongly felt, original, compact, and hardly ever dull: which makes it a rarity in its genre."[4] Naipaul's failure to get near to the spirit of India, however, according to him, lies in his wrong choice of form. Fiction or poetry would have been far better than the orthodox travelogue. But he is quick to realize that the book "is not exactly about a journey, a country, but largely about himself [Naipaul], a hybrid production, part novel, with himself as hero, villain, at times clown." Surprisingly, Narasimhaiah seems to be in agreement with Enright when he says: "We can deal with the book under the broad classification of belles-lettres."[5] Later, he curiously adds that from belles-lettres we must demand "an interest in man, society and civilization." But, once again surprisingly, the article has absolutely nothing to say about the book as 'belles-lettres.' "The present undertaking," the article sets out to warn us, "is not intended to be a defence of India." But even after reading the article over and over again one cannot help feeling that it is nothing but "a defence of India" and that contrary to his presumption its writer is "a spokesman of the Ministry of Information" of the government of India.

Forgetting the commonly accepted principle that in "belles-lettres" what matters most is the writer and not the subject, Narasimhaiah laments: "to understand India, one must understand Mr. Naipaul. Hardly the way to understand a country." He finds Naipaul lacking spirituality, wisdom, humility, sympathy and inner illumination. He finds in him callousness, heartlessness, perversity and "the arrogance of a sponsored visitor." He is very much worried about Naipaul's "deceptive appeal to the skeptical among us." To him Naipaul seems to have been on "the look-out for material for a best-seller." While granting that Naipaul is a gifted writer and that "his English is remarkable," he finds Naipaul's feelings terribly detestable. Naipaul's negation, disgust, and horror of the unclean, unsettle him thoroughly. To him the book is "tantalizing mixture of first-rare literary sensibility along with what should belong to pot-boilers, namely a morbid obsession with filth, dirt, defecation, and an extraordinary lack (in one so gifted) of sympathy, penetration and concern for people as people."

That D.J. Enright's review, mistakenly hailed by Narasimhaiah, failed to be a trend-setter is once again seen in Nissim Ezekiel's rather half-hearted, and yet characteristically light-hearted, attack on *An Area of Darkness*. While frankly confessing that he sees "India in most ways as Naipaul sees her," Ezekiel expresses his "dissatisfaction with his mode of argument, his falsifying examples." 'To him Naipaul is a 'hypersensitive person' showing little humility. Though Ezekiel praises "Naipaul's special gift for the telling detail," he finds the book "heavily flawed in detail."

Knowing fully well that "Naipaul's cultural base is not national but humanist, not a territory or even a culture but a complex of values which cuts across all historical divisions," Ezekiel, surprisingly, adds: "my quarrel is that Mr. Naipaul is so often uninvolved and unconcerned. He writes exclusively from the point of view of his dilemma, his temperamental alienation from his mixed background, his choice and his escape."

Is this valid criticism? From the point of view of whose dilemma, whose temperamental alienation, whose choice and escape should Naipaul write so that Ezekiel forgets his quarrel and makes friends with Naipaul? Ezekiel's? What dilemma, what temperamental alienation, what choice and what escape does Ezekiel have? In spite of being "a natural outsider" doesn't Ezekiel tell us in the same breath "in India I am an Indian"? How could Naipaul have written like Ezekiel? How could Naipaul's India be like Ezekiel's? And if Ezekiel is not interested in Naipaul's India why should people be interested in Ezekiel's? Well, Ezekiel's self-elevating anecdotes, only overtly modest, do make amusing reading, but they hardly offer any critical insight into Naipaul's book.

I.K. Masih's article appeared much later, runs more or less on the lines of Nissim Ezekiel's except that it displays a "more loyal than the king" attitude more emphatically than Ezekiel's. Following Jill Hugh-Jones, who charges Naipaul of a "holier than thou" attitude,[7] one can hardly resist the temptation of charging both Masih and Ezekiel of a "more loyal than the king" attitude. Like Ezekiel, who tells us only "circumstances and decisions (of not leaving India for good) relate me to India," Masih says "even I, a Christian, an alien in many ways, feel at home and a chip of the same block" in India.[8] The reason for this is, of course, that "the cosmopolitan Hindu society of modern India has its roots in the soil." Well, that gives Masih an excuse to take Naipaul, and to a much lesser extent Ezekiel, to task for not conforming to his perception of India.

H.H. Anniah Gowda would have been happy if only Naipaul had written about "the India which is not defecating." Calling *An Area of Darkness* "Naipaul's personal testament" he tells us that "as a record of his personal reactions, the book has value; but he is writing about himself, not India."[9] The book falls short of the idea of making people dream (which is what according to Flaubert, Gowda reminds us, a great book should do). It is a readable but negative book about India. It is charged with prejudice and it makes painful reading to an Indian.

Anand Rao Thota finds faults with the book because Naipaul, according to him, due to his mixed background, is "incapable of confronting Indian reality of the twentieth century." To Naipaul India is an enigma because "India has always been an enigma, particularly to the West."[10]

Even as late as 1983 we find Shyamal Bagchee displaying an unforgivably cavalier attitude towards both of Naipaul's books on India. The topic he is going to talk about, he tells us, "creates a peculiar problem for me because of the two subjects that intersect here, India and Naipaul, one is of the utmost significance to me; about these books by Naipaul on the other hand, I care very little."[11] So once again we have an article dealing with his India, finding fault with each and every detail of Naipaul's peculiar perception of India, ignoring even the need to probe into the writer's dilemma.

The list of Indian critics who have responded to *An Area of Darkness* more or less in the manner indicated so far can be further extended. But that would not add anything significant to what has been said so far. The risk of monotonous repetition is not worth taking.

It is refreshing to discover a couple of critics who have something different and more profound to say about *An Area of Darkness*. K.

Narayan Kutty's brilliant article, though essentially about Naipaul's second book on India, has this to say about *An Area of Darkness*: "*An Area of Darkness* was more about Naipaul than about India, it was also amusingly apocalyptic in its vision of India." Though K. Narayan Kutty does not elaborate upon this searching remark of his (for that is not what his article intends to undertake) he tells us how Naipaul is distinct from the two great myth-makers, favourite among Indians: E.M. Forster and Ruth Prawer Jhabvala:

> One of the few writers that I have read who do not create myths about India is V.S. Naipaul. If anything, he is a destroyer of existing myths. Naipaul is angry at the way things are in India and angry with Indians for making things the way they are, that is, a mess. He is not interested in India's spiritual heritage, he is not taken in by Western fascination with India's holiness; he takes nothing about India for granted.[12]

We may safely presume that what K. Narayan Kutty says about *India: A Wounded Civilization*, he would not mind saying about *An Area of Darkness*:

> Undoubtedly, his book will infuriate Indians who have been nurtured on the notion that India is the greatest of countries. But to respond negatively to Naipaul's criticism is to be intellectually touchy; to reject it totally is to be naively smug. I find his trenchant expose of India, in spite of its many flaws, invigorating. I prefer it to mindless adulation India receives from sentimental and self-indulgent western visionaries who wax eloquent about India's gods and goddesses, mantras, and tantriks without understanding them. Actually, Naipaul's diatribe against India reveals a truer concern for India than the hollow admiration of its devotees abroad.

Indeed, "If the plight of the country of his ancestors can enrage Naipaul, why can't it do the same of its natives?"

P.C. David is another Indian critic whose analysis of *An Area of Darkness* makes interesting reading for, in spite of its limitations, it attempts to look at *An Area of Darkness* from a formalistic point of view. He starts with the assurance of taking a fresh look at the work and of keeping aside "the uncritical and often unbalanced stances of its early critics and reviewers." He promptly reminds us how the book rubbed "the national pride on the wrong side." He hails the essays of Narasimhaiah and Nissim Ezekiel as "fine and perceptive criticism."[13] Isn't it astounding to see how quickly P.C. David forgets and probably forgives "the uncritical and often unbalanced stances of its early critics and reviewers?" And yet, we are happy to note, he goes on to say that his "humble attempt is to look at the work as a specimen of literary writing which seeks to reverify the formal resources of the conventional travelogue." He proclaims his verdict on the book by calling it "an artistic fiasco" and "an artistic failure." After giving us half a dozen confused reasons of why he thinks so, he concludes that *An Area of Darkness* falls "between two stools" of travelogue and novel. Thus far, and no further!

It is really a sad thing that *An Area of Darkness* should have defied being properly analyzed by some of the best critical minds in the country. Understandably, the failure of its early critics to come to grips with the book is partly due to the limitations imposed upon them by their nearness to the book in terms of time. Their peculiar perspective prevented them from taking a look at the book as something demanding an altogether different kind of response. Most of them joined issues with Naipaul, blaming him of falsification and at times of ignorance. They did not take into account that *An Area of Darkness* was Naipaul's seventh book showing a remarkable continuity with his earlier works, notably, *The Middle Passage*. But sadly, even later critics also blindly followed the great masters's path and failed to place the book in a proper perspective. With the arrival of Naipaul's twentieth book, we are today in a better position to place *An Area of Darkness* in the context of the Naipaul canon.

It was a foreign critic, Alastair Niven, who in 1978, while comparing Nirad C. Chaudhari's *A Passage to England* and V.S. Naipaul's *An Area of Darkness* for the first time pointed out: "No study of his [Naipaul's] fiction would be complete without the complement of his other work and amongst that his account of the Indian sojourn [*An Area of Darkness*] has a special pathos."[14]

In 1980 the selection committee for the Bennett Award viewed all Naipaul's work as one integrated whole and found him to have "risen to the challenge of a great subject—the wreckage of empire and the emergence of the Third World."[15] In his Bennett Award acceptance speech, Naipaul said: "I liked the terms of the award. It was for one's work as a whole. So it didn't just acknowledge one book, one piece of luck; it acknowledged the vocation."[16]

A couple of years later Helga Chaudhary, a West Indian critic, perceived in *An Area of Darkness* a candid appraisal of the author's problem of alienation and psychological ambience, both in relation to the Caribbean and to India. It is because of this, she tells us, that "the book is widely regarded as an important mile-stone in West Indian literature."[17] Much earlier, in 1976, Naipaul had said: "I feel that any statement I make about my work would be misleading. The work is there: the reader must see what meaning, if any, the work has for him. All I would like to say is that I consider my non-fiction an integral part of my work."[18] This view of Naipaul of his own work as a whole seems to have been rightly shared by Dom Moraes, who hails Naipaul as "a writer of our times."[19] Moraes views *An Area of Darkness* in a larger perspective and laments that it "has come in for much unwarranted criticism in India." He finds it "not only a brilliant piece of literature but an interesting psychological study of Naipaul by Naipaul." What he probably suggests is that much of the early Indian criticism of *An Area of Darkness* be ignored because "nowhere he [Naipaul] went . . . did he escape whipping from the local intelligentsia." Today Naipaul "has become international in the fullest possible sense" and "he is no longer obsessed with parts of the world relevant to him." Naipaul never wanted to prettify his reactions, as he is on record to have told Adrian Rowe-Evans. He is "more concerned with thought, meaning, philosophy" expressing himself in a writing which is "perfectly transparent."[20]

But in the final analysis even the relevance of the whole world itself becomes irrelevant to him. His Hinduism, unlike that of most of his unsympathetic critics, is not just "skin-deep." When Andrew Robinson asked him the following searching question: "What aspects of yourself do you feel to be specifically Indian?" Naipaul answered: "I think the philosophical aspect—Hindu I would say. Speculative and probably also pessimistic. What I mean by pessimism is not things turning out badly but a pessimistic view about man's existence: that men just end." Like all other recurrent metaphors such as decaying house, ship-wreck, sexual violence, aridity and wound etc. 'darkness'" of the book's title fits into that pessimistic view of Naipaul of man's existence, the exploration of which would be the topic of another paper for another ocassion.

NOTES

1. "Gallery," *The Sunday Observer*, 18 Dec. 1988, p. 19.
2. "Current Topics: Naipaul's Turn: Society Saviours," *The Times of India*, 26 Dec. 1988, p. 12.

3. Meher Dastoor, "The Elusive Master," *The Illustrated Weekly of India*, 5 July 1987, p. 12.
4. D.J. Enright, "Who is India?," *Encounter*, Dec. 1964, pp. 59-64.
5. "Somewhere Something Has Snapped," *The Literary Criterion*, 6, 4 (1965), pp. 83-96.
6. "Naipaul's India and Mine," *New Writing in India*, ed. Adil Jussawalla (Penguin, 1974), pp. 71-90.
7. "Seeing the Obvious," *Quest*, 45, April-June 1965, pp. 103-5.
8. "India: Theirs and Mine," *Osmania Journal of English Studies* (V.S. Naipaul Special Number), 1982, pp. 125-34.
9. "Naipaul in India," *The Literary Half-Yearly*, 11, No. 2 (1970), pp. 163-70.
10. "V.S. Naipaul and the Confused Hindu Sensibility," *Osmania Journal of English Studies*, 1982, pp. 37-45.
11. "Naipaul in India: The Mocker's Holiday," *New Quest*, 41, Sept.-Oct. 1983, pp. 285-97.
12. "Naipaul and India," *New Quest*, 9, May-June 1978, pp. 167-73.
13. "Between Two Stools: Naipaul's *An Area of Darkness*," *Alien Voice*, ed. Avadhesh K. Srivastava (Lucknow: Print House, 1981), pp. 226-34.
14. "Crossing the Black Waters: Nirad C. Chaudhari's *A Passage to England* and V.S. Naipaul's *An Area of Darkness*," *ARIEL*, 9, No. 3 (1978), pp. 21-36.
15. "The Bennett Award, 1980," citation, *The Hudson Review*, 33, No. 3 (1980), the opening page of the issue.
16. *The Hudson Review*, 33, No. 4 (1980-81), the opening page of the issue.
17. "V.S. Naipaul's Changing Vision of India: A Study of *An Area of Darkness, India: A Wounded Civilization*," *The Literary Half-Yearly*, 23, No. 1 (1982), pp. 98-114.
18. "Naipaul V(idiahar) S(urajprasad)," *Contemporary Novelists*, ed. James Vinson (London: St. James's Press, 1976), p. 1002.
19. "A Writer for our Times," *Gentleman*, Feb. 1984, pp. 36-39.
20. "An Interview with V.S. Naipaul," *Quest*, 78, Sept.-Oct. 1972, pp. 47-55.
21. Andrew Robinson, "The Weekly Cover Story" (An Interview with V.S. Naipaul), *The Illustrated Weekly of India*, 5 July 1987, p. 13.

V.S. Naipaul and the Demythologizing of El Dorado

R.K. KAUL

> Wondrous is this wall-stone; broken by fate, the castles have decayed; the work of giants is crumbling.[1]

The above extract is from an Anglo-Saxon poem of the 8th century. "We may imagine," says the translator, "the poet walking about the overgrown streets" of a deserted Roman city. The Anglo-Saxon did not have the architectural skill to repair the Roman walls and castles, let alone build new ones. Typically the Anglo-Saxon had an elegiac temper. The sight of the broken-down walls and castles confirmed their world-view: "To the Christian Anglo-Saxon poets, these tangible signs of the decay of a civilization more magnificent than their own provided an opportunity for moralizing on the theme of the transience of earthly splendour."[2] So marvellous did the remains of Roman buildings seem to them that they called them "the work of giants."

I have approached V.S. Naipaul through this unfamiliar route. The context of this quotation will make my reason clear, "The West Indies," says Naipaul, are "so completely a creation of Empire that the withdrawal of Empire is almost without meaning."[3]

The equation of the British Empire with ancient Rome is taken for granted. It had a civilizing mission. What is more, it fused the subject people into a nation. It invested them with history. The withdrawal of the Empire will leave the natives more or less in the condition of the Anglo-Saxons of the seventh and eighth centuries. They are devoid of all the skills which make civilization possible. Consider for instance what happens when colonial rule is withdrawn from the African state in *A Bend in the River*. The narrator Salim informs us, "Pedestals had been defaced, protective railings flattened, flooded lights smashed and left to rest."[4]

Naipaul is not so naive as to imagine that the initial motive of the colonial powers was benevolent. In *The Loss of El Dorado* (1969) he traces the history of expeditions to Trinidad, Guiana, Venezuela and the neighbouring islands from 1592 when de Vera landed in Trinidad. The earliest conquerors viz. de Berrio from Spain and Walter Ralegh from Britain had chiefly one motive. In fact all the colonial powers, including the French, the Dutch and the Portuguese, like the British and the Spaniards, laboured under the delusion that there were gold mines in this region. They did not scruple to lure the native Indians into deathtraps, to subject African slaves to unspeakable cruelty or treat the rival colonial power with treachery. Naipaul does not gloss over any of these facts which he has gleaned from learned works of history.

Nevertheless both his fiction and non-fiction assume that the withdrawal of the colonial power would spell chaos. This foreboding, however, is systematically suppressed by the ambitious politician, black or brown, who is eager to take over. He succeeds because of the "liberal" whites who control the media in Europe and America.

Four of Naipaul's works of fiction have their setting in countries liberated from European rule viz. *The Suffrage of Elvira* (1958), the title story of the volume *In a Free State* (1971), *Guerrillas* (1975) and *A Bend in the River* (1979). In this paper only the last three will be discussed because the first is a comic account of how the very first elections took place immediately after the grant of independence to a West Indian island. It does not relate to the theme of this paper.

The other three are more grim in tone. They expose the hollow rhetoric of the new leadership that has emerged in the third world. The native dictators, military or civilian, who succeeded to the colonial rulers in the West Indies and Africa, showed no real interest in the welfare of their people. They were power maniacs whose efficiency consisted chiefly in liquidating all opposition to their governments. But no individual dictator lasted very long. They were soon overthrown by equally ruthless rivals. Their subjects had to suffer alternating spells of tyranny and anarchy.

Naipaul directs his wrath especially against the Western media which treat the coloured people as playthings. For example when the Big Man took over the government of the African country in *A Bend in the River* the Western press was irresponsible in its reporting. Some of the newspapers found good words for the butchery on the coast. (34) The explanation given by one of the characters is that "people are like that about places in which they aren't really interested and where they don't have to live." (34)

Naipaul's outlook is anti-primitivist. He values the amenities of civilization. He is unapologetic about preferring the highway to the bush. Presumably he considers the Western conservationist sentiment irrelevant to the undeveloped regions of Africa and the West Indies. When Roche in *Guerrillas* visits Stephen's area he has to find his way through an unpaved road and an irregular dirt track. The sight of chickens does not occasion a pastoral rhapsody. Instead they were "open beaked, clucking in the heat." They "roosted in hollows in the thick, dry, dingy dust about the pillars."[5]

The anti-pastoral sentiment of Naipaul is understandable. The interior of the bush is not the kind of place in which a Wordsworth or a Thoreau can find a refuge from the clamour and the crowds of city life. It is the ideal setting for crimes of violence. "The bush," he tells us in *A Bend in the River*, "muffled the sound of murder, and the muddy rivers and lakes washed the blood away." (58) Altogether the landscape has a frightening character.

The novelist who has fully succeeded in suggesting the ineffable horror of this landscape is Conrad. In *Heart of Darkness* he calls the smell of mud "primeval." The forest is "virgin." It is silent but its silence contains such exuberant fertility as the following:

> The great wall of vegetation, an exuberant and entangled mass of trunks, branches, leaves, boughs, festoons, motionless in the moonlight, was like a rioting invasion of soundless life, a rolling wave of plants, piled up, crested, ready to topple over the creek, to sweep every little man of us out of his little existence. And it moved not. A deadened burst of mighty splashes and snorts reached us from afar, as though an ichthyosaurus had been taking bath of glitter in the great river.[6]

It is not until we come across the comparison with "an ichthyosaurus . . . taking bath of glitter in the great river" that we fathom the full meaning of the "primeval mud" in the heart of Africa.

Conrad's vision, in my view, is close enough to Naipaul's to explain why the protagonist of *A Bend in the River* wishes to be dissociated from the life of the bush around him. Africa had been the home of his family for centuries and yet he insists that he and his ancestors did not take root in the soil. (17) This forms a fairly close parallel to Naipaul's own situation. The only difference is that his family migrated only two generations ago.

The settlers in *A Bend in the River* are appalled by the proximity of the bush. The bush threatens to over-run the feeble attempts of man to build the highway, the rock garden and the floodlit hotel. During the mutiny in *In a Free State*, "the grinning soldiers threw away their guns and tore off those uniforms and ran off naked into the bush." (216) They truly belong to the bush. In Naipaul's view, and Conrad's, they are a species apart from the settlers.

And yet Conrad who had not studied the writings of the more upto-date anthropologists could see beneath the exterior. "The prehistoric man" that Marlow confronts is still extant in the African heartland. Marlow and his sailors "were travelling the night of the first ages." A suspicion passes through his mind that they were inhuman. "They howled and leaped, and spun, and made horrid faces." (96) But Conrad adds the disturbing reflection:

> What thrilled you was just the thought of their humanity—like yours—the thought of your remote kinship with this wild and passionate uproar. Ugly. Yes, it was ugly enough; but if you were man enough you would admit to yourself that there was in you just the faintest trace of a response to the terrible frankness of that noise. (96)

Now Naipaul is not, in Marlow's words, "man enough" to acknowledge his kinship with primeval man. This is how he describes such a specimen, "a wild man of the hills was asleep. His matted hair was done in long pigtails, reddish brown in places and with a kind of thick blue grease." (59) Naipaul's fear is that after losing contact with the civilizing force of Europe or America the whole of society will revert to primitive savagery.

It does not occur to Naipaul that we are all descended from the "wildman of the hills." More representative of the modern sensibility is the poet R.S. Thomas who sees in the half-witted grin of the Welsh peasant his own and his reader's prototype.[7]

Naipaul's reactions are strictly pragmatic not poetic. Once the foregin capital is pulled out, the coffee and cocoa plantations will relapse into the bush that was pervasive before colonizing.[8] "The derelict old cocoa drying houses," the "little rattling shacks" were insulated from the "weekend holiday traffic." Very lyrically the author adds, "charmed villages stranded in time, belonging to another era" but surprisingly concludes, "an era which contained no possibility of a future." (155) To be cut off from civilization is to be without a future. Needless to say Naipaul does not recognize the possibility of any civilization other than one based on capital investment, mechanization and modern managerial organization. Even the Marxist alternative is not considered, let alone the Tolstoy-Gandhi utopia.

Naipaul sets out systematically to demolish the myth of the noble savage popularized in post-Rousseau Europe. The Western reader brought up on a romanticized view of tribal rites and rituals would be shocked by Linda's denunciation in the title story of *In a Free State*: "They are going to swear their oaths of hate. You know what that means, don't you? You know the filthy things they are going to do? The filth they are going to eat? The blood, the excrement, the dirt."[9]

While Naipaul seeks to deglamorize all the flattering myths about primitive cultures his focus understandably is on myths pertaining to the West Indies. Among the numerous popular versions of the idealized West Indian perhaps Aphra Behn's *Oronooko* (1688) was one of the first. The poeple of Surinam, it is claimed, "understand no vice, or cunning, but when they are taught by the *White Men*."[10] Oronooko himself already at the age of 17 was endowed by nature with "real Greatness of Soul . . . refined Notions of true Honour . . . absolute Generosity, and . . Softness that was capable of the highest Passions of Love and Gallantry." (153)

The popularity of the fictitious West Indian apparently did not decline in the next century in spite of widespread awareness of the condition of the Negro slaves on the sugar plantations. Richard Cumberland's play *The West Indian* (1971) was performed for 28 successive nights to appreciative audiences in London. Although the hero's English origin is revealed at the very outset to one character by the father, in the eyes of the other characters he passes for a native of that "warm sunny region, where naked nature walks without a disguise." (IV, x) In contrast to the simplicity, candour and nobility of the West Indian the English are condemned as cold and contriving. (IV, x) Belcour is blessed with strong animal spirits, a high principle of honour and an uncommon benevolence.[11] (III, v)

Naipaul, however, in his West Indian novels and stories is more concerned with deflating the myths current now about the West Indian. One of them is their supposed frivolity, conviviality and partiality for music. In *Guerrillas* one of the characters, Harry de Tunja, is critical of the West Indian reputation for music, dance and fun-making. In Toronto they call him Calypso Harry. He is bitter enough about this to observe: "If I had my way I would ban music. And dancing. . . . This is a country that has been destroyed by music." (129)

Jimmy's friend Roy writes to him from London, "I am beginning to feel that we are an incurably frivolous people and as a nation we seem resigned to giggling our way to oblivion." (165) The word "oblivion" occurs where we would normally expect "heaven." To abjure all sense of responsibility is to risk an eternity of oblivion. It certainly will not earn for the "japers" and jesters a place among the blessed.

In *Guerrillas* Naipaul also exposes the persistence of the Western intelligentsia in seeing not what is there but imposing their own preconceptions on West Indian and African reality. The abstract presentation of the theme goes hand in hand with the concrete presentation.

The two presentations converge in Jimmy Ahmed who is at the centre of the novel. Jimmy tells us himself that he was born "in the back room of a Chinese grocery." (27) In other words he is both a bastard and a mongrel. He is the leader of a gang consisting of "boys spawned by the city." They are "casually conceived, and after the backyard drama and ritual of their birth gradually abandoned." They attack themselves to certain groups and through the groups to certain houses that offered occasional shelter or food. (34) This is how Naipaul debunks the ideology of Che Guevara.

Jimmy Ahmed's so-called Community Farm is, as Jane immediately perceives, bogus. She complains very justly that the fields are in an appalling state and yet. "Everybody is pretending that something exists that doesn't exist." (30) She immediately suspects that it is a perfect cover for the guerrillas. And she turns out to be right.

According to Naipaul not only Jimmy's farm but the very idea of agricultural communes is unsound. The most articulate advocate of the idea in the novel, i.e. Roche, is made to admit that it was anti-historical: "All over the world people are leaving the land to go to the cities. And they know what they want . . . more excitement, more lights . . . richer . . . brighter." (204) By implication the Chinese model as an alternative to capitalism is rejected.

Now the interesting thing is that while Jane sees through Peter's self-deception she is herself a victim of Jimmy's meritricious charm. This aspect of the situation is presented novelistically.

To begin with, Jimmy calls his farm Thrushcross Grange. Peter simplistically remarks to Jane, "I don't think it means anything. I don't think Jimmy sees himself as Heathcliff." (10) About 50 pages later we notice that Jane, in describing Jimmy, quotes Catherine's tribute to Heathcliff: "Your mother was an Indian princess and your father was the Emperor of China." (62) She confesses that Jimmy possesses her. In her imagination his body is lithe like that of a panther. His presence casts a spell on her. She is a mesmerized rabbit. And yet the author lets us know that Jimmy has homosexual relations with Bryant, the most repulsive character in the novel. What is more, Jimmy treats her with contempt, calling her "rotten meat."

While Jimmy's self-deception is exposed, Jane's is treated with brutal irony. Instead of being compared with Catherine, Jane is frequently referred to as a prostitute. The culmination of her passion for Jimmy is pathetic. She is buggared by Jimmy and butchered by Bryant at the behest of the black panther (i.e. Jimmy Ahmed). It would not be too far-fetched to suggest that her murder in the neighbourhood of a lavatory is meant to be a parody of Othello's sacrificial murder of Desdemona.

The demythologizing of El Dorado thus reaches its culmination.

NOTES

1. Quoted in *The Middle Passage* (1962; Penguin, 1978), p. 155. For the Anglo-Saxon poem, see *The Earliest English Poems*, trans. Michael Alexander (Penguin, 1966), p. 30.
2. Dorothy Whitelock, *The Beginnings of English Society* (Penguin, 1952), p. 17.
3. *The Middle Passage*, p. 153.
4. *A Bend in the River* (1977; Penguin, 1982), p. 32.
5. *Guerrillas* (1975; Penguin, 1976), pp. 105-6.
6. *Heart of Darkness* (Oxford: the World's Classics, 1984), p. 86.
7. While Thomas has direct racial links with the Welsh peasants, Naipaul has none with the African tribals. But when Naipaul visited his father's home, the village of the Dubes, he found both the people and the place repulsive. See *An Area of Darkness* (1964).
8. *Guerrillas*, p. 123.
9. *In a Free State* (1971; Penguin, 1978), p. 122.
10. *Shorter Novels*, Vol. II, *Jacobean and Restoration* (Everyman, 1930), p. 150.
11. See *Eighteenth Century Plays* (Everyman, 1946).

Looking Back in Anger: The Transformation of Childhood Memories in V.S. Naipaul's *A House for Mr. Biswas* and Jamaica Kincaid's *Annie John*

GILLIAN DOOLEY

Anger, for all its negative aspects, can provide creative urges which produce works of art of great power. The anger of the adult writer is often directed against the forces which tried to control and repress that writer as a child, so that the novel written in anger is frequently in essence, even if not in detail, autobiographical. Dickens's novels, for example, often deal with the child victim of industrialization—dramatizing again and again his own unhappy childhood. And another great feature of the European ascendancy, imperialism, spread conditions across the world which created more anger among the colonized peoples of the world. Ironically, however, the means to express this anger was also often provided to those who had the intelligence to use it. Perhaps it represents a triumph of western liberal education, over those who tried to use it as a weapon of oppression, that it could produce writers as articulate and subtle as V.S. Naipaul and Jamaica Kincaid.

Jamaica Kincaid said in an interview in 1990 that at school:

> she was considered bright but troublesome. "I was sullen. . . . I was always being accused of being rude, because I gave some backchat. . . . I wasn't really angry yet. I was just incredibly unhappy." Her anger came on slowly, but once upon her, it never let her go. Gradually she became aware that she and all Antiguans were subservient to the British. . . . Her family and friends appeared to accept their inferior status, and that confused and infuriated her.[1]

We recognize this confused, unhappy child in *Annie John*. In *A House for Mr. Biswas*, it is often Anand's anger we see and feel, and, reading this novel with the awareness that Anand is in many ways the young Naipaul, and that Mr. Biswas is based on Seepersad Naipaul, his father, it becomes clear why this happens. For example, after the extraordinary scene in which he chooses to stay behind at Green Vale with his father, Mr. Biswas asks Anand why he stayed. He replies, "'Because—' The word came out thin, explosive, charged with anger, at himself and his father. 'Because they was going to leave you alone.'"[2] Naipaul said in an interview in 1987, "When I was young . . . I was always amazed that out of such profound rage, one could end by writing quite calmly. One reacts rather strongly, but, as a writer, one distils that down. If those responses were not strong, probably one would not be a writer."[3]

Kincaid's anger is clearly a reaction to her status as a colonial subject, and even her troubled, ambivalent feelings for her mother are bound up with the tension between her true nature and the demands of her mother that she become a "lady" in the English style. In *A House for Mr. Biswas*, anger and rebellion are not so obviously directed against the imperial power. However, Gordon Rohlehr makes a convincing case for regarding Hanuman House and the Tulsis as potent symbols of colonial power:

> There is something archetypal in the organization of Hanuman House. Mr. Tulsi is a powerful mother-figure, and rules through an understanding of the psychology of slavery. . . . Mrs. Tulsi, good colonizer as she is, justifies her exploitation with the explanation that she is really doing her subjects good. Her argument is that which ex-colonial peoples most bitterly resent, and also the one which gives them pause.[4]

Anand and Mr. Biswas are both victims of the imperialism of the Tulsis. Mr. Biswas experiences it at the height of its power, and Anand is particularly affected by its decline and disintegration, which is in its way as damaging as its ascendancy. Like a country that has been colonized, exploited and then abandoned, Shorthills and the Port of Spain house become run-down, disorganized and overcrowded, with no proper facilities, so that the effort required just to carry on a normal life is almost overwhelming.

In *Annie John*, poverty is not a problem. If anything, Annie is overprotected rather than neglected, and as she matures she feels more and more rebellious against the closed, well-ordered world of her parents. The family is not rich, but her father has been able to build their house, and make furniture, and her mother sews, and cooks nutritious meals. At the time of transition from childhood to adolescence, the very way they have provided material security for her begins to oppress her, so that she rebels secretly by making friends with the Red Girl, who is free of the kinds of restrictions her mother places on her, and by playing marbles. By the time she leaves home for England, she completely rejects her parents' world:

> Everywhere I looked stood something that had meant a lot to me, that had given me pleasure at some point, or could remind me of a time that was a happy time. But as I was lying there my heart could have burst open with joy at the thought of never having to see any of it again.[5]

This feeling of rebellion is typical of the creative adolescent from a sheltered background. Her mother's insistence that she conform to an ideal of, in this case, English womanhood makes Annie all the more aware of her distance from that ideal; and the close supervision and the constant attention which are the lot of the only child makes her adept at lying and stealing to fulfil her need for creative freedom and her thirst for a different kind of life. What makes this experience particularly a colonial one is that the ideal imposed on Annic is a foreign one, and makes little sense in the small island on which she lives. The outrage of her teacher, for example, at what she wrote under the picture of Columbus in her history book, seems outrageous to the postcolonial mind, and the punishment of having to copy Books I and II of *Paradise Lost* seems entirely bizarre. This was a punishment the author herself underwent, as well as, on another occasion, having to "write over and over, 'Ignorance is bliss; it's folly to be wise'." As Leslie Garis remarks, "It was a perfect colonial punishment." Nevertheless, however restrictive the colonial education system was, it did provide Kincaid with the language and the intellectual means to escape that world and eventually become a successful writer.

The rituals of punishment in *A House for Mr. Biswas* are, if possible, stranger still. At school, Mr. Biswas himself undergoes typical canings and humiliations, but he manages to turn one penalty into a subtle undermining of the teacher's authority. In this case, the teacher "didn't flog Mr. Biswas. He ordered him to write I AM AN ASS on the blackboard. Mr. Biswas outlined stylish, contemptuous letters, and the class tittered approvingly." (40) His home life is so disorganized that it seems discipline is not an important issue: nobody really cares about him enough to punish him. Pundit Jairam inflicts probably the cruellest punishment on him by making him eat seven bananas because he stole two, thus ruining his digestive system for life. But his children grow up in Hanuman House among the Tulsis, where the ritual floggings mothers give their children are much more than a corrective for bad behaviour. The Tulsi sisters beat their children to communicate messages to other family members, especially their brothers-in-law. Sumati's reaction to Mr. Biswas's complaint that her child had broken some bottles in his shop is to beat the child, but the flogging is accompanied by a ritualistic chanting:

> "*This* will teach you not to meddle with things that don't belong to you. *This* will teach you not to provoke people who don't make any allowances for children." She caught sight of the marks left on the boy's collar by Mr. Biswas's fingers, sticky from the tin-lid. "And *this* will teach you not to let big people make your clothes dirty. *This* will teach you that they don't have to wash them. *You* are a big man. You know *right*. You know *wrong*. *You* are not a child. *That* is why *I* am beating *you* as though you are a *big* man and can take a *big* man's blows." (154)

The unfortunate child, probably without realizing it, is merely an instrument of his mother's desire to humiliate her brother-in-law and make him feel guilty and excluded from the family circle. The perverse psychology of this is minutely observed by Naipaul, who no doubt is writing from personal memories. The strong impulse to conformity in the Tulsi household—the propensity of the sisters to crush any type of individuality, which causes Shama to destroy Savi's doll's house—forces Anand into a particular form of self-defence:

> Though no one recognized his strength, Anand was among the strong. His satirical sense kept him aloof. At first this was only a pose, and imitation of his father. But satire led to contempt, and at Shorthills contempt, quick, deep, inclusive, became part of his nature. It led to inadequacies, to self-awareness and a lasting loneliness. But it made him unassailable. (412-13)

Annie John develops a similar satirical method of defending herself:

> If someone behaved toward me in a way that didn't meet with my approval, without saying a word I would look at them directly

> with one eyebrow raised. I always got an apology. If someone asked me a question, I would begin my answer with the words 'Actually' or 'As a matter of fact.' It had the effect of allowing no room for doubt. I left people's company if they said or did something I did not care for, and I had made my presence so felt that when I removed myself my absence was felt, too. Many girls wanted to show me up, and tried, but all attempts failed. I could see that everything about me aroused envy and discontent, and that made me happy—the only happiness I knew then. (129)

Both Anand and Annie, alter egos for their authors, develop the detachment from their everyday lives which is essential for the novelist. As Naipaul says, the feelings have to be strong for the impulse to write to exist; but without the ability to stand aside and analyse those feelings, the writer will not have the strength and calmness to channel and shape experience into literature which rises above mere self-indulgence.

These two novels, so different in many ways, show some interesting similarities. It is unlikely to be insignificant that each mentions death in its first sentence, for example. This cool mention of mortality in both cases sets the tone for the novel. Annie John starts off her first-person account with the statement, "For a short while during the year I was ten, I thought only people I did not know died." (3) This level, adult voice continues throughout the novel, resisting shock tactics, but conveying the full range of emotions—the confusion, anger, unhappiness and ambivalence—that the child experiences. This is very much a novel focussed on the changes in the mother-daughter bond as Annie passes from childhood to adolescence, with intense and often unexpected emotions all the more powerfully conveyed by the detachment of the tone. *A House for Mr. Biswas* is in every sense a larger novel, covering the whole lifespan of the protagonist. It has a stronger commitment to the narrative conventions than *Annie John*, which concentrates on capturing the child's feelings at various stages of her childhood, rather than narrating a chronological series of events. Nevertheless, Naipaul also strongly resists such devices as suspense. The first sentence of the novel gives away several facts that would be difficult to predict from the humble birth of Mr. Biswas: "Ten weeks before he died, Mr. Mohun Biswas, a journalist of Sikkim Street, St. James, Port of Spain, was sacked." (7) Before we know he has been born, we find out that he has died. The interest of the novel thus lies in the details of his life as it progresses—in finding out how these circumstances came about, rather than what will happen in the end. This technique is used throughout the novel. We are never left to wonder what will happen—whether Mr. Biswas will find a house at last, how long he will live, whether he will become rich: this is all covered on the very first page. The novel works on several levels. It can be seen as a richly comic vision of life in a parochial society; a homage to a father the author belatedly came to appreciate; or an allegory for the colonial situation. But in the end, the breadth of the novel's scope, combined with its profound understanding of relationships and emotions, and Naipaul's resistance to any sentimentality or simplification, is what gives it its power.

Both these novels, despite their avoidance of obvious shock tactics, show an interest in exploring beyond the expected and conventional. This is not surprising when we realise how badly the expectations and conventions of, for example, the education system were adapted to the children's situations. In *Annie John*, the children are expected to admire and respect Christopher Columbus, whereas an intelligent child like Annie can see the difficulty this involves.

> Of course, sometimes, what with our teachers and our books, it was hard for us to tell on which side we really now belonged—with the masters or the slaves—for it was all history, it was all in the past, and everybody behaved differently now; all of us celebrated Queen Victoria's birthday, even though she had been dead a long time. But we, the descendants of the slaves, knew quite well what had really happened, and I was sure that if the tables had been turned we would have acted differently; I was sure that if our ancestors had gone from Africa to Europe and come upon the people living there, they would have taken a proper interest in the Europeans on first seeing them, and said, "How nice," and then gone home to tell their friends about it. (76)

In her later novel, *Lucy*, also written in the first person about a young woman with a very similar life story to her own, Kincaid writes of the hatred she feels when confronted in America with daffodils, flowers she had been forced to celebrate by memorising poetry about them in her school days in Antigua. Such an incident reveals the ambivalence Kincaid feels about her education. She hated having Wordsworth and Milton forced upon her, but she loved the English novel: *Jane Eyre* was her favourite novel as well as Annie John's.

One of the funniest passages in *A House for Mr. Biswas* describes Mr. Biswas's experience with the Ideal School of Journalism, based in England. The subjects suggested for Mr. Biswas to practise on include

"The Seasons," "Characters at the Local," and "Some Village Superstitions." The point is made with a light touch, but it is nevertheless clear how this Anglo-centrism has suppressed Mr. Biswas's confidence in his obviously quite remarkable writing skills. As a child he has been glibly taught about oases and igloos, things he never has a chance of seeing in real life, and history, to his teacher, was "simply a school subject, as unreal as the geography, and it was from the boy in the red bodicé that he [Mr. Biswas] first heard, with disbelief, about the Great War." (46) Anand's schooling, although it takes him to success in the overseas scholarship stakes, is similarly divorced from the reality of his situation:

> Childhood, as a time of gaiety and irresponsibility, was for these exhibition pupils only one of the myths of English Composition. Only in compositions did they give delirious shouts of joy and their spirits overflowed into song; only there did they indulge in what the composition notes called "schoolboy's pranks." (392)

And Mr. Biswas finds fault with the reader Anand uses at school, with its non-Hindu sentiments: "'The cow and the goat give us milk and we eat their flesh when they are killed.' You hear the savage?" (340) The compositions the children are encouraged to write contain stories of trips to the seaside in cars most of their parents are unlikely ever to own. Creativity is discouraged in preparing for the exhibition exam—education is a matter of memorisation and regurgitation, rather than intellectual training individual minds. Both Annie John and Anand Biswas, however, receive special recognition for autobiographical compositions which describe, coincidentally, incidents involving their parents and the sea. Annie reads out her piece to her new classmates, and earns their adoration as well as the teacher's approval. Anand is given twelve out of ten for his highly personal account of his narrow escape from drowning. The education system is not entirely committed to crushing individuality: obviously in the case of Naipaul and Kincaid, it produced or at least failed to suppress two angry, articulate and aware individuals, amply equipped to convey their message to the world.

The differences between these two novels are as illuminating as their similarities. Annie John's world is closed, secure and suffocating. Mr. Biswas and his children are adrift in an uncaring world, and the course of events that lead to their final achievements seems random and tenuous. Seepersad Naipaul wrote a story called "They Named Him Mohun," in which his sense of alienation and insignificance is clearly displayed. The first sentence reads, "Mohun's coming into the world was not an occasion of joy for anyone."[6] V.S. Naipaul wrote in his Preface to the collection which includes this story, published in 1976 for the first time outside Trinidad:

> It was the only piece of autobiography my father permitted himself, if autobiography can be used of a story which more or less ends with the birth of the writer. But my father was obsessed by the circumstances of his birth and the cruelty of his father. I remember the passion that preceded the writing; I heard again and again the forty-year-old stories of meanness and of the expulsion of his pregnant mother from this father's house; and I remember taking down, at my father's dictation, a page or two of a version of this sketch. (8)

The story of Mohun Biswas's birth in *A House for Mr. Biswas* is another version of this story, but the inauspicious signs are undercut by a sceptical narrator. The midnight birth, for example, which is mentioned without comment as uniucky in "They Named Him Mohun," is tempered in *A House for Mr. Biswas* with the comment that the child's grandmother "had no means of telling the time, but both she and the midwife had assumed it was midnight, the inauspicious hour"[7] and the unfortunate sixth finger falls off undramatically in the novel, whereas the Mohun of the story remains six-fingered. There is little room for superstition in *A House for Mr. Biswas*. Mr. Biswas has a reputation for atheism, but as he grows older he shows more and more respect for the Hindu faith, and one of his running arguments with Mrs. Tulsi is her adoption of Catholic, and possibly even obeah, customs: her elder son leaves for his examination with all the charms and protective devices she can think of from any religion—including "crucifix, sacred thread and beads [and] a mysterious sachet," (125) reminiscent of the "little black sachet, filled with something that smelled abominable," (127) that Annie was given by the obeah woman when she was ill. Obeah in *Annie John* is not ridiculed or dismissed. Ma Chess is a skilled obeah woman, as well as a beloved grandmother. Anand, on the other hand, is a determined sceptic, and resists as far as possible his mother's efforts to load him with good luck tokens on his examination day.

These two novels, between them, have a great deal to say about the colonial experience in the islands of the Caribbean. Culturally, they depict two separate worlds. The Afro-Caribbeans, descended from the slaves of the European imperialists, had little sense of a continuing African culture of their own. Kincaid said in an interview, "The connection

I have to Africa is the colour of my skin," and this may be why the world of *Annie John* seems so closed and isolated, with little reference to an outside world other than an unreal image of England. The Indians of Trinidad, on the other hand, feel very strongly about their heritage and culture, and try to a ridiculous degree to continue with their customs. The Tulsis regard their stay in Trinidad as "a stage in the journey that had begun when Pundit Tulsi left India." (390) This sense of being adrift in the world seems to be characteristic of Naipaul, who vowed to leave Trinidad as soon as possible, and feels rootless and out of place wherever he lives. Both Kincaid and Naipaul had to leave their Caribbean homes before they could write: Kincaid in America, where she feels that she has been given "a place to be myself—but myself as I was formed somewhere else" (Jamaica Kincaid, Oct. 1993); and Naipaul in London, which he wrote in 1958 was "the best place to write in,"[8] despite or even because of its drawbacks as a place to live.

The postcolonial writer thus becomes the expatriate writer, looking back with anger balanced with detachment and a cool, sometimes ironic, gaze at his or her own childhood; making sense of it and at the same time creating some of the most compelling fiction written in English this century.

NOTES

1. Leslie Garis, "Through West Indian Eyes," *New York Times*, 7 Oct. 1990, Late ed. Final: 6/42. *New York Times Online*. Online. Nexis. 1 Sept. 1995.
2. V.S. Naipaul, *A House for Mr. Biswas* (London: Penguin, 1969), p. 279.
3. Mel Gussow, "Enigma of V.S. Naipaul's Search for Himself in Writing," *New York Times*, 25 April 1987, Late City Final ed., 116; *New York Times Online*. Online. Nexis. 7 September 1995.
4. Gordon Rohlehr, "Character and Rebellion in *A House for Mr. Biswas*," *Critical Perspectives on V.S. Naipaul*, ed. Robert D. Hamner (Washington: Three Continents Press, 1977), pp. 87-88.
5. Jamaica Kincaid, *Annie John* (New York: Plume, 1983), pp. 131-32.
6. Sreeprasad Naipaul, *The Adventures of Gurudeva, and Other Stories* with a foreword by V.S. Naipaul (London: Deutsch, 1976), p. 124.
7. Allan Vorda, "I Come from a Place That's Very Unreal: An Interveiw with Jamaica Kincaid," *Face to Face: Interviews with Contemporary Novelists* (Houston: Rice University Press, 1993), p. 90.
8. V.S. Naipaul,"London," *Times Literary Supplement*, 15 August 1958, Rpt. Robert O. Hamner, p. 12.

'Island' as a Metaphor of Creativity: A Study of V.S. Naipaul's *A House for Mr. Biswas* and *The Mimic Men*

RAMA NAIR

"All the arts without exception are imitative," says Coomaraswamy. This concept that all the objects of life or Nature are represented in art through a process of "mimesis" or "imitation" was, perhaps, first propounded by Plato. Reality, which is associated with the principle of Nature, has been interpreted variously in art and literature. The subject of Reality is such a vast one, that no philosopher has been able to give an adequately satisfactory interpretation of it. Nevertheless, it is this attempt to capture "reality" either in language, colour or stone that has led to some of the most exquisite creations in art and literature. Man's urge to express concretely the result of his imaginative perception led to the birth of the creative impulse in him. Very often he attempted to represent some ideal that he had intuitively visualized. And of all the arts, creative literature is that in which the process of idealization can take place more freely. Idealization does not mean that the things represented are either real or unreal in the literal sense. It cannot be examined logically. We can only accept them as they are.

The "reality" of colonial and postcolonial societies as represented in the novels of V.S. Naipaul, himself a postcolonialist, has often evoked mixed responses from his critics. The West Indies, to Naipaul, according to many of his critics, has never been his home. Yet the West Indies has been the subject of most of his fiction and non-fiction. Naipaul has acknowledged the influence of his background: "I imagine that one is really shaped by everything that occurs when one is young. I think I was greatly made by my childhood and by my background, and naturally, therefore, by Trinidad."[1] Naipaul's own life was characterized by rootlessness and alienation. As an East Indian in Trinidad, or as an East Indian West Indian Englishman in India, or as an East Indian West Indian in England, Naipaul has always been restless and displaced, a condition which his unique East Indian West Indian background can explain. Living in isolation in London, through necessity, Naipaul remains twice displaced—from India (the land of his forefathers), and the West Indies (to which his ancestors were brought as indentured labourers). Yet Naipaul remains a citizen of the world, his novels being a telling testimony of the universal predicament of disorder that governs the Third World postcolonial societies today. In this context, "Naipaul's present identity is not so much that of an exile, which would presume a home to be exiled from, as a permanent alien."[2] Naipaul's disordered existence in Trinidad, his apparent detachment from the political upheavals of his "island home" led him to attain the status of a "secluded alien" in England. It was through his writing here that he attempted to overcome the creative sterility of his circumstances. But, here again, Naipaul was reviled for having betrayed his motherland in favour of his adopted motherland. In *Writers in Exile*, Andrew Gurr stresses that writers moved voluntarily from the colonies to the metropolis in search of artistic freedom and intellectual expansion which their own conservative, traditional, and conformist small communities did not provide or allow.[3] In the West Indies itself, as Bill Carr observes, such an emigration was viewed unsympathetically. "Unfortunately," he says, "the exile has been greeted with minority sympathy in the West Indies itself. Far too much assertive language is heard about 'sell-out,' 'betrayal,' 'doing us an injustice,' and so on a purely nationalist reaction, which has nothing to do with genuinely critical engagement with what the writers have attempted."[4]

Naipaul's indictment of the moral, social, cultural and political corruption that existed in these postcolonial islands in the absence of any viable alternative forms of governance, earned him the epithet of 'a prophet of doom and gloom' in Trinidad. The reality of the harrowing history of the Caribbean as seen by Naipaul as it is. A new identity based on order and creative regeneration can emerge only if these existent facts are acknowledged and remedied.

Place and displacement are recurrent themes in postcolonial literature. The crisis of identity, one can conclude, is related more to placelessness than to rootlessness. "A valid and active sense of self may have been eroded by dislocation resulting from migration, the experience of enslavement, transportation, or 'voluntary' removal for indentured labour. Or it may have been destroyed by cultural denigration, the conscious and unconscious oppression of the indigenous personality and culture by a supposedly superior racial or cultural model."[5]

This paper attempts a comparative analysis of this search for belonging and identity in Mr. Biswas and Ralph Singh, the central protagonists of Naipaul's *A House for Mr. Biswas* and *The Mimic Men*. The common denominator is that both lived on islands—Mr. Biswas in the West Indies and Ralph Singh in Isabella. The historical, ideological, and cultural circumstances that entrap Mr. Biswas and Ralph Singh in closed worlds of despair and loneliness are re-examined and realigned to symbolize the beginning of a creative process. In these two novels, Naipaul's vision of reality is as cutting as ever. But in this framework, the question and definition of identity is analyzed in terms of a creative endeavour that enable Mr. Biswas and Ralph Singh to transcend the 'island' of their mind. The hostility and cultural alienation that existed between the blacks and the East Indians during indentureship continued even after the British left the colonies. For the East Indian to carve a respectable niche for himself in such a society was almost as impossible as was their inability to merge with the mainstream Creole culture renouncing their cultural and religious heritage.

Mr. Biswas and Ralph Singh are both East Indians. The island each one lives on is not a mere geographical entity. The island as a metaphor is connotative of cultural insularity—breeding instability, insecurity, and a desperate quest for 'freedom.' Physical attempts at transcending alienation are futile, as is evident in these two novels. The island in these novels is interiorized. It is the interior landscape of the mind that has to be reset and re-patterned. The Caribbean islands, once dominated by British imperialism, are not only culturally distanced from the imperial Centre, but also, metaphorically, stand at the periphery of civilisation, marginalized, overlooked and trivialized. For many West Indians, migration became an easy solution to their political and economic problems characterized by physical insularity, racial and political divisions, economic and educational dependence, the island to many became a symbol of creative sterility and cultural stasis.

On the other hand, the identification of England with an island is, according to prominent critic Gillian Beer, a fiction. She states: "In English cultural imagining, the island has seemed the perfect form—defensive, secure, compacted, even paradisical—a safe place; a safe place too from which to set on predations and from which to launch the building of an empire."[6] If England could hold within it the creative tension needed to create an empire, then, by implication, the island far from being a stock metaphor for creative sterility could also hold within itself the potential for creative regeneration.

Naipaul's *A House for Mr. Biswas* and *The Mimic Men* are set against this colonial backdrop. Critics have remarked on Naipaul's tendency towards nihilism. Apparently, Naipaul finds disorder and anarchy wherever he goes. But Naipaul's contention is that these societies never even try to escape from their chronic condition of degradation and existential despair. Naipaul's constant depiction of decline and disintegration are a reminder that these negative forces can be overcome. All creative activity springs from the tragedy of negation and destruction. Naipaul proved it through his writings. Nihilism and negation precede affirmation and remain a part of it. Naipaul's interpretation could be an attempt to create a new culture—a culture based on both negation and affirmation.

In *A House for Mr. Biswas* and *The Mimic Men*, there is precisely this personal quest for meaning in a world that is perverse and alien. Self-knowledge cannot be based upon theoretical assumptions. The object of self-knowledge is the individual himself. Mr. Biswas and Ralph Singh, through their unique individual experiences, arrive at the means by which they discover their individuality and dignity. Naipaul's Mr. Biswas and Ralph Singh have shown that cultural displacement and dispossession need not necessarily lead to a pathological state of negation. Banishment can be creative as in the case of Shakespeare's Caliban in *The Tempest*. *The Tempest* has, perhaps, been the most important text to establish a paradigm for postcolonial readings of canonical works. In one such reading, George Lamming (1960) dismantles the hierarchy of Prospero, Ariel, and Caliban. Caliban is no longer seen as a creature outside civilisation, but as a human being whose human status is derived by the European claims to an exclusive human condition. *The Tempest* is also read as a political allegory where the injustice of Prospero's dispossession of Caliban's inheritance, the island, bequeathed to him by his mother, Sycorax, is emphasized.[7] But Prospero justifies his stance claiming that he had given Caliban the gift of language, *his* language, in return. But Prospero's gift is rightly, though ironically, rejected by the enslaved Caliban. Caliban's response is, 'and my profit on this, I know how to curse.' (I.ii.425-26) Subversion is a psychological trait that exists in the unconscious of the colonized. When Caliban spurns the gift of language, he is, in effect, spurning that powerful weapon which reduced him from a free 'unlettered savage' to a colonized prisoner. But, paradoxically, it is through this very language that he articulates his anguish and bitterness at his changed plight. Through his creative expression, Caliban is rescued from being a total nonentity. He retains his individuality, and his weapon to protect it becomes his language: a language that is potentially critical, subversive and radical. In Mr. Biswas and Ralph Singh, this aspect of creativity is exemplified.

The crisis of identity that Mr. Biswas experiences in Trinidad is compounded of many factors—one of them being the destitute culture of which he is a part. The 'Prologue' to the novel encapsulates Mr. Biswas's uneventful life. "Weeks before he died, Mr. Mohun Biswas, a journalist of Sikkim Street, St. James, Port of Spain, was sacked. . . . Mr. Biswas was forty six and had four children. He had no money. His wife, Shama, had no money. On the house in Sikkim street Mr. Biswas owed, and had been owing for four years, three thousand dollars. . . . It gave Mr. Biswas some satisfaction that in the circumstances Shama did not run straight off to her mother to beg for help. Ten years ago that would have been her first thought. . . . Now she tried to comfort Mr. Biswas."[8]

On the surface, it might appear that Mr. Biswas is the archetypal failure. But the opening sentence invests Mr. Biswas with a distinct identity. Mr. Biswas was a journalist and this is interesting and enlightening. Mr Biswas had created himself and his world out of nothing. How empty this world could be, can be understood by an insight into Mr. Biswas's earlier existence. Mohun Biswas was born into a poor orthodox Hindu family at an inauspicious and inappropriate hour. He was born at midnight in the wrong way, and with six fingers. Born with this burden of guilt, Mr. Biswas (so called from birth) married Shama, a girl who belonged to the rich Tulsi joint family. He is compelled to stay there due to his poverty. The caste rigidities, the religious rituals, and the stiff orthodoxy of a conventional Hindu expatriate society is evident in Hanuman House. Hanuman House, to Mr. Biswas, becomes a symbol of oppression and inhuman bondage. Mr. Biswas is marginalized, and subjected to innumerable humiliations in this depressing atmosphere. Yet, in spite of being a rootless East Indian caught between the hypocrisies of a decaying culture, and the sterility of a colonial society, Mr. Biswas struggles to maintain his independence and self-respect. After his abortive attempt to build a house for himself, Mr. Biswas moves on to Port of Spain. In this world, education was the only protection. Mr. Biswas, who was now a journalist of the *Sentinel* clung to his independence. His duties brought him into contact with Indian farmers, who being illiterate, treated him "as an incredibly superior being." But these farmers were rich, and "from this money, despite Marcus Aurelius and Epictetus, despite Samuel Smiles, Mr. Biswas found himself barred." (438) Despite the system, he defies the forces that compel him to confirm. Mr Biswas evolves as a self-made man. He is soon appointed as an investigator at the *Sentinel*. The *Sentinel* had begun a Deserving Destitutes Fund, and it was Mr. Biswas's duty to "read the applications from destitutes . . . and then, if the circumstances warranted it to write harrowing accounts of their plight harrowing enough to encourage contributions for the Fund." In the course of his job, Mr. Biswas visited the "mutilated, the defeated, the futile, and the insane living in conditions not far removed from his own: in suffocating wooden kennels, in sheds of box-card, canvas and tin, in dark and sweating concrete caverns." Exposure to the horror and misery of these broken and listless people increased his own sense of helplessness. He could only investigate, write and move on. But this job gave him respect, status, and an identity of his own. Writing provided him with a creative outlet. In writing about the destitutes, Mr. Biswas was, perhaps, unconsciously venting his own frustrations at being a "deserving destitute" himself. His position was one of responsibility and power, and he was given a by-line and described as "Our Special Investigator." After this, he bought a house of his own, his family life improved, and he died, a journalist at the age of forty-six. To get one's name and occupation mentioned in an English newspaper even if it was in the nature of an obituary, is not a hope that every destitute, coloured, colonial can fulfill. But Mr. Biswas dies an individual with a distinct identity, and not as an unknown deserving destitute which he could have easily become. To achieve it, Mr. Biswas overcame two great obstacles: he conquered the fatalistic attitude of his ancestors, and he broke away from a stifling traditional society, to realize his own self. Language, in his hands, becomes a mode of liberation, even though it is used radically to expose the rottenness of decadent society.

Written in 1967, *The Mimic Men* explores the dilemma of a postcolonial writer. Forty-year-old Ralph Singh is a displaced East Indian West Indian. A disillusioned former Cabinet Minister from the newly independent multi-racial island of Isabella, Ralph Singh flees to London, the metropolis, to seek refuge. In London, he reflects on, and reevaluates his whole life. The result is an autobiographical work which depends mainly on the narrative technique of flash-back and flash-forward. The work becomes an expository socio-political novel which underlines the pathetic hollowness of postcolonial states. Unlike the language used by the characters in *A House for Mr. Biswas*, the language used by Ralph Singh approximates the Standard English of the Centre. This once again brings into conflict the distance between the marginalized peripheries of colonial power and the Centre, as in Mr. Biswas, and the desperate need to conform to the accepted and privileged stance of the colonizer, as in Ralph Singh. Language, in postcolonial states, becomes a tool to mimic the 'original' and the 'true.' But this only creates an illusion of power, and the end is the perpetuation of disorder. Ralph Singh's view of his own short-lived career as a colonial politician is revealing in this context. He remarks, "The career of the colonial politician is short and ends brutally. We lack order. Above all we lack power, and we do not understand that we lack power. We mistake words and the acclamation of words for power; as soon as our bluff is called, we are lost."[9] Ralph Singh is representative of those men, who after independence from colonial rule, can only mimic their erstwhile masters, thus denying themselves the authenticity of their own selfhood. The chaos that follows the birth of new states is symptomatic of the fragmented consciousness of the colonized. Still economically dependent on foreign investment, these states continue to disintegrate under a new type of neo-colonialism. As Bruce King observes, "Singh feels that history has left him shipwrecked. What is he, an Indian, doing on a 'slave island'? In contrast he admires England with its folk tales, long history, and comforting nursery rhymes. . . . But the comforting, orderly England of his imagination does not exist."[10] Yet this self-imposed exile is the creative source for a rich and incisive reconstruction of post-colonial life. His marriage to an English woman, and his flight to England can be read as a deliberate attempt to be absorbed into English culture and tradition. But this proves to be futile, and Ralph Singh remains as much an exile in England, as he was in Isabella.

Politics at Isabella comprised of empty promises, its independence was nominal, and the 'mimic men' were incapable of handling its problems. The oppressed now became the oppressors. As a failed politician, Ralph Singh's only desire was to escape. London offers no solution either. In *The Mimic Men* the dispossessed colonial remains dependent and displaced. It is against this background of racial, cultural, and political disorder that Ralph Singh prepares to order his own disjointed experiences through the writing of his autobiography. His exile in London, in his own words, turned out to be the most fruitful period of his life. In the eighteen months he took to write the book, Ralph Singh discovers the value of order, sequence, regularity. As he confesses: "It never occurred to me that the writing of this book might have become an end in itself, that the recording of a life might become an extension of that life." (244)

Through the ordering of their experiences as a reporter and as a writer, respectively, both Mr. Biswas and Ralph Singh come closer to life, and writing becomes not just a symbol of identity. It becomes the identity itself. This creative act enables them to come to terms with the reality of their own socio-cultural situation. It also prevents them from being condemned to the worst kind of provinciality, that is, creative sterility.

Like the use of language by Caliban in *The Tempest*, the language of power is subverted in the hands of the oppressed to become a potent device to indict the brutalities and indignities inflicted on them by the oppressor. In this context, George Lamming points out that while identity is crucial, just to assert a different identity is never enough. The main thing is to be able to see that Caliban has a history capable of development, as part of the process of work, growth and maturity to which only Europeans had seemed entitled.[11] Whether it is Mr. Biswas's portrayal of the distressing plight of Trinidad's forgotten destitutes, or Ralph Singh's forthright acknowledgement of the 'mimic men' colonialism had created, both strike out independently at the wretched effects of colonialism.

Many reviewers have identified Biswas's life with the life of Naipaul's father, and Naipaul's own childhood days. Others have considered Ralph Singh to be Naipaul's alter ego. But Naipaul, in these novels, vividly recreates his own experiences in the fictional world of art. If art is imitative of reality, then these two novels need not be merely considered as onslaughts on colonialism. It can also offer a positive approach. With an awareness of, and an open acknowledgement of the existent evils, art can reveal the path to order as it did in the case of Mr. Biswas and Ralph Singh. Fiction (or the story-shaped metaphysics), gives one aspect of reality, while philosophy provides another. But both are necessary for a unified sensibility. By creating an alternative language of discourse, even if it is diffuse and ambivalent, Mr. Biswas and Ralph Singh provide an 'ethically sensitive' response to the existing political and social theories. The culture of colonialism suppresses dissent, but here, the inner resistance of the protagonist is worked out within the psychological limits set by the former. And so, in the words of Salman Rushdie, '*The Empire Writes Back* to the Centre. '

But in an interview, Naipaul made the observation that "the truth about India wasn't what I thought about India, it's what they are living through. That is the great discovery; it moved to it slowly."[12] If this is kept in view, 'island' is both negative and positive; if the truth of thought does not match the actuality of experience there is nothing surprising about it. But what in Naipaul is reassuringly surprising is his constant balancing of the 'island' of his creative responses with the realities surrounding it. Structurally therefore, fiction in his case is followed by travel accounts, but neither is privileged nor hegemonised. Islands and continents exist, but the creative writer transcends both because he keeps a constant tension between the two. Escape is not possible, as nothing is exclusive. Islands exist within the sight of the mainland. One is the definitional counterpart of the other. Disorder exists everywhere, and the Centre keeps changing according to needs. A frozen Centre festers in its own isolation. Therefore, disorder is a necessary condition of order, as dissociation is no longer possible.

To sum up, 'island' in Naipaul is the "house" that one builds: if it is imaginary only mimic men can inhabit it; but at the same time, if real, the very stifling nature of reality imitates a movement towards balancing. To rescue Caliban from his colonial hatred without assuming something else—the Other—as solidly ordered elsewhere, is the new paradigm of 'island' in Naipaul.

NOTES

1. Dolly Zulakha Hassan, *V.S. Naipaul and the West Indies*, American University Studies Series (New York: Peter Lang, 1989), Vol. 18, p. 68.
2. *Ibid.*, p. 69.
3. *Ibid.*, p. 73.
4. *Ibid.*, p. 74
5. Bill Ashcroft, Gareth Griffiths, Helen Tiffin, *The Empire Writes Back: Theory and Practice in Post-Colonial Literature* (London: Routledge, 1990), p. 269.
6. Gillian Beer, "The Island and the Aeroplane: The Case of Virginia Woolf," *Nation and Narration*, ed. Homi K. Bhabha (London: Routledge, 1990), p. 269.
7. *The Empire Writes Back*, p. 189.
8. V.S. Naipaul, *A House for Mr. Biswas* (New York: Penguin: Rpt. 1992), p. 7.
9. V.S. Naipaul, *The Mimic Men* (England: Penguin, 1967), p. 8.
10. Bruce King, "V.S. Naipaul," *West Indian Literature*, ed. Bruce King (London: Macmillan, 1979), p. 171.
11. Edward W. Said, *Culture and Imperialism* (London: Vintage, 1994), p. 257.
12. "Delivering the Truth, " *An Interview with V.S. Naipaul*, Aamer Hussein, *TLS*, Sept. 2, 1994, p. 3.

The Theme of Selfhood in V.S. Naipaul's *A House for Mr. Biswas*

S.S. SHARMA

A House for Mr. Biswas is considered V.S. Naipaul's masterpiece. Critics find a number of strands in the novel and label its protagonist Mohun Biswas in a variety of ways. Some critics have seen it as a Dickensian novel, others as a Dostoevskian. Mohun Biswas is seen by some as an anti-hero and by others as an absurd protagonist. Despite this diversity of opinion, one thing stands out. More than anything else, *A House for Mr. Biswas* is the portrayal of a single individual's search for identity, his struggle to arrive at authentic selfhood.

It is by no means an easy struggle. The odds are against Mr. Biswas right from the start. Life to him has been a series of big and small disasters, each designed to underscore the fact that he was necessary to no one and dependent on everyone. His poor physique as a child and later as a boy adds to his absurdity and to the poor self-image that he has. He has "the smallest of chests, the thinnest of limbs, a soft rising belly."[1] (22) He is very nervous too. The nervousness decreases a little as he grows up but not the grotesque aspect of many of his actions. From a rudimentary education which he receives (along with his quota of flogging) from one Mr. Lal, Biswas moves over to the house of Pandit Jairam. Here he comes across an abstract and high-minded cruelty which is as unsettling as the flogging. Next there is Ajodha's rumshop where Biswas is a big eyesore for Bhandat, the person who runs the rumshop. He moves on to become a sign writer but work is very irregular in coming to him. While painting signs in a shop of the Tulsi family, he makes a clumsy advance to one of the Tulsi daughters—Shama. He is promptly accepted as the girl's suitor and the next thing he knows, he is married to her already caught in the Tulsi trap.

Biswas's relationship with the Tulsi clan (with Tulsidom, that is) goes a long way in defining his struggle for selfhood. There is the matriarch Mrs. Tulsi; Mr. Seth, her brother-in-law who manages the Tulsi estate; the two sons of Mrs. Tulsi. Shekhar and Owad; Govind and Chinta;

and later the Tuttles, Tulsidom is a system that provides subsistence and shelter in return for total devotion and the abdication of one's self. The relationships and transient alliances within this system are quite complex. The proceedings are often made lively by Mr. Biswas's refusing to be either a suave or mild victim of this system. His clowning, his querulousness and his blasphemies are all, at one level, the flutterings of a trapped self, caught in a world from which there is no easy or lasting escape for him. His clowning especially is a defence against his being turned into a puppet of deterministic forces, and ridicule also is used by him as a defence in situations which he cannot otherwise control or dominate. His genuine inability to belong either to the original Indian culture or to the new Caribbean culture compounds his problems.

The "glory" of Tulsidom is its capacity to induce conformity among its members. Pitted against this, Mr. Biswas revels in non-conformist acts and words. His resistance to being totally absorbed between "them" and himself takes a variety of forms. His speaking Creole English, for example, when he is in Hanuman House is a deliberate, calculated act. Then there is the nicknaming of people which he is so good at. It comes to be at its malicious best where the Tulsis are concerned. The marriages of Tulsi daughters are termed "car-in-bag" transactions. Mrs. Tulsi is "old queen," "old cow" depending upon the intensity of his reaction. Shekhar and Owad are called "little gods" and Mr. Seth is let off with just "Big Boss."

This kind of nicknaming and Mr. Biswas's wry humour are his ways of hitting back at the system which reduces him almost to subhuman levels of irrelevance. These very traits later help him to find an outlet in journalism. It makes no difference that his early attempts at journalism are cliche-ridden. The important thing is that his exploitation of the potential of language (as a weapon in the form of nicknames and as a means to a living through journalism) is a very significant step in his journey toward authentic selfhood.

The same is true of his reading of the Meditations of Aurelius, and his brushes with the work of Samuel Smiles. This for him is another way of trying to be different. He sees that most other people around him seem to exist just to fulfil a function rather than to be a person. His reduction of the roles offered to him—the dutiful son-in-law, the resident sign-painter, the obedient shopkeeper—means that his endeavour is always to be on his own. It is not surprising, therefore, that in his assertion of independence he decides to write.

Role-playing and self-image have a lot to do with each other. Biswas's self-image suffers a lot as a result of his being taken into the grinding machine that is Tulsidom. At one stage, his crisis of identity is extremely acute and real. Looking at himself in a mirror, he says to Shama: "I don't look like anything at all. Shopkeeper, lawyer, doctor, labourer, overseer—I don't look like any of them." (159)

The venture into journalism comes for Biswas at a time when his self has taken a lot of beating from all quarters. Hemmed in from all directions, moving from job to job and one kind of habitation to another, he has been reduced to being a passive victim of circumstances. His relationships with others are becoming intolerable, more so with his wife. A stage comes when he is on the verge of distintegrating altogether. Objects lose their neutrality for him and become a source of menace. People and figures frighten him. His personality (or whatever there is of it) undergoes disorientation. His lucidity keeps decreasing day to day. A kind of darkness envelops him. His "self" faces total dissolution.

Journalism saves him. More than that, it is the city (Port of Spain) that saves him. In Tulsidom and in Green Vale Mr. Biswas felt smothered. The city brings about a refreshing and invigorating change in his being. There is an openness and an impersonality about the city which offers to Biswas's damaged inner life that measure of detachment which accelerates his return from the "wall of flawless black" to daylight of consciousness. Above all, the city gave him the possibility of establishing relationships on terms very different from those available to him in Tulsidom.

Most of Naipaul's protagonists come nearer to the sociologist's view of the self rather than the philosopher's. 'Self' in this sense is an entity that arises and develops in the process of an individual's social experiences and activities. Port of Spain helps Biswas to evolve as a social self on terms which are not very far from those on which he wants to relate to others. The terror of disintegration which bothers Biswas so much around this time is dispelled greatly by the unending succession of the city's moods, its complexity of classes, places, institutions. The wet cinema posters, the crowded pavements and the continuous traffic all help much in his recovery as he comes to be part of a sea of humanity that manages to ward off disintegration in the face of menaces and disasters both personal and financial. Port of Spain helps Biswas to bring about a re-centring of the displaced impulse and the restructuring of his self in the context of the racial and urban pressures of Trinidadian society as a whole.

Biswas now finds himself face to face with a whole new range of possibilities of relating with others. All this comes upon him all of a sudden. He finds a job which gives him both dignity and pleasure and helps him to further humanize the context of his whole being. The ultimate expression of such attempt is of course the search for a habitation where one can be one's own self. Biswas's semi-independent occupation of the house in Port of Spain begins the long process of recovery for his damaged self which culminates in his coming to have a house of his own on Sikkim Street.

As a boy, Biswas had moved from one house of strangers to another; and since his marriage he had always felt that he had lived nowhere but in the houses of the Tulsis—at Hanuman House in Arwacas, in the decaying wooden house at Shorthills, in the clumsy concrete house in the Port of Spain. The urge to have his own house, strengthened by his awareness of his children's emotional needs now comes upon him in a big way. His coming to have a proprietory pride in his children (especially in Anand) has a lot to do with this. Going in for a house of his own is for Mr. Biswas a kind of investment in the future, in the continuity of his own self after his death. The Epilogue at one point tells us: "Living had been a preparation a waiting. And so the years had passed; and now there was nothing to wait for." This could sound pretty gloomy but pat come the words: "Except the children." (586) These three words are extremely significant in indicating Mr. Biswas's having arrived at authentic selfhood. His investing in the children's happiness is a sign of his having travelled a long way from the restlessness and lack of focus of the Tulsi-dominated days. How much the house in Sikkim Street means to the children, despite all its shortcomings can be seen in: "Soon it seemed to the children that they had never lived anywhere but in the tall square housed in Sikkim Street. From now on their lives would be ordered, their memories coherent." (581) Once in his own house, Biswas's relationship with Shama too undergoes a positive transformation:

> He didn't now care to do anything against his wife's wishes. He had grown to accept her judgement and to respect her optimism. He trusted her. Since they had moved to the house Shama had learned a new loyalty to him and to their children; away from her mother and sisters, she was able to express this without shame, and to Mr. Biswas this was a triumph almost as big as the acquiring of his own house. (8)

This is from "The Prologue" of the novel and in Naipaul's hands "The Prologue" is a really helpful gloss on the whole novel. It is in fact the key to our understanding of the novel. It beautifully sums up Mr.

Biswas's having arrived at authentic selfhood and helpfully provides a rationale for his final move it refers to "The wonder of being in his own house, the audacity of it; to walk into his own front gate, to bar entry to whoever he wished . . . to hear no noises except that of the family, to wander freely from room to room." And the rationale

> How terrible it would have been at this time, to be without it: to have died among the Tulsi, amid the squalor of that large, disintegrating and indifferent family; to have left Shama and the children among them in one room; worse, to have lived without even attempting to lay claim to one's portion of the earth; to have lived and died as one had been born, unnecessary and unaccommodated.

From a total non-entity (first the trouble with the birth certificate, later difficulty of making an entry in the column—'profession') to 'somebody' (a journalist—the tag used by *The Sentinel* for reporting his death); from a person always being shoved around to someone with a place of his own ("one's portion of the earth") is a remarkable progress both in terms of selfhood and in terms of worldly advancement. To have done that without conforming (or conforming as little as possible) makes Biswas an archetypal figure. Some have seen him as a tragicomic figure, others as a part of the overall grotesque satire which Naipaul is attempting. Some have stressed the element of the absurd protagonist in Biswas. None of these views is very far from the truth but seeing Biswas as a pathetic figure is. Far from that, he is a character in whose portrayal Naipaul brings into play tremendous humanity. It is this that makes *A House for Mr. Biswas* as rich and moving a novel as it is.

The best summing up of Naipaul's extraordinary achievement in his handling of the theme of selfhood in *A House for Mr. Biswas* comes from William Walsh, a perceptive critic of Naipaul's work: "The members of the community in *A House for Mr. Biswas* . . . carry about them in their attitude and posture, in their management of life and feeling the indelible mark of the slave, who is supremely the unnecessary man. All are impelled by the desire to demonstrate, to themselves even more than to others, their human necessity. In the earlier novels they did this by bruising themselves absurdly and ineffectively against an indifferent universe. Mr. Biswas constructs the proof of his necessity in both a comic and a most moving way. Saturated as he is with the ethos of the given place, maltreated by its peculiar deficiencies and cruelties, he is nonetheless realised with such complete conviction, so living a reality, that he becomes a model of man just as the history and situation which formed him see to be a metaphor of the process which constitutes any man."[2]

A House for Mr. Biswas, then, has universality as well as contemporaneity. It spares nothing in judgement, neither in representation nor reaction. And the whole matter of the novel is informed with a fullness of human sympathy. The important thing to note is that the deficiencies, the pretensions and cruelties of the society which Mr. Biswas is caught in are recorded as effects of our common humanity, not as the operations of an alien or inferior nature. That, in itself, is a great triumph for the novelist. It makes his artistic vision remarkably inclusive and gives to *A House for Mr. Biswas* a unique position within his own work.

NOTES

1. *A House for Mr. Biswas* (Penguin).
2. William Walsh, *V.S. Naipaul* (Oliver and Boyd, 1973), pp. 30-31.

Samuel Selvon's Short Stories: A Survey

NIRUPA RANI

West Indian novelists of this century have made it their prime concern to focus their attention on the evils of their social and economic system. The pervasive consciousness of a majority was of race and colour, lack of a history to be proud of and the absence of settled values. The amalgamation of the European, African and Asian in an environment where none had deep roots is probably the reason for this uncertainty of a cultural identity and thus became a dominant note in West Indian writing. Many writers in the Third world have made attempts to retrieve cultural dignity, an imaginative mediation between the old and the new to reconstruct and affirm cultural values. Some of the writers felt that they have to assume the role of a prophet and some have taken on the garb of a teacher. It is quite evident that they have recognized the responsibility of the writer in a new nation.

Most of the writers who have felt quite committed to their nations have faced the problem of publication and as a result they were forced to address their literature not to traditional society but to an English-speaking and reading audience. In the process the writers were estranged from their own past and the result is 'how-for-do' writing. This commercial restraint is one of the major reasons for the importance of the short story in the development of the new literatures.

In West Indian writing one finds a number of small regional literatures that have many common features and interests. Local journals have helped the writers to form the identity of the Caribbean. The most influential journals were *The Beacon* in Trinidad, the place from where V.S. Naipaul and Samuel Selvon started their career, *Bim* in Barbados, the region which was celebrated in George Lamming's writings, *Kyk-Over As* in British Guyana which claims Wilson Harris as its pioneer, and in Jamaica, *Focus* which asserts the sensitive Edgar Mittlehotzer as its writer who has reflected the divided consciousness which is the result of mixed racial origins.

Of these *The Beacon* was the most ambitions literary journal in the

Carribbean and it covered both creative writing and regional and international politics. The Russian Revolution and Indian national movement have both had influence on the writings of the journal and the result was a sense of new 'realism.' The short story emerged from this new realism, its sense of social responsibility and commitment. The editors were firm that creative writing should not imitate the west but accurately reflect the West Indian condition, the speech patterns, characters, conflicts and situations. The creative writer realized the necessity of capturing the dialect of the Caribbean to explain the West Indian life. The journals have helped a climate of obvious and literary awareness and the BBC's programme Caribbean Voices (1945-58) has enhanced the cultural awareness and regional consciousness among the people.

Of the writers from Trinidad mention may be made of Samuel Selvon (b. 1923) and V.S. Naipaul (b. 1932) who are of Indian descent domiciled in London since 1950. Though both are of East-Indian origin and are from the same island, there is not much common ground of interests between them. Probably this could be because of their different religious and social backgrounds. Selvon has recorded his observations of social change through his peasant sensibility with a consistent love for the peasant. He has tried his best to understand the quest for harmony in his young protoganists, whether they are in Trinidad or exiled in London. Naipaul on the other hand made no effort to conceal his contempt for the island and its inhabitants. He reviewed his Trinidadian background and experience time and again with irony and detachment. "I had never wanted to stay in Trinidad . . . for many years afterwards, in England, I had been awakened by the nightmare that I was back in tropical Trinidad."[1] His resentment for the Island which has offered him a possibility to write and get world acclaim as a 'world class writer' is enough to prove that he is not fair to his people.

Samuel Selvon who was born in 1923 in Trinidad had started his career in the 1950s as a writer with love for recording social change. In the short span of twenty-seven years of stay in Trinidad, he had been exposed to many changes both in his personal and professional life. He very keenly observed the change in trends of social life and recorded them with enthusiasm against a historical perspective. The values established in 1920s and 1930s by 'Beacon group' as social realism as a mode and commitment impressed Selvon and inspired him to explore the human landscape. The spirit of 1940s and 1950s looked around for the quest for meaning—the meaning of a people's life and struggles in a social and historical context. This period encouraged the writers to go deep into the human need for subsistence. Just before the declaration of war, Trinidad had seen immigration of Jews and Germans into Port of Spain. This influx brought about rapid social changes and the crisis reached a peak when the Americans started building bases connecting roads in the villages to the capital. When the island was going through the turbulent throes of the world war, the peasant community remained ignorant and insulated against the consequences of war and the subsequent predicament. The Yankee dollar had lured many from rural areas; the complacence of the village was shaken; it prompted the villagers to show preferences for the power block. When peace was declared in 1945, people expected change in their lives and society but nothing happened. It is during this time that Selvon joined the Communications Division. He recorded these experiences in his non-fiction which is essential to understand him as a writer and as an individual.

The parallels between the writer and his society can be demonstrated by the popularity of autobiographies. In the process of establishing his own bearings and identity, the writer divulges the dilemma of his society. The recurring personal and subjective note in a writer's work, be it a novel or a short story, demonstrates how quickly autobiography can metamorphose into fiction. The impressions made on the psyche of an individual as a child and juvenile hold on for a long time till it gets deep rooted in the ethos. Many writers cope with recurring themes to provide greater insights into human nature. The habitat may change but the distress and delight, ambition and setback are the same for one and all. Maybe to create profound historic perspective, Selvon limits his writing to either Trinidad or London, though he has been a domicile of Canada for the last so many years.

By the time Selvon started publishing his works, Trinidad could boast about few magazines like *Guardian Weekly* and *Trinidad Guardian* for which he worked as a journalist immediately after Second World War. His familiarity with urban style and rural folk ways, city speech and country talk; East Indian peasants and creolised Africans in assorted jobs in urban areas have made his writings quite interesting and pleasant to read, without ironic humour which is typical of V.S. Naipaul. In 1950 Selvon sailed to England and in 1978 he left England for Canada, where he now lives with his family. So far he has published ten novels, two volumes of short stories, besides children's books, poems and plays.

The short stories of Samuel Selvon have to be understood against this background. His first collection of short stories, entitled *Ways of Sunlight* was published in 1957 and subsequently reprinted in 1979. The book is divided into two parts—Part one 'Trinidad' deals with stories about East Indians working in sugarcane fields and Part two 'London' deals with his immigrant stories. There are altogether nineteen stories in this collection—nine in 'Trinidad' stories and ten in 'London' stories—all published after he left for England except 'Cane is Bitter' which he published in 1950, before he left for England. As a boy scout Selvon observed the peasants at work and shared the warmth of their company at social level. He deals with them with a compassionate attitude in his fictional world.

The next collection of short stories appeared in 1989 under the title *Foreday Morning*—selected prose 1946-1986, edited and introduced by Kenneth Ramchand. This book is also in two sections—part one 'Trinidad 1946-50' comprising non-fiction and short stories written and published before Selvon left for London and part II 'Abroad 1950-1986,' consists of short stories he wrote after 1950 either abroad in Britain where he lived until 1978 or Canada, where he now lives, or on subsequent visits to Trinidad. There is an epilogue—'Three into One can't Go—East Indian, Trinidadian and West Indian.'

Between 1946-1950 Selvon worked as a journalist with *Trinidad Guardian* and editor of the literary section of *Sunday Guardian* weekly which used to provide the richest literary source of material relating to the early fiction, poetry and drama of Trinidad and Tobago. Whenever he used to feel shortage of material for the journal he supplied poems, short stories, articles and editorials by using a number of pen-names including Michael Wentworth, Esses, Ack-Ack, Big Buffer etc. The pen-names have nothing to do with the contents of the work and point of view of the author.

The non-fiction section in *Foreday Morning* discloses the ambition of many a young natives to be part of a greater action in war, not out of patriotism but enthusiasm. The articles in this section can be grouped into three categories. The first part deals with Selvon's personal experience of war. "We Join the Navy" is about how Selvon joined the communication division in 1946; "The Last Outpost" about the pleasant memories the writer had gathered on an outpost writing in the wireless room and how he experienced the affection of the local people and immediate superiors, though he kept away from the village and how sad the narrator was when peace was declared. Despite the hardships of the punishment of running in the loose sands, the never-dying mosquitoes, the desolations, there was a quietness about the last outpost which will never fade from my memory." "A Man I Remember" was one of the first persons to see and encourage Selvon's writing and with a florid memory he remembers about him.

The next group of stories are autobiographical. "The House We

Lived in Holidays at Aunt Polly" have strong autobiographical notes. The fond memories of childhood on San Fernando are captured with a philosophic note: "Time is no healer: events only appear in a different light because we grew older and think back on them." "The Story of a Tree" is a moving memorial of Selvon's first wife Draupadi who is now no more.

The third group of essays are quite interesting and meditative. "From Trinidad Birds" is about birds in West Indies—the bird is identified with happy-go-lucky West-Indian. "The Life of a Day" and "He is Going to Die" are sad and meditative, discussing truth about life and death and the necessity of expression. "Michael Wentworth Contends" is an essay in which Selvon defends the cause of the artist against the 'elitist' conception: "It is because many people do not fully appreciate art. They must be taught to value valuable things, they must be taught to read and write—what a spur it would be if schools used the works of Trinidadians—experience is a better teacher." The last piece in the non-fiction is almost a story dealing with a virtual manifesto for the West Indian writer. The realization of the writer to take the deported crooks, criminals, defeated Royalist gentlemen fleeing from Europe, slaves from the West Coast of Africa, East Indians etc. surrounded by splendour and misery as subjects.

Of the short stories "The Christmas Gift" is the first story that appeared in print in *Guardian Weekly* in 1946. Since then Selvon has published many stories in various journals and many of them are not incorporated in the short story collections. He was active as a short story writer till 1957 after which he has written very few. Between 1966 to 1977, Selvon has not published any short stories except few extracts from his novels in journals. In 1980 he published one short story, in 1982 three and in 1987 one story entitled "Turning Christian" which is more or less an extract from the novel that is in progress and is set in Canada. He has written just two short stories based on Canada: "Ralphie at the Races" about an immigrant in Canada and "Her Achilles' Heel" a love story about a person and a place at the same time. The remaining stories in *Foreday Morning* are all written and published in 1957. Four of the stories that are published in this collection—"Johnson and the Cascadura," "The Great Drought," "Five Rivers," "Colypsonian"—are the earlier versions of the stories published in *Ways of Sunlight*.

The stories of Selvon can be grouped into four categories. Immigrant stories; personal stories dealing with love and personal reminiscences set either in Trinidad or London; stories set in rural Trinidad containing characters of Indian origin, stories set in the city or suburbs containing characters of African origin—Creole world. Irrespective of the setting, almost all characters are poor in search of something. There may be a reason behind this preference—it could be because of Selvon's identification with the poor of his country or there might be a greater and deeper reason for it. Probably Selvon understood that the poor are the least affected by anything except poverty and he must have decided to study the deeper ròots that colonialism has taken as far as human consciousness is concerned. The attempt of the Creoles and Indians to be like the whites is understood by Selvon with compassion.

> By the time I was in my teens I was a product of my environment as Trinidadian as anyone could claim to be, quite at ease with a cosmopolitan attitude, and I had no desire to isolate myself from the mixture of races, that comprised the community.

For him colonial indoctrination has no meaning and he is not conscious about it, either at home or at school. The inevitability of westernization both in personal and public life has been accepted without much ado, change is inevitable and acceptance is the only alternative to keep pace with the times.

The first group of stories—immigrant stories—are quite interesting ones as the stories talk about individuals that have migrated to London in search of better living conditions and the difficulties faced by them to get used to the climate; indifference of the white man, poverty and loneliness. All these stories are written during the period 1952-1957 and Selvon must have experienced some of the problems personally as narrated by George Lamming in *Pleasures of Exile*. Some of the stories in this group like "Erasers' Dilemma" and "Waiting for Aunty to Cough" are hilarious but at the same time the stories tell us about the value of honest approach to life in an alien world. "Finding Piccadilly Circus" is a story of social reality of the 1950s—a blackman's strange encounters in London, like finding a white man in menial job and the ignorance of a blackman thinking Piccadilly Circus is real circus. The shifted superstitions, pollution in London, the conditions of hospitals, the value of an immigrant's life in London are few of the many themes that he dealt with.

The second category of stories—the personal stories set either in Trinidad or London—are the stories that deal with the private worlds of individuals alienated from his immediate surroundings. These are the stories that deal with the large questions of Time, Death, Friendship and the meaning in life. These stories are philosophic not in the sense of exposing philosophy but approach the perennial issues afresh as they arise out of one's personal experience in the world. The reading of philosophic texts of East and West are not required to understand human predicament.

> Do you know, sometimes in reading the learned sages I have discovered that I held the same thoughts but never worried to put them on paper or thought of writing a book? Deep in their hearts all men think alike, it's only that some cannot express how they feel. (Epilogue)

"Christmas Gift" deals with the return of a war hero with an amputated leg and how he is received by his immediate family. "Rhapsody in Red" deals with an artist and his search for an inspiration and finally how he dies with disillusion, when the source of inspiration destroys the music composed by him (Great Drought—passing clouds etc.).

The third category of stories is set in Trinidad having characters of Indian origin. War had not directly affected the rural Trinidadians, but they were made aware of their role in society because of war. Selvon has recorded those moments of awareness both in his novels and short stories. The exodus made by the peasants leaving their fields to urban areas is one such trend, and the other is how life had been affected by war, disrupting the daily routine. "Cane is Bitter," "Holidays in Five Rivers," "Wartime Activities" are the best examples to show how change has crept into social life, without the protagonists realizing it.

The fourth category of stories deal with the Creole people working in the city or suburbs, the theme being how the blacks try to cope up with the situation they have created for themselves as a class by themselves. The Creole community is a much-discussed community in Selvon's novels, though according to order the blacks and the Indians live in harmony socially in the works of Selvon. They may have different political ideology but the harmony deserves appreciation.

In Selvon's world nothing is ignored. The superstitions, the beliefs and sentiments of the people are honoured. One striking feature of his writing is that neither he has gone into minute details about cultural issues nor he made pretence about things he is not aware of. His writing is a good example of honest and sincere writing and very close to reality. Myth is discussed at length in the three versions of the same theme about Cascadura fish in Johnson and the Cascadura as short story and as a novel but in no single instance he tries to convince his readers. He leaves it to the discretion of the reader. The story is set in the 1930s in the short story and in the fifties in the novel. Johnson in the *Foreday Morning* stories comes to Sansonce in 1926 to visit his friend, eats Cascadura fish and returns to the same place to die. In the novel Johnson comes into contact with a peculiar disease and falls in love with the village beauty Sarojini and leaves place after eating Cascadura. Of all the three stories the story included in *Ways of Sunlight* is dear to the heart of the readers as the story ends on a happy note.

Selvon's fictional world has characters who keep hopping from one story to the other performing stereotyped roles. The names of the streets, places recur again and again making us feel at home with Selvon's writings. So also the language and beginnings of the stories. Most of the stories begin with a typical traditional way of expression, "why I tell you about the legend is because it may have a bearing on the story I'm going to tell you. One time in Trinidad during the war one set of thing happens that afterwards I had to hold my head and bawl. I mean, it going to sound I making up the story, but if I lie I die. Now I suppose you want to know what is eh? you know where Barbado is don't? Well that is your hard luck you want to know what them doing up in the tree eh?" But he takes the reader along involving him in the action of the story. The omniscient way of narration is characteristic of Selvon. There is unity of action and the stories are complete with perfect endings. Regarding the language of the stories one can say the Trinidadian dialect used by the different communities and the language registers used by him are appropriate to the theme.

If the themes of alienation, frustration and pessimism dominate the work of Naipaul, the theme of compassionate understanding is the striking principle in Selvon's work. Naipaul has given satanic dimensions to his individuals. However, compassionate understanding devoid of satire is the trait of Selvon. What is lacking from humanistic point of view in Naipaul the classic writer is compensated in Selvon's work which is from the same Island.

As a short story writer Samuel Selvon cannot be classed on par with world writers like Guy de Maupassant, O'Henry or Chekhov. His speciality is that he is able to steep himself in the place and capture its spirit. He also reveals himself as a poet of nature and the human heart—a national philosopher thinking his way into life. His technique is the normal method adopted by all short story writers. As he himself has admitted, he does not claim to be an innovator in the field of creative writing and he has no pretensions to greatness. He has authentically and faithfully recorded his own experiences and observations. What Browning says in his poem *How It Strikes a Contemporary* is an apt description of Samuel Selvon as a writer.

> He took such cognizance of men and things
> If any beat a horse, you felt he saw
> If any cursed a woman, he took note
> Yet stared at nobody—you stared at him.
> And found, less to your pleasure than surprise.
> He seemed to know you and expect as much.

Innocence and Experience: Colonial Consciousness in Two Caribbean Stories

S. RAMASWAMY

> When a writer is writing, it should be approached with a certain amount of innocence and when a writer loses that innocence he ceases to be a writer as far as I am concerned. Therefore deliberately cultivate a certain measure of ignorance about everything in order to allow the innocence to feel its way into a situation or issue.[1]

> The old prejudices against coloured people have not yet died in the Caribbean, particularly in the islands nearest to a colonial past.[2]

I

Andrew Salkey, writing about the West Indian short story, says:

> West Indian short story writers wear the comic mask with more assurance than the tragic. We are still without our prophets; but it is unlikely that the short story is the form in which to look for them, or to expect promise of their coming. If self criticism and, in certain instances re-evaluation are going on, then the form of the short story lends itself admirably to just that sort of situation. Often the themes are passionately serious, themes of protest and revolt; and when not of them, inspired by them. But with Samuel Selvon, Stuart Hall, John Figueroa, Geoffrey Dayton, Barnabas G. Ramon Fortune, and George Lamming . . . wit and humour are used as effective weapons for a serious purpose.[3]

The complex attitudes, intentions and the sensibilities of the West Indian writers reveal the diversity within the unity of the Caribbean colonial consciousness, "The Trinidadian's irreverent wit, wry humour and at the same time, his obtrusive sentimentality; the British Guianese and his penchant for mysticism, legend and jungle lore; the Barbadian's regard for rhetoric and his overbearing seriousness; the Dominican's inventiveness and easy belief in superstition and myth; the St. Lucian's lyrical melancholy and brooding resentment of 'small islandism'—a feeling of inferiority shared by most of the 'small islands' and the Jamaican's restlessness, class consciousness and intolerable arrogance."[4] What is being attempted here is a very limited approach to two short stories—one from Jamaica and the other from Trinidad. In "Jamaican Fragment"[5] by A.L. Hendricks, what we find is the world of innocent children and the adult's complex attitude towards that innocence in the light of experience. In Samuel Selvon's "Brackley and the Bed,"[6] the experience of adults who have emigrated to the colonial capital is explored through an apparently innocent comic attitude. This comparative perspective reveals two aspects of colonial consciousness.

II

"Jamaican Fragment" is an extraordinarily simple and straightforward story—almost an allegory, where the white consciousness—the white man's burden and black consciousness—black is beautiful—are integrated into a colonial consciousness which is no more a bitter experience but one of integration. The narrative is so completely lucid that it reflects the innocence of childhood which is pictured through a game—the game of master and slave—played by two children. The narrator is black.

> The game, if it could be called a game, was not elaborate. The little white boy strode imperiously up and down and every now and then shouted imperiously at his bigger playmate. The little brown boy shuffled along quietly behind him and did what he was told.
> "Pick up that stick." The dark boy picked it up.
> "Jump into the water." The dark boy jumped.
> "Get me some water." The dark boy ran inside.
> The white boy sat down on the lawn. (144-45)

This is paralleled in the description of what the narrator of the story saw the next morning:

> To my utter astonishment the little dark boy was striding imperiously up and down the lawn while the white youngster walked ab-

> jectly behind him.
>
> "Get me a banana!" The little white boy ran into the house and reappeared shortly with a banana. "Peel it for me." The little white boy skinned the banana and handed it to his dark master. (145-46)

The neat reversal of the situation here makes the black narrator muse to himself, "How silly grown-ups are, how clever we are, how wonderfully able we are to impose deep motives to childish actions! How suspicious we are when we have been warped by prejudice!" (146) This realization comes to the narrator especially as he was a victim of colonial consciousness in his reaction to the situation on the previous day when he contemplated:

> Was there an indefinable quality in the white man that enabled his baby, smaller and younger than his playmate to make him his slave? Was there really some difference between a white man and a black man? Something that made the white superior? I could find no answer. I could not bring myself to believe such a thing, and yet with my own eyes I had seen a little dark boy take orders from a little white boy—a little white boy obviously his social equal, and younger and smaller. Were we as a race really inferior? So inferior that even in our infancy we realized our deficiencies and accepted a position as the white man's servant? (145)

This intellectual cerebration and theorizing is a part of racial/colonial consciousness. C.L.R. James in talking about "the intelligence of the Negro" says, "Racial psychology is a mere matter of commonsense based on personal pride when all is said. When this pride is absent or vitiated the accompanying psychology must of necessity go wrong. Do not stamp upon an impressionable mind that which would result in an inferiority complex. This point ought to be obvious to any thinking intelligence."[7] The thought-process of the narrator here is an example of "personal pride" which is a result of his experienced "thinking intelligence" and it "goes wrong" because the inexperienced innocent "impressionable minds" of the children at play do not admit complexes—either that of superiority or inferiority. The narrator's contrition on jumping to conclusions on the first day is more than compensated on the second morning when he sees a reversal of the situation. However, this is not the end of the story. When on the second morning the black narrator sees a white man standing at the gate of the house and tries to hoist on him his own feelings of the previous day and wants to console him that the boys alternate as servant and master, the white man smiles "surprised at my outburst" (146) and explains:

> "I know all about the game," he said. The boys are brothers—my sons. He pointed to a handsome brown woman on the verandah who had just come out to call in the children. "That's my wife," he said. (146)

However, the purpose of commenting on this story has been to bring home the point about the nature of colonial consciousness in the Jamaican context, "I smiled. My spirit laughed within me. This is Jamaica. I said in my heart, this is my country—my people." (147) This is the triumph of "Innocence" over "Experience."

III

In the second story that we are going to look at, a very different attitude is presented—the experience of the "innocents abroad," the West Indians in London. In Samuel Selvon's story "Brackley and the Bed," the London setting is used in a limited but very precise way and the London winter and the poverty of accommodation for the black man in the city make the "bed" more than literally significant. The narrator of the story is "wearing the comic mask" despite the serious implications under the facade of laughter, behind the ballad and the episode. As Kenneth Ramchand points out: "The narrator of this story takes up a colloquial idiom and the stance of the calypsonian ballad-maker."[8] In fact the narrator uses the word "ballad" and sets the tone for the narration in the opening lines of the story: "One evening Brackley was cruising around the Embankment looking for a soft bench to rest his weary bones and to cogitate on the ways of life. The reason for that and the reason why the boys begin to call him Rockabye, you will find out as the ballad goes on." (151)

This is the "ballad" of the blacks in London—colonials in the capital city. It is a ballad about a bed and a man called Brackley. In keeping with the "ballad" form, the speaking voice of the oral tradition is maintained throughout the story with the result that the authentic Trinidadian dialect is used. To quote Ramchand again:

> He [Selvon] seems to be placing himself deliberately in an oral tradition. We must remind ourselves that a literature begins long

> before it begins to be written. Before there is a written literature and after, along with it, there is a body of traditional songs and stories transmitted from generation to generation without the aid of writing. This oral literature is closely related to the daily lives, the beliefs, the superstitions and the fears of the people. Such would be the Anancy stories and West Indian folk tales and the Calypso before its commercialization. A great deal of this material is lost to us, but we cannot afford to pretend it never existed or that it had no influence.[9]

This context for the analysis of the story has been given partly because "in the writings of Samuel Selvon, the colloquial idiom which is associated with the speaking voice and oral literature is exploited more fully than in any other West Indian author"[10] and partly because I intend this to be feeble explanation for the unsatisfactory way in which he is able to read the extracts from the story as the beauty of the dialect is especially important in the oral tradition. This point is made very clear in the interview with the author of the story by Ramchand.

KR: It is good to know a writer who does not wish to conscript us and it is a relief to know that if we close the book he will not pursue us with his microphone. But still I must ask, would foreigners benefit as readers from hearing you or a Trinidadian read your work aloud?

SS: Yes, but I would like to be the one to read it. (Laughter) I think that I am the best reader of my work and I have been told so very often.[11]

It is this aspect of not having any experience in reading West Indian dialect that makes the present writer take advantage of his innocence and attempt to impart the true tone of the story as best as he can.

> Brackley hail from Tobago, which part they have it to say Robinson Crusoe used to hang out with Man Friday. Things was brown in that island and he make for England and manage to get a work and was settling down when bam! he got a letter from his aunt saying that Teena want to come England too.
>
> Teena was Brackley's distant cousin and they were good friends in Tobago. In fact, the other reason why Brackley hustle from the island is because it did look like he and Teena were heading for a little married thing and Brackley run. (151)

The marvellous mixture of motives and the unobtrusive serious element in the essentially comic situation is the hall-mark of this delightful story. As soon as Brackley sees Teena alighting from the boat-train at Waterloo, he asks more with the trepidation of a man whose fate has caught up with him than of a man who is greeting his "fiancee":

> 'What you doing in London' Brackley ask as soon as Teena step off the train. 'What you come here for, eh? Even though I write home to say things real hard?'
>
> 'What happen, you buy the country already?' Teena sheself giving tit for tat right away, 'you ruling England now? The Queen abdicate?'
>
> 'You know where you going?' Brackley say. 'You know where you is? You know what you going to do?'
>
> 'I am going straight to the Colonial Office,' Teena say.
>
> 'What you think the Colonial Office is, eh? you think they will do anything for you? You have a god-father working there?'
>
> Well, they argue until in the end Brackley find himself holding on to Teena suitcase and they go on the way to the little batchy he have in Golders Green at the time. (151-52)

Now arises the comic situation which is the central point of the story justifying the title, "Brackley and the Bed."

> 'Ah well,' he say, stretching by the fire, 'that wasn't a bad meal. Look, I will give you some old blankets and you could wrap up that coat and use as a pillow—you could sleep on the ground in that cover. . . .'
>
> 'Me? On the floor? You not ashamed?'
>
> 'Well, is only one bed and here as you see. . . .'
>
> 'I using the bed.'
>
> 'Girl, is winter and if you think I going to sleep in the corner with two old blanket and wake up stiff. . . .' But in the end, was Brackley who crouch up in the corner and Teena sound asleep in the bed. (153)

Teena roundly takes Brackley to task calling him a 'lazy feller.' She tells him "Well six o'clock tomorrow morning, bright and early as the cock crow." The protest of Brackley 'you don't hear cock crowing in London' (153) goes entirely unheeded by her. Teena rudely wakes him up with the refrain 'Get a job, Get a job,' and by ten o'clock Brackley finds himself 'washing dishes in a cafe,' where he got work. (153) The comic vein continues:

> One night when frost was forming on the window pane Brackley wake up and find he couldn't move.
> 'Teena.'
> 'What?'
> 'You sleeping?'
> 'Yes.'
> 'Teena, you want to get married?'
> 'Married? To who?'
> 'To me.'
> 'What for?'
> 'So-I-could-sleep-in-the-bed—I mean, well we uses to know one another good in Tobago and now that you here in London, what you think?'
> 'Well, all right, but you have to change your ways.'
> 'Yes, Teena.'
> 'And no foolishness when we married. You come home straight from work. And don't want you looking at no white girls.'
> 'Yes, Teena.'
> No sooner said than done. Brackley hustle Teena off to the Registry Office as soon as things was fixed, thinking only how nice the bed would be after the hard floor and the cold. (154-55)

However, this is not the end of the story. Brackley's obsession with the bed has to remain an unfulfilled ambition for the present as the story ends with the twist so characteristic of the comic mode.

> 'What about honeymoon?' Teena say after the ceremony.
> 'In the summer,' Brackley say 'Let we go home I am tired and feel I could sleep for weeks.'
> 'Bracks,' Teena say as they was coming away, 'I have a nice surprise for you. Guess who coming to London, this evening?'
> 'Father Christmas,' Brackley says yawning.
> 'No, Aunty, I write telling her to come up. . . .'
> 'But Teena,' he say quietly, 'We ain't have no place for Aunty to sleep?'
> 'Don't worry,' Teena say, 'She can sleep with me until we find another place.' (155)

It is clear that the use of the "bed" here in the comic context is not without the serious implications of a black man, a colonial, not finding a proper place to stay in London, his difficulties in finding a job and all the attendant miseries that he has to encounter if he decides to emigrate to London. As Coulthard points out, "The West Indian emigrant leaves his country because of economic frustration resulting from overpopulation in relatively small under-developed territories."[12] The adult "experience" of the "innocent" colonials is taken into account by Ramchand when he comments, "Teena and Brackley behave as they would in their own country and speak a West Indian dialect. But these features perform another function as well. They combine with the absence of English characters in the story to suggest the West Indian Londoner's loneliness—his isolation both from his own country and from English life and people."[13] Thus the themes of loneliness, isolation and alienation in a story that is essentially comic—even farcical—takes one from "Innocence" back to "Experience."

IV

Thus in these two stories which are, in a way complementary to each other we see the essence of the West Indian colonial consciousness. However, the contribution of the West Indian short story writer to the English language may also be mentioned. It is in this spirit that an extract from the dialogue between Samuel Selvon and Kenneth Ramchand is given here:

SS: When a writer is writing it should be approached with a certain amount of innocence and when a writer loses that innocence he ceases to be a writer as far as I am concerned. Therefore I deliberately cultivate a certain measure of ignorance about everything in order to allow the innocence to feel its way into a situation or issue.

KR: Would you say that you cultivate this innocence in your use of language?

SS: To the extent that it does not worry me if I invent a turn of phrase or word and interpolate it into what is commonly accepted as Trinidad dialect. . . .

KR: This sounds very much as if you are saying that if you did not have to think of a non-Caribbean reading public you would have written differently. Do you mean that?

SS: No, because I am a writer and language is a tool, I do not think I

> could have said what I wanted to say without modifying the dialect. And if I had not done this modification the dialect would have been Greek to a lot of people. . . . In spite of the modification I consider what I do to be dialect. . . . The point I want to make is that archaic form is a kind of dialect. So I am combining two kinds of dialect. Another thing that a lot of people forget is that standard English or "proper English" is also used as part of our dialect in certain phrases or words. For instance if I rudely interrupt a creolized[14] Trinidadian and he or she turns to me, looks me up and down and says in Queen's English "I beg your pardon," I would consider that to be part of the Trinidad dialect.[15].

We started with a reference to the variety of approaches and complex attitudes by the West Indies writers to their colonial experience. It is in this context that perhaps we should agree with Andrew Salkey when he says:

> To the West Indies, with its uncertain roots and highly original racial mixtures, with its scattered islands and its doubtful yet enthusiastic claims to nationhood, with its turgid colonial history part rejected and part unconsciously absorbed, England has been a sort of necessary common denominator, a link holding all its constituent parts together. Out of seeming contradictions, a partnership has been established on more levels than one.[16]

NOTES

1. "Sam Selvon Talking: A Conversation with Kenneth Ramchand," *Canadian Literature*, Number 95 (Winter 1982, "Caribbean Connections"), pp. 56-64.
2. G.R. Coulthard, *Race and Colour in Caribbean Literature* (London, New York, Toronto: Oxford University Press, 1962), p. 103.
3. Andrew Salkey, ed., "Introduction," *West Indian Stories* (London: Faber and Faber, 1960), pp. 11-12.
4. *Ibid.*, p. 11.
5. A.L. Hendricks, "Jamaican Fragment" in *Andrew Salkey*, pp. 144-47.
6. Samuel Selvon, "Brackley and the Bed" in *Ways of Sunlight* (London: Longman, 1957), pp. 151-55.
7. C.L.R. James, "The Intelligence of the Negro" in *From Trinidad: An An-*

thology of Early West Indian Writing, ed. Reinhard W. Sander (London, Sydney, Auckland, Toronto: Hodder and Stoughton, 1978), p. 239.

8. Kenneth Ramchand, *West Indian Narrative: An Introductory Anthology* (Nelson, Caribbean, 1966), p. 100.
9. *Ibid.*, pp. 99-100.
10. *Ibid.*
11. "Sam Selvon Talking," p. 64.
12. Coulthard, p. 105.
13. Kenneth Ramchand, pp. 99-100.
14. Born and naturalized in the West Indies out of European (or African) origin.
15. "Sam Selvon Talking," pp. 60-61.
16. Andrew Salkey, p. 10.